Eat Yourself Full

Eat Yourself Full

by

RUTH R. TYNDALL

DAVID McKAY COMPANY, INC.

New York

EAT YOURSELF FULL

Copyright © 1967 by Ruth R. Tyndall

Library of Congress Catalog Card Number: 67-18205

MANUFACTURED IN THE UNITED STATES OF AMERICA

VAN REES PRESS • NEW YORK

For

BARBARA AND ROY

My own Feinschmeckers

Contents

Introduction

As visitors to the Pennsylvania Dutch country well know, the variety and quantity of foods served there has to be seen to be believed. Frequently, as many as thirty different dishes, including the well-advertised seven-sweets-and-sours, appear on the table. But in the restaurants, where tourists are most likely to end up, except for a very few, quantity rather than quality is apt to be the rule, far different from the true Dutch home cooking, which is as delicious as it is abundant.

The seven-sweets-and-sours custom is observed at home as well as outside. Tradition has it that a well-set Pennsylvania Dutch table should include seven sweet and seven sour dishes, which means that the table is sure to be well covered with all sorts of jellies, jams, sauces, and pickles. In my childhood, we never actually counted them, but a rough estimate gave us an idea of how big a meal would soon be served. All foods for a Dutch meal are placed on the table at once, including dessert, "else how could abody know whether there would be room for all, still?"

Pennsylvania Dutch cookery is indigenous to those areas of southwestern Pennsylvania which were settled by "The Plain People," the Mennonites, Amish, and Dunkards, who came to the New World at the invitation of William Penn, to seek freedom to worship as they pleased. They came from the Palatinate, or Rheinpfalz, to join other early German settlers on the rolling fertile land whose rivers teemed with fish and whose forests abounded with game.

The term "Plain" was coined by the settlers themselves and is one of pride, never contempt. It is used to distinguish those religious groups the "Plain People" consider as belonging to "The Church" from their more worldly neighbors who are designated as "Fancy" or "Gay." To an outsider the chief difference is one of costume. Although the various sects may worship differently and even have different habits of dress, they all wear some form of old-fashioned garb.

On coming to this country the early settlers retained their Pfalz speech, which contained some French. They slowly began adding numerous English words, and soon their speech (then, later, they themselves) became known as Pennsylvania Dutch, a corruption of Deutsch. As time passed and they attempted to translate their own language into English, their efforts were somewhat awkward. Verbs still began sentences. V's and w's, b's and p's, were readily interchanged. The cadence of their speech retained a distinctly German lilt. "Essen Sie sich," became "Eat yourself," as in "Eat yourself full." "Was für," became "What fer," as in, "What fer pie vould you like?" Many of these expressions are still in use, as is the accent, even among the tenth generation, because even now many of them speak only "Dutch" at home.

In this new world, the Dutch put up small limestone farmhouses. Bakehouses, springhouses, and smokehouses soon followed. In the beautiful rolling country of Lancaster, Berks, York, and Lebanon counties one can still see these small buildings clustering around the farmhouses. Many of them are no longer used, except by those sects of the Plain People to whom electricity is still forbidden. Until the advent of supermarkets and freezers, however, most farmers not only butchered, but cured their own meats, baked in the old stone ovens, and kept things cool in the springhouse.

Farms were widely scattered at first, roads all but impassable, and there were few towns, so it was not always possible to locate the ingredients needed for favorite recipes brought from Europe. Substitutions had to be contrived, and they were shared in the community, which is one of the reasons why the Dutch cooking differs from the more traditional German cuisine found in other parts of the United States. Many dishes made from handed-down recipes are still aromatic with the kinds of spices and herbs the New World housewives grew in their kitchen gardens with seeds brought from Europe—parsley, sage, thyme, dill, and even the little autumn crocus, whose stamens give us that rare spice, saffron.

These dishes are not for calorie-watchers nor for the cholesterol conscious! Dutch housewives used lard, butter, cream, and eggs with a lavish hand, for these ingredients were always readily available to them. The early settlers were farmers and needed energy to cope with the backbreaking work of pioneer days, and the eating habits they established endure to this day. Although the Gay people are sometimes considered better cooks, I have enjoyed many mouth-watering meals in "Plain" homes. The only real distinction lies in the fact that the Gay people use more sophisticated seasonings. In fact, good food is one of the few pleasures the Plain People permit themselves, since most forms of recreation that others take for granted are prohibited. For pleasure they visit, and when they visit they eat! In some Plain homes, an hour or so after a company dinner, a large pitcher of "bread soda," dissolved in water or lemonade, is served, and it is no doubt needed.

Most of the recipes in this book have been collected over the years and have not appeared in any publication, but have been handed down or taught from generation to generation. Some of my own grandmother's recipes are included. At times, in order to get these recipes, it was necessary to stand over a famous cook while she worked, since her directions consisted solely of "a pinch of this," "enough flour to make the dough," or "throw in a little of . . ." Wherever possible, I have adapted the recipes to include the use of convenience foods, and since

Pennsylvania Dutch home cooking is often a little too sweet, I have sometimes reduced the sugar content.

The "Feinschmecker" to whom I address this book is, in Pennsylvania Dutch terms, "someone who knows what good is." The implication is more gourmand than gourmet. "Schmeckt es gut?" means, "Does it taste good?" A Feinschmecker is one who knows, appreciates, and consumes good food in large quantities. (The idea of lip-smacking is implicit in schmecken.)

Eat yourself full!

QUANTITIES

The number of people which each of these recipes serves can vary greatly. None of the older recipes gave quantities, because we cooked "by guess and by God," and much depended upon what else was being served, and how big "fressers" one was serving. Many of the new recipes which indicate four servings are barely enough for two of us, I'm sorry to say! People are constantly amazed at the extent of my meals, but they are really barren compared to those we used to serve on the farm. Although I have indicated the number of people each recipe will feed, the reader should keep in mind the appetites of her family and guests.

SPIDER

A spider is a heavy iron skillet particularly favored by Pennsylvania Dutch cooks. For most of the recipes in the book, any good frying pan will do, but in one or two instances I have suggested that only a very heavy one be used.

Eat Yourself Full

CHAPTER I

From the Soup Pot (Soups)

Soup making went on all year around in our Pennsylvania Dutch home. An old iron pot frequently stood on the back of the stove, and a batch was cooked up. "Soup to stick to the ribs gives a body strength, not?" It was usually served for supper, in dishes deep enough to be used nowadays for serving vegetables. If there were no crackers to "go vis," there were usually hot hunks of homemade bread and butter, muffins, or biscuits. Mom dished up each plateful from the kettle, at the range, and then fished out the meat from which the soup was made, sliced and served it, with either horseradish or mustard sauce, or some kind of gravy, plus the usual complement of potatoes, slaw or red beets. After the soup was consumed, one ate the rest of the meal out of the same plates.

The varieties of soup were endless—from chicken corn to pretzel. Sometimes, after a particularly heavy dinner, or when supplies ran low, Mom would make mock oyster stew for supper. This was simply hot milk, aromatic with thyme, fresh pepper, with a dab of yellow butter floating on the top, "ohne" (without) oysters. Served with crackers to be broken into it, one could imagine it was the real thing.

Soup is still a mainstay of farmers' meals in the Pennsylvania Dutch country. How else would you use up all the leftovers? In the wintertime it is especially hearty—bean, lentil, dried pea, pepper pot, and the like. There is nothing quite like the sight

1

and smell of a big kettleful of soup to greet one on a bitterly cold winter's day. A bowl of it, and homemade bread, can make any man coming in from out of doors feel as if he has reached a truly secure haven.

Ingredients and garnishes are the secrets of good soup. The Pennsylvania Dutch housewife prides herself on these, and each generation hands on its special touches to the next.

Mittgehe für Sup
(TO SERVE WITH SOUP)

All sorts of things were put into soup and added to the hearty flavor. The extras also "stretched the soup," when there were many mouths to feed. Noodles, of course, went into chicken and some beef broths, but dumplings were a mainstay as well.

Spätzele
(EGG DUMPLINGS)

2 eggs
2 teaspoons baking powder
Pinch of salt

Flour to make a very stiff batter —about 1 cup.

Beat eggs until light and add to dry ingredients, adding more flour if needed. Batter must be very stiff. Drop by spoonfuls into meat broth; cook for 5 minutes. Dumplings are light and fluffy and delicious.

Rivels

The name of this thickener probably comes from *reiben*, which means "to rub, mash, or grate." Rivels are a component of chicken corn soup but are also used to thicken any soup which appears to be too thin.

Pinch of salt
Enough flour to make mixture crumble between fingers—about ¼ cup.

One egg, beaten

Add salt to beaten egg. Work in flour until it becomes crumbly. Crumble into boiling soup, and cook just until it thickens.

Noodles

Whenever we had some free time we made our own noodles, cut into different widths and stored in cans. These homemade ones are light and delicate, but I really can't see much difference between them and the better "boughten" ones nowadays.

2 eggs
1 cup flour
2 teaspoons baking powder
½ teaspoon salt

Beat eggs and add to dry ingredients. Place on floured surface and knead gently to mix well. Roll out as thin as possible. Fold dough over and over into 1-inch strips. Let stand for several minutes, then cut crosswise into desired width. Spread noodles out on floured surface to dry, fluffing them apart with your fingers. My recipe says "dry in a clean wind, if possible!"

Buttery Egg Noodles

3 cups sifted flour
1 teaspoon salt
3 eggs, slightly beaten
1 tablespoon melted butter or cooking oil

Sift flour and salt onto waxed paper. Make hollow in center. Beat eggs with butter, just enough to mix, and pour into hollow. Work flour into this mixture until dough is formed. Then knead until smooth and elastic, about 10 minutes. Cover with bowl, and let dough rest for 15 to 20 minutes.

Roll dough as thin as possible on lightly floured surface. Fold into four thicknesses, over and over, somewhat like a jelly roll. With sharp knife, cut noodles into desired width (narrow, medium, or wide). Separate and spread on clean towel or napkin. Let them dry for 50 minutes to an hour.

Short Cut for Making Noodles:

Take ⅓ of the ingredients of a pie-crust mix. Roll thin, fold, and cut as above.

Ein Lauf

This is another thickener from an old recipe. *Einlauf* means "to pour in," so you pour this into soup!

1 egg, mixed with ¼ cup water   3 tablespoons flour
⅛ teaspoon salt   1 teaspoon chopped parsley

Add egg beaten with water to rest of ingredients. Pour slowly from spoon into boiling soup. Cook for 3 or 4 minutes.

Suet Dumplings

½ cup finely chopped beef suet   Cold water
2¼ cups flour   ½ teaspoon parsley, chopped
⅛ teaspoon salt   (optional)

Using fingers, mix suet with 2 cups flour and salt. Add just enough cold water, a little at a time, so that mixture can be shaped into tiny balls. Roll in rest of remaining flour, and drop into soup. You may add parsley to mixture, if you wish.

Pretzels

Pretzels are of Germanic origin, so that it is appropriate that they reached their acme in the Pennsylvania Dutch country. We children were thrilled when a neighboring Mennonite farmer opened a pretzel factory, and we loved to walk up the hill just to watch him. The dough was deftly mixed, rolled, and bent into the pretzel shape, dipped into a mixture of lye and water, then into rock salt and placed in a huge oven on a wooden peel (a spadelike object). What a mouth-watering odor as the pretzels turned a delicate light brown! We could scarcely wait for them to cool. They were thick and salty and shattered into crunchy bits when you tasted them. You can buy pretzels all over America nowadays, and they are delicious, but fresh from the oven they are incomparable.

There were also soft pretzels—great, thick hunks of chewy goodness, which are seldom available now. We used to buy them from the pretzel man in the Square in Lancaster, and I've occasionally seen them vended in large cities. They don't keep or ship well, and they should be eaten on the same day that they are baked. Sometimes you can find so-called soft pretzels at beach resorts, but they are doughy and tough, while the true Dutch soft pretzels are light and chewy.

We nibbled pretzels with ice cream; we spread them with butter or cheese; we munched them "so"; and we even used them in soup. "There's nosing like a good dish of pretzel sup to settle the stomach," it was said, and here is the recipe:

Pretzel Soup

3 tablespoons butter	1 quart milk
3 tablespoons flour	½ pound pretzels

Combine butter and flour, thinning mixture with a little of the cold milk. Add slowly to rest of milk, being careful to avoid lumps. Heat to boiling. Break pretzels into soup just before serving.

Serves 3 to 4

Wegetable Soup

1 shin bone or large beef soup bone, with meat on it	1 small turnip, diced (optional)
Water to cover	4 potatoes, peeled and diced
1 cup barley, rinsed in cold water	1 cup cooked soup beans
3 stalks celery with leaves	(may be canned or leftover)
1 onion, diced	1 pint canned tomatoes, or
Salt and pepper	5 or 6 tomatoes, diced
1 quarter small cabbage	Any leftover vegetables—peas,
4 carrots, sliced	string beans, limas, or corn
	Grated cheese (optional)

Cover soup bone with cold water and bring to boil. Skim off fat, and add rinsed barley, celery, and onion. Add salt and pepper to taste. Simmer until meat falls off bone, about 1 hour. Remove bone, slice meat, and put slices back into soup. Simmer 1 hour. Add uncooked vegetables, and boil about half an hour until soft. Add cooked vegetables and boil a few minutes to blend flavors. Correct seasoning. *Serves 3 to 4*

We sometimes sprinkled a little cheese over the top of each bowl before serving—delicious, especially Parmesan, which we didn't have in what my children call "the olden days."

Mehlsup
(FLOUR SOUP)

This was sometimes called "poor man's soup," since the ingredients are available in almost any home, no matter how low the larder. It's amazingly good.

4 tablespoons bacon or ham fat
8 tablespoons flour
4 cups water (approx.)
Few drops onion juice or
⅛ teaspoon very finely minced onion

Salt and pepper
Grated cheese, 1 teaspoon per person

Melt fat in bottom of large kettle. Add flour and stir over low heat until flour turns brown. Slowly add water, stirring constantly to avoid lumps. Add onion juice, salt, and pepper to taste. Cover and let simmer for at least an hour, stirring every so often to keep soup from scorching. Serve hot, adding about 1 teaspoonful of grated cheese to each bowl. *Serves 4*

Chicken Noodle Soup

We usually made this when we were having fried chicken, using the tips of the wings, the back, and all the giblets except the liver. If you want a little more soup, use a small whole chicken. You can also buy parts of chickens very economically nowadays.

Backs, necks, and gizzards of two chickens, or 1 small frying chicken
Water to cover, about 2 quarts
1 onion, sliced thinly

3 stalks celery
½ package medium-broad noodles
Salt and pepper to taste
Pinch of saffron (optional)

2 tablespoons chopped parsley

Cover chicken with water and add onion and celery. Bring to a boil and let simmer until meat falls off bones—about 2 hours, or less, depending upon age of chicken. Skim off fat. Take out meat, discard bones, and cut meat into small pieces. Add noodles to stock and boil for 20 minutes. (If you use homemade noodles, add them slowly to stock, about three handfuls—and if that doesn't sound like my mother!) When noodles are done add chicken and seasonings. If soup gets too thick after noodles are added, just pour in a little boiling water. Taste for seasoning, sprinkle with parsley, and serve.

Serves 4 to 6

Chicken Corn Soup

This is still the best soup I've ever tasted. I make it frequently, and it is really a meal in a pot, although my mother served it for supper, accompanied by the usual cold meats, and all the rest.

1 stewing chicken or	2 quarts of fresh corn, or
2 pounds necks, backs and giblets	1 can cream-style corn, or
	1 can whole-kernel corn
Water to cover	2 hardboiled eggs
Salt to taste	Pinch of saffron
½ onion, sliced very thin	Dash of pepper
2 stalks celery, diced	⅛ teaspoon paprika
2 tablespoons chopped parsley	½ cup noodles, or rivels (see Index)

Cover chicken with water, salt to taste, and bring to a boil. Add onion, celery, and parsley, and simmer gently until meat begins to fall off bone. Remove chicken, and cut into bite-sized pieces. Strain broth, if you wish. (I prefer the vegetables left intact, but be sure to remove all small bones.) Add corn, chopped hardboiled eggs, saffron, pepper, and paprika. Taste to check seasoning. Cook together for at least 10 minutes until well blended. While soup is boiling, add the rivels, or ½ cup noodles, and boil 20 minutes more.

Serves 4 to 6

Split Pea Soup

2 cups split peas	1 tablespoon butter
About 2 quarts of boiling water	1 tablespoon flour
1 ham bone, or	Salt and pepper to taste
3 smoked ham hocks	Dash of thyme
1 onion	1 knockwurst sausage, cut into
3 sprigs parsley	1-inch pieces (optional)

Wash and pick over peas, cover with boiling water, and bring back to the boil. Let stand 2 hours. Add ham, onion and parsley. Bring to a boil again, and simmer 2 hours or until peas are tender. Take out 2 cupfuls of peas, put them through a food mill or coarse sieve, and return to broth. (If you don't like whole peas in the soup, put them through a sieve, but it's not necessary.) Take out ham bone or hocks, and cut meat into bite-sized pieces. Rub butter and flour together with a spoon, until completely smooth. Add a little soup stock to blend, then place in soup with salt, pepper, and thyme. Add cut-up knockwurst, if you wish, and boil gently 5 to 10 minutes, to blend flavors.

This is a good hearty soup, wonderful for cold winter evenings. It freezes well, but be sure to allow head space of at least an inch in container. *Serves 4 to 6*

Lentil Soup

This is made exactly as the split-pea soup, substituting 2 cups dried lentils (they don't have to soak overnight any more) for the peas, and omitting the knockwurst.

Bean Soup

2 pounds dried white beans (navy or home-grown)	2 teaspoons chopped parsley
4 cups water (approx.)	½ cup chopped onion
3 smoked ham hocks, or leftover ham bone, or 1 pound butt end of ham bone	2 tablespoons butter or margarine
2 celery stalks, leaves and stems, chopped	Pinch of thyme
	Salt and pepper
	Pinch ground cloves

Wash beans and pick over carefully, removing any damaged ones. Place in water and bring to boil. Turn off heat and let stand at least 2 hours. (For home-grown dried beans, soak overnight.)

Brown onion in butter in fairly deep skillet for 5 minutes—do not allow to become dark. Take a cupful of the beans, mash them through a sieve or food mill, and add to onions. Add this to rest of soup and stir. Add thyme, cloves, salt, and pepper to taste. Soup should be quite thick. Now add ham bones, celery and parsley. Bring to boil and simmer 2 hours or until beans are tender.

This soup tastes even better on the second day. It also freezes well, so take out a pint for future use, and keep it in the freezer, being sure to allow 1 inch of head space in the container.

Serves 4 to 6

Grumbere Sup
(POTATO SOUP)

This is another wonderful cold-weather soup, rich, hearty, and nourishing.

6 or 8 potatoes, diced
1 onion, diced
Water to cover
1 quart of milk
1 tablespoon chopped parsley
Salt and pepper to taste
Paprika

1 tablespoon butter or margarine
1 egg, lightly beaten
Flour and water if needed to thicken
1 hardboiled egg

Pare and dice potatoes, add onion, cover with water and boil until good and soft, but not mushy. Drain; add milk, parsley, salt, and pepper to taste, and butter. Beat egg, add some of the soup to it, and pour mixture into pot. This soup should be quite thick. If it isn't, blend a couple of tablespoons flour with equal amount of water and add to pot. Cook a few minutes to blend flavors. Cut up hardboiled egg and distribute pieces in soup plates. Pour soup over egg, sprinkle with paprika, and serve.   *Serves 4*

Calf's Head Soup

This is a whole day's project, it would seem, but it's not as difficult as it looks. Although you can buy it under the name of "mock turtle soup," because the flavor is reminiscent of turtle, the homemade kind is simply luscious. If you plan to freeze some of it, omit the hardboiled eggs and wine, and add them after you have thawed the soup. Some people used to add a piece of tripe to this, but we never did. If you use the tripe, add it to the calf's head or veal at the beginning, then cut it up into small squares and add them to the soup.

1 calf's head, or
  1 large veal knuckle (4 or 5 pounds), with meat on it
2 pounds honeycomb tripe (optional)
Water to cover
1 onion, stuck with 10 or 12 cloves
1 bay leaf
2 teaspoons Worcestershire sauce

Salt and pepper to taste
2 medium-sized potatoes, cubed
2 carrots, scraped and sliced
2 tablespoons butter
2 tablespoons flour
2 hardboiled eggs, sliced
1 lemon, sliced very thin
4 tablespoons sherry or currant wine

You will have to order the calf's head in advance, since most butchers no longer carry them. Have him cut the head in half, skin it for you, and remove the ears. (It's easier to use a veal knuckle, and you can't taste the difference!)

Wash calf's head, or veal knuckle, and tripe if you use it, removing all gristle. Put it into a deep kettle, and cover with cold water. Bring to boiling and skim. Cover and simmer for about 3 hours, or until meat falls from bones. Add clove-studded onion, bay leaf, Worcestershire sauce, salt, and pepper. Boil for 20 minutes. Strain. Fish out meat and cut into bite-sized pieces. Add potatoes and carrots, and boil for 20 minutes more, or until vegetables are tender.

Make a roux with butter and flour—mixing them together thoroughly. Add a little of the soup to roux, then place in soup kettle, stirring until soup thickens. Correct seasoning. Slice hardboiled eggs and lemon and add to soup, together with wine. Serve at once.   *Serves 6 to 8*

Snapper Soup

Such excitement as prevailed at our house one summer! While draining the pond, the men found a huge snapping turtle. They were afraid of it, but kept tempting it with sticks, which were pretty long, I can assure you. When my father learned what was going on he said, "Don't bother it, I've heard

tell that they make wonderful sup! Somebody fetch me the axe."
He managed somehow to get close enough to it to cut off its
head, which was a feat in itself, and hung it in the woodshed.
My mother tried to refuse to cook it, saying she didn't know
how—she couldn't bear to touch the horrible thing—so he said
he'd cook it himself. At that threat to her domain, she weak-
ened, and said that if he cleaned it, she would try cooking it.
Whereupon he set off in the wagon to see our next-door neighbor, Chake (a mile away!) and find out how to do it. This old
man, then in his eighties, said they often used to cook turtles
in the old days, and volunteered to come over. "But you must
let it hang for a day, anyvays," he said.

On the morrow, over he came, and he and Pop threw the
turtle into Mother's copper wash kettle, and put it on to boil in
the summer kitchen. After a while they removed it, took off the
shells, and took out whatever didn't look fit to eat, and brought
it in to Mom. Old Chake came in to supervise. They put the
well-washed shell into the bottom of the soup kettle, placed
the meat, cut into small portions, on top, and covered the
whole with water. To this they added sliced onion, some whole
cloves, a couple of bay leaves, some peppercorns, and a tablespoonful of salt. Then they allowed it to simmer for two hours.
By now the smell was so tantalizing that we all hung around.
Mom fished out the meat and the shell, strained the soup, and
put the cut-up meat back into the broth. Then she thickened
it with butter and flour, and got up enough nerve to taste it.
"Ach," she said, "it's chust like calf's head sup," whereupon
she added some sliced hardboiled egg, small pieces of lemon,
and a little wine, tasted it again, and smacked her lips. "Yes
vell," she grumbled, "vhen I make avay all this dreck—I never
in all my life had such a schmutzy (messed-up, dirty) kitchen!
Then ve'll eat." And so we did, with gusto.

After that we watched in vain for more snappers, but we
never did find another. So if you ever find a snapping turtle
you'll know just how to proceed!

Pepper Pot Soup

This is sometimes called "Philadelphia Pepper Pot," so it probably originated in Philadelphia, but it is equally popular among the Pennsylvania Dutch.

4 pounds tripe (honeycomb or plain, or half and half)
1 veal knuckle (about 4 pounds), with meat on it
Water
1 onion, chopped
2 carrots, sliced
1 bay leaf
3 stalks celery, diced
2 tablespoons chopped parsley
Salt and pepper
Dash of Tabasco
3 or 4 potatoes, cubed

Wash tripe thoroughly, cover with cold water, and simmer at least 4 hours. (You can't overcook tripe, the French say, so cook it longer if possible. You could do this the day before.) Cool tripe and cup it into ½-inch squares. Wash veal knuckle, cover with cold water and bring to a boil. Keep skimming the soup until all scum is removed. Simmer about 2 hours or until meat falls from bone. Remove meat and cut into bite-sized pieces. Strain broth, add chopped onion, bay leaf, celery, and parsley, reserving 2 teaspoons parsley for garnish. Add salt, pepper, and Tabasco to taste. Simmer about 1 hour, then add cubed potatoes and sliced carrots. Cook gently until vegetables are soft, but not mushy—about 20 minutes. Return veal and tripe to pot and simmer to blend flavors. Taste and correct seasoning.

We usually made suet dumplings or plain ein lauf (see Index) to go into this. They are dropped into the hot soup and simmered for a few minutes. Garnish each soup plate with a little of the chopped parsley and serve at once. *Serves 4 to 6*

Lamb and Barley Soup

1 lamb bone with meat on it, or 1 pound shoulder of lamb
Water to cover
1 medium onion, sliced
3 stalks of celery, leaves and root, sliced
1 cup barley, rinsed in cold water
1 12-ounce can tomatoes
⅛ teaspoon basil (optional)
1 teaspoon salt
⅛ teaspoon pepper
Pinch of thyme

Cover lamb with cold water. Add onion, celery, and rinsed barley. Bring to a boil. Skim frequently until scum is removed. Simmer about 2 hours, or until meat falls off bone, stirring occasionally, to keep barley from sticking. Remove meat from broth, and cut it up, discarding bones and gristle. Place meat back in pot with tomatoes and seasonings and cook on low heat 15 minutes longer.   *Serves 4*

Salmon Soup

1 can salmon	1 tablespoon butter
1 quart milk	Salt and pepper
	Pinch of thyme

Pick over salmon, removing skin and bones, and break fish into very small pieces. Add milk, butter, and seasonings. Heat to boiling, and serve at once.   *Serves 4*

Baked Bean Soup

We made this soup from leftover baked beans and it was surprisingly good. Sometimes we eked it out with a can of tomatoes, but usually we made it "chust so."

1 quart baked beans, or	2 tablespoons butter
1 can baked beans	2 tablespoons flour
1 onion, minced	Salt and pepper to taste
6 to 8 cups water	1 or 2 frankfurters, sliced
	Butter for browning

Combine beans and onion, cover with water, and cook until beans are completely mushy. Strain, or put through a food mill. Mix butter and flour well, add a little of the soup to the paste and then place in pot. Season with salt and pepper, heat just to boiling and serve.

Brown frankfurter slices in butter, and float on top of soup.
                                                          Serves 4

CHAPTER II

From the Butcher's Wagon (Meats)

In Pennsylvania Dutch country a loud, clanging bell used to announce the arrival of the butcher's wagon two or three times a week. This was a signal for the children to gather around the tailgate, in anticipation of a snitch of bologna, Lebanon or plain, or even perhaps a slice of liverwurst. Since butchering on the farm took place only during the cold seasons of late fall and early winter, the fresh meat and spicy sausages were a welcome supplement to the menu.

Pork sausage, headcheese, scrapple, and blood sausage were made at home, and either canned or smoked, but the butcher's wagon carried different sausages. In addition to the Lebanon bologna, he often carried Thuringer, Bratwurst, salami, ham sausage, Cervelat, summer sausage, and the most delectable of all, Buckwurst. The small, white veal sausages called Buckwurst do not ship well, and freezing robs them of their delicately blended flavors of veal, parsley, chives, and milk, so that they have seldom been seen outside of the Dutch country, even to this day. They are still procurable at market in Lancaster during the winter months, and in a very few German neighborhoods in large cities. Brought to a simmer in a little water, and then delicately browned and served on toast, they are a gourmet experience.

Along the sides of the butcher's wagon were huge hooks, on

14

which the varied carcasses were displayed, as well as a rack holding the knives, saw, and cleavers. The floor of the wagon served as the butcher's block, and the "aufschnitt" (cold cuts) were temptingly displayed on a shelf at the rear. The children's mouths watered at the sight of these, while the butcher carefully sharpened his knife and patiently awaited the housewife's decision.

In the spring, veal and lamb were abundant, since every farmer could get "cash money" by selling off some of the calves and lambs which he had not time to butcher himself. The beef was tough, since it was newly killed and not hung, but beef with a little "chaw" in it tasted fine after the soft canned and salted meats of the winter. Then too, panning, stewing, and pot roasting have always been the preferred ways of cooking beef in the cuisine of the region, so the toughness wasn't a problem. It is almost unbelievable to us now, but liver, sweetbreads, kidneys, or heart were frequently "thrown in" for good customers, since they were not much in demand.

There was no refrigeration on the wagon, and during the late spring and early autumn, as well as during the summer, the flies clustered around as soon as the butcher removed the cheesecloth covers to permit the viewing of his wares. Chicken was never on the wagon, because any self-respecting housewife raised her own, even if she lived in the town or village.

The butcher wagon no longer visits the towns, since every supermarket and grocery store carries either fresh or frozen meats, but a few old-timers still make the rounds of the outlying farms, especially those farms of the Plain People who do not own automobiles. Even they, however, find meat at the markets and there is little call for door-to-door services. But whether the food be bought at the supermarket, at market or at the local grocery, it is still prepared in the old ways, with the special care and the seasonings which give Pennsylvania Dutch cookery its unique flavor.

BEEF

Pot Roast with Potato Pancakes

2 tablespoons lard or other shortening
Flour
3 to 4 pounds chuck or brisket of beef
½ teaspoon pepper
2 teaspoons salt
1 large onion, sliced
2 stalks celery with leaves, sliced

1 clove garlic, crushed
3 carrots, sliced
1 quart stewed tomatoes (may be canned)
1¼ cup water
⅛ teaspoon each (optional): basil, thyme, rosemary, and marjoram
¼ teaspoon ginger
1 tablespoon sugar

Melt lard. Flour the meat, add pepper and salt, rubbing in well. Brown meat on all sides in fat along with sliced onion, celery, garlic, and carrots. Add tomatoes, 1 cup water, herbs, ginger, and sugar. Cover and simmer for 35 to 40 minutes per pound of meat. Remove meat to warm platter. The gravy should be cooked down, but if not quite thick enough, add 1 tablespoon of flour mixed with ¼ cup cold water and stirred until smooth. Taste, and correct seasoning. (You may need more salt.) Serve vegetable gravy in large gravy boat or soup bowl to pour over the potato pancakes, a traditional accompaniment to this dish.   *Serves 6 to 8*

Raw Potato Pancakes:

These are now available in a packaged mix which makes delicious pancakes if you add a little grated onion to them. If you want to start from scratch, here is the recipe:

3 large potatoes
1 egg, beaten
4 tablespoons flour

½ teaspoon baking powder
¾ teaspoon salt
¼ teaspoon grated onion

Shortening for frying

Peel and grate potatoes, then drain in sieve. (You should have about a cup of potato.) Beat egg, add rest of ingredients, except shortening, and let stand for about ten minutes. Mixture will darken, but this doesn't matter. Fry by teaspoonfuls in about ¼ inch of hot fat, keeping pancakes very thin. (I usually use a fork to spread them out.) Brown on both sides, and serve at once.   *Serves 4*

Sauerbraten mit Grumbere Kloess
(SOUR BEEF WITH POTATO DUMPLINGS)

4 or 5 pounds beef (chuck or rump)
½ cup vinegar
1 onion, sliced
1 bay leaf
3 or 4 peppercorns
Water

Flour
Pepper and salt to taste
Dash of nutmeg
Shortening for browning
2 large onions, sliced
4 or 5 carrots, sliced
1 tablespoon sugar

10 to 12 gingersnaps, crumbled

Place meat in glass or china bowl. Add vinegar, onion, bay leaf, peppercorns, and enough water to cover meat. Keep in refrigerator at least 2 days, turning once or twice in the marinade. Remove meat, dry, rub with flour, pepper, salt, and nutmeg, and brown on all sides in shortening. Add onions and carrots, and brown slightly. Then add about 2 cups of marinade. Cover and simmer for 40 minutes per pound of meat, or until tender. When tender, remove meat. Add sugar and crumbled gingersnaps to liquid. Correct for seasoning—you may need more sugar or salt. Cook, stirring constantly, until gravy thickens. Serve immediately, sliced and surrounded by the following:

Grumbere Kloess
(POTATO DUMPLINGS)

6 large potatoes
3 eggs
1 cup flour
½ cup bread crumbs

2 teaspoons salt
⅛ teaspoon nutmeg
Croutons (½-inch squares of bread fried in butter), optional

2 quarts salted water (approx.)

Boil potatoes, and put them through a ricer or a food mill. Beat eggs well, combine with flour, bread crumbs, salt, and nutmeg. Shape potato mixture into dry balls around croutons. (They should be stiff enough to hold their shape.) Add more bread crumbs if they are not quite dry. Drop balls into slowly boiling salted water. They will sink to the bottom, and then rise. After they rise to the surface, boil for about 3 minutes. (If you are at all in doubt about the dryness, try one ball first.) *Serves 6 to 8*

Geschtuffte Kraut mit Noodles
(STUFFED CABBAGE WITH NOODLES)

Sauce:

1 onion, chopped
2 tablespoons butter or margarine
1 teaspoon salt
1 teaspoon pepper

⅛ teaspoon basil (optional)
1 quart tomato sauce
4 tablespoons sugar
¼ cup lemon juice, or vinegar
⅛ teaspoon thyme

Simmer chopped onion in the butter until soft but not browned. Add rest of ingredients, and let simmer for 30 to 40 minutes.

Short Cut:

Add 4 tablespoons sugar and ¼ cup lemon juice or vinegar to 1 10½-ounce can of meatless spaghetti sauce.

Cabbage:

1 head cabbage
Water to cover
1 pound ground beef (chuck or round)
1 teaspoon salt
¼ teaspoon pepper
1 tablespoon onion, chopped very fine
1 teaspoon parsley, chopped

2 slices bread, soaked in 3 to 4 teaspoons milk
1 teaspoon Worcestershire sauce
Dash of Tabasco or hot pepper sauce
1 cup cooked rice (may be instant type)

Remove hard core of cabbage with sharp knife, leaving leaves intact. Place whole head in boiling water in large pan or pressure cooker and steam just enough to wilt leaves. Peel off 10 or 12 leaves.

Mix rest of ingredients. Lay cabbage leaves on flat surface, and divide stuffing among them—about 2 teaspoonfuls to each. Tightly fold each leaf over filling. Place the little bundles in large skillet or electric fry pan, seam side down. Pour sauce over packages, cover, bring to a boil, and simmer for 50 to 60 minutes, or until tender.

Serves 5 to 6

Geschmeltze Noodles:

Most "boughten" noodles are as light and delicate as the homemade ones used to be. Cook the noodles according to the package directions. While they are cooking, crumble a few raw noodles (about 2 tablespoonfuls) and fry them in butter until they are brown and crisp. Sprinkle over the top of the boiled noodles for a true Dutch flavor, and you'll have "geschmeltze noodles."

Klopps
(MEAT BALLS)

1 pound hamburger or ground beef	1 small onion, chopped
3 slices stale bread, soaked in milk	1 egg
	Pepper and salt to taste
	Butter or lard for frying

Place hamburger in medium-sized bowl. Squeeze out bread, and mix thoroughly with meat. Add rest of ingredients except butter and form into patties. (If mixture is too moist, add a few bread crumbs until it holds its shape.) Fry in butter or lard.   *Serves 4 to 6*

Fricadellen

2 or 3 cups leftover beef or veal	2 or 3 slices bread, soaked in water
½ small onion, chopped	Butter or lard for frying
1 egg	Dash of Worcestershire sauce or
1 tablespoon chopped parsley	1 teaspoon catsup (optional)
Salt and pepper	

Grind beef or veal, or combination of both. Add onion, egg, parsley, salt, and pepper to taste, and enough soaked bread to shape. A little Worcestershire sauce or catsup may be added to give them zip. Mix thoroughly. Fry in butter just long enough to brown both sides.   *Serves 4*

Rundestik mit Zwievele
(ROUND STEAK AND ONIONS)

2 tablespoons flour
Salt and pepper to taste
1 teaspoon paprika
1 slice round steak
(about ½ inch thick)

2 large onions
1 can tomatoes
Lard or other shortening for
browning

Mix flour with salt, pepper, and paprika. Using edge of a saucer, or your hands, pound flour into meat until well covered. Brown meat on both sides in lard or other shortening. Add sliced onions, and cook until the onions are brown but not burned. Pour tomatoes over meat, cover closely, and cook at low heat until meat is tender —about ½ hour, stirring occasionally.   *Serves 4 to 6*

Stuffed Flank Steak

1 flank steak (about 2 pounds)
Meat tenderizer
4 slices bread, torn into small
pieces
1 tablespoon melted butter, or
margarine
½ teaspoon salt

⅛ teaspoon pepper
½ cup chopped celery
1 small onion, minced
1 egg
Flour
Shortening for browning
Water

Trim off tail of steak, and freeze for stewing or soup. Score surface of steak on both sides in a diamond pattern, and sprinkle with tenderizer, as label on container directs.

Mix bread, melted butter, salt, pepper, celery, onion, and egg and spread evenly on steak, leaving about one inch at sides. Roll up like a jelly roll; secure with skewers or toothpicks. Sprinkle lightly with flour, and brown in large kettle with tight lid. Add 1 cup water, cover and simmer for about 1½ hours, or until tender, Remove toothpicks or skewers.

Mix 1 tablespoon flour with 1 tablespoon water, stir into liquid in kettle, and cook, stirring constantly until thickened. Use more water if necessary to achieve proper consistency.

Sometimes this recipe was varied by laying several hot sausages of the knockwurst variety in the very center of the steak before rolling. When sliced, this makes a very appetizing-looking dish.

Serves 4 to 6

Baked Elephant's Foot

This dish was usually concocted from the meat left over after making vegetable or chicken soup. Where the name elephant's foot comes from I have no idea.

4 medium-sized raw potatoes, diced
2 medium-sized onions, diced
1 carrot, diced
1 can peas (my recipe says "or not"—meaning optional!)

2 stalks of celery, chopped
Salt and pepper to taste
2 pounds any kind of boiled meat or chicken
2 cups broth

Put potatoes in greased two-quart casserole; place other vegetables on top, seasoning to taste. Pour meat broth over raw vegetables, place meat on top, and bake at 350° for 45 minutes, or until potatoes are soft. (If you have no broth, dissolve two bouillon cubes in two cups of water.)

Serves 4 to 6

Süss un' Sour Ox Zunge
(SWEET AND SOUR TONGUE)

1 smoked tongue
4 bay leaves
1 teaspoon peppercorns

1 teaspoon whole cloves
1 slice onion
Cold water to cover

Wash tongue, place in deep kettle with seasonings, add water, and let simmer until tender—2 to 4 hours, depending on size of tongue. (Much less time in pressure cooker! 55 minutes with steam at Cook position.) Remove tongue from brine, pull off outer skin, cut off root, and put back in brine to cool. Slice on diagonal, and serve with the following sweet and sour sauce.

Sauce:

½ cup sugar
1 tablespoon flour
1 cup of the tongue stock brought to a boil

¼ cup vinegar
½ teaspoon salt
⅛ teaspoon pepper
½ cup raisins

Melt sugar in frying pan, simmering until it caramelizes, or turns a light brown. (The easiest way to do this is to rock the pan gently.) Using wooden spoon, add flour and stir. Remove from fire and very gradually add boiling liquid, then vinegar and seasonings. Sauce will tend to lump at first, but never mind. Put it back over a slow fire and stir until all lumps are melted. Taste and correct seasonings. Add raisins and stir again. If sauce is too thick, add a little more stock. Pour sauce over tongue and serve.   *Serves 8 to 10*

Beef Schtew mit Kloess
(BEEF STEW WITH DUMPLINGS)

3 to 4 pounds beef (shoulder, rump, or steak ends)
Flour to dredge—about ¼ cup
1 teaspoon paprika
Salt and pepper to taste
2 tablespoons shortening (vegetable or beef fat)
1 small onion
1 small turnip
3 stalks (and leaves) celery

4 carrots, sliced
1 quart tomatoes, or 1 can tomatoes
1½ to 2 cups water
6 potatoes, peeled and quartered
⅛ teaspoon basil
⅛ teaspoon garlic salt
⅛ teaspoon thyme
1 teaspoon parsley

Cut beef into cubes about 1½ to 2 inches. (Do not discard bones.) Dredge meat with flour, paprika, pepper, and salt. Brown on all sides in fat. Add onion, turnip, celery, and carrots and brown with meat, stirring frequently, until vegetables turn a golden brown. Add tomatoes and bones, lower heat and let simmer about 1½ hours until meat is well cooked and tender. Add enough water to keep meat well covered and to have enough broth for dumplings. Remove bones and discard. Add potatoes, basil, garlic salt, thyme, and parsley and boil until potatoes are tender—about 25 to 30 minutes.

Check level of broth. Be sure it comes about 1 inch above meat and vegetables—if not, add more water and simmer to blend. About 15 minutes before serving, correct seasoning, add dumplings, and boil 15 minutes longer. Stew should now be quite thick. If not, after removing dumplings, meat, and vegetables, thicken with 2 teaspoons flour dissolved in ¼ cup cold water. Bring to boil, pour over stew and serve at once.

Dumplings:

1 egg	½ cup cold water
1 teaspoon salt	1½ cups flour

Beat egg, add salt and water, and mix with flour, beating until batter is smooth. Drop by tablespoonfuls onto hot stew. Do not cover. Cook for 15 minutes.   *Serves 8 to 10*

Bouva Shenkel
(SHANK OF BEEF)

Bouva shenkel is always accompanied by potato dumplings— potatoes enclosed in dough and steamed. Small wonder that there are so many stylish stouts among the Pennsylvania Dutch!

Meat:

3 to 4 pounds shank or rump of beef

Cover beef with cold water, add salt and pepper to taste, and half an onion, diced. Cook slowly until tender, about 1½ hours, depending upon size of cut. While meat cooks, make the filling for the dumplings.

Dumpling Filling:

4 or 5 potatoes, pared and sliced	2 tablespoons parsley, chopped
Salted water to cover	½ onion, minced
1 tablespoon butter	Salt and pepper to taste
3 eggs	

Cook sliced potatoes in salted water until soft. Drain and place in bowl. Add butter, parsley, onion, salt, and pepper. Beat eggs slightly and add to mixture. Mix well and let cool.

Dumpling Dough:

Make up 1 pie-crust recipe (may use packaged mix). Roll out, not too thin, and cut into circles 8 to 10 inches in diameter. Spread potato mixture over the circles, wet edges with a little cold water on your fingers, press together and crimp edges closed with a fork.

Skim as much fat as possible from meat, bring to a slow boil, and drop in dumplings, one at a time, taking care to keep broth boiling. Cover closely and boil for 20 minutes.

Gravy:

In a little butter, brown the cubes of bread made from two slices with crusts removed. Add about ½ cup of milk and stir together.

Slice meat, surround it with the little half-moon dumplings, and pour gravy over all. *Serves 6 to 8*

Sour Hash

2 or 3 cups leftover beef, any kind
Shortening for browning
2 large onions, sliced
Water to cover
1 tablespoon vinegar

2 teaspoons sugar
Pepper and salt to taste
Dash of Tabasco, or hot pepper sauce
1 tablespoon flour, mixed with a little water

Chop leftover beef and brown in skillet with hot fat. Add onions and about 1 cup or more of water to cover. When liquid reaches the boil, add vinegar, sugar, pepper, salt, and Tabasco. Pour in mixture of flour and water. Boil till thickened.

Note from the donor of the recipe (spelling and punctuation unchanged): "Make mashed potatoes with this, and you'll have a good dinner for a change, as well as useing up left over meat. You don't need very much meat to make this as sometimes I only had ½ cup or a little more whatever you have left if there isn't much fat use a little butter." What she meant was that the dish would be a change, not that I'd have a "good meal for a change," I trust!

Sauerkraut Dutch Pie

Shortening for browning
1 pound ground beef, made into patties
1 quart fresh or canned sauerkraut

1 cup sliced olives
1 quart stewed tomatoes
¾ pound sausage meat, made into patties

Brown meat patties, and layer as follows: make a layer of beef patties, spread over it the sauerkraut, then olives, and finally tomatoes. Top with sausage patties. Put dish in oven and bake at 350° about 1 hour, until all flavors are blended. We often served scalloped noodles with this. *Serves 6 to 8*

Mohn Noodles
(SCALLOPED NOODLES WITH POPPY SEEDS)

1 cup cream	½ teaspoon celery salt
1 cup milk	2 tablespoons minced onion
¾ teaspoon salt	1 12-ounce package broad
1 teaspoon pepper	noodles, cooked in salted water
½ teaspoon poppy seeds	for 15 minutes

Mix all ingredients except noodles. Put noodles in an oblong, shallow baking dish. Pour milk mixture over them. Bake 25 minutes at 350°.

Serves 4

Beef and Horseradish Sauce

In my childhood we grew our own horseradish roots down near the trickle of water that ran off from the springhouse. The roots, of all shapes and sizes, were dug, scrubbed, peeled, and then grated. Such weeping when the fiery fumes arose, and such an ouching when knuckles were scraped! Most of the grated horseradish was dried for the winter, but some of it was mixed with vinegar, water, and a smidgen of sugar, and placed in a special jar for the table. "Pass auf!" (look out)—it was strong!

3 pounds beef—brisket, round, or rump	1 medium-sized onion, sliced
Water to cover	1 teaspoon salt
2 stalks celery, sliced	⅛ teaspoon pepper
	1 head cabbage

Wash meat, cover with cold water, bring to boil. Add rest of ingredients, except cabbage; lower heat, and simmer about 3 hours, or until meat is fork tender. Skim frequently during first hour. Cut cabbage into eighths, and add during last hour of cooking. Serve with boiled potatoes and horseradish sauce.

Serves 6 to 8

Horseradish Sauce

2 tablespoons butter or margarine	1 cup liquid from boiled beef, or water
2 tablespoons flour	2 to 4 tablespoons horseradish

The amount of horseradish used depends upon the strength of the horseradish, as well as your own taste.

Melt butter, add flour, remove from heat, and slowly add liquid from boiled beef, stirring constantly to remove all lumps. Return to fire and cook until sauce is thick and smooth. Add horseradish, and serve hot.

Scrambled Brains

1 pair brains	3 eggs
Water	2 teaspoons milk
½ teaspoon lemon juice or vinegar	2 tablespoons butter
	Salt and pepper to taste

Remove all membrane and blood from brains and soak them in cold water about 1 hour. Parboil in fresh water, to which has been added the lemon juice or vinegar. Let liquid just come to boil, then drain brains.

Break meat in small pieces into a bowl, add eggs and milk, and beat together lightly. Heat butter in a spider, add mixture, lower heat, and cook as for scrambled eggs. Sprinkle with salt and pepper and serve at once. *Serves 2 to 3*

Baked Hash

2 cups raw potatoes, chopped	½ onion, minced
3 or 4 cups cold cooked beef, ground	1 teaspoon salt
	⅛ teaspoon pepper
2 eggs	⅛ teaspoon paprika

Peel and chop potatoes; stew them in water for 5 minutes. Do not drain. Add meat together with more water if needed to make a good moist mixture. Stew 10 minutes longer. Remove from fire, add beaten eggs, onion, salt, and pepper. Put hash into baking dish, and bake for 20 minutes at 400°. Sprinkle with paprika, and serve.

Serves 6 to 8

PORK

Souse or Sulz
(PICKLED PIG'S FEET)

Sulz in German means "pickled or salted meat," which became *souse* in Pennsylvania Dutch.

3 or 4 pig's feet
Water
1½ cups vinegar
12 peppercorns
1 bay leaf

6 whole cloves
½ to 1 tablespoon salt
2 pimientos, diced, or
   8 stuffed olives, chopped

Have butcher split pig's feet. Scrub them thoroughly and cover with cold water. Bring to boil, pour off water, and cover again with cold water. Add rest of ingredients, except pimiento, and simmer slowly for 2 hours. Remove pig's feet, and cut meat into small pieces, discarding bones. Strain broth, and put meat back into liquid, together with pimientos or olives, "for pretty." Pour into a loaf pan and refrigerate. Slice and serve cold. I never cared very much for this, but some people "vould hang themselves for it," and it looks nice when served with other cold meats.   *Serves 4*

Baked Leberwurst

1 pound liverwurst
1 medium onion, minced very
   fine
1 cup bread crumbs

½ teaspoon salt
½ teaspoon pepper
¼ to ½ cup water
2 slices bacon

Mix first 5 ingredients. Then add water slowly until mixture is fairly stiff. Line a bread pan with 2 halved slices of bacon. Add liverwurst mixture. Bake at 350° for 30 minutes. May be served hot or cold. (If you prefer a hotter dish, add a dash of Tabasco or hot pepper sauce.)   *Serves 4 to 6*

Pork Sausage

5 pounds lean pork
1 pound pork fat
2½ tablespoons salt
2 tablespoons freshly ground
pepper

1½ tablespoons powdered sage
½ teaspoon powdered ginger
(optional)

Put meat and fat through meat grinder on finest blade several times until very finely ground. Add seasonings. If you like a good hot sausage, be sure to include the ginger. Mix thoroughly, and form into patties. Put in small plastic bags for freezing. Makes 8 large or 10 small patties.

Rack of Pork with Cider Sauce

1 loin of pork
Salt and pepper to taste

12 whole cloves
3 tablespoons brown sugar

1 cup of cider, fresh or frozen

Season meat with salt and pepper. Score fat on pork and insert cloves, about 1 inch apart. Cover with brown sugar, and place in roasting pan. Pour cider in bottom of pan. Bake at 350° for 45 minutes per pound. During last half hour, baste frequently, to glaze.

Serves 6 to 8

Schnitz un' Knepp

Schnitz un' Knepp is a mixture of dried apples, brown sugar, ham, and little buttons of dough. "Knepp" is the dialect form of the German word for buttons, *Knöpfe*. ("Knepp" is spelled in many ways. Pennsylvania Dutch is a spoken, not written, language, and spellings, as well as pronunciations, differ in Berks, Lancaster, York, or Lebanon counties. I have tried to spell the words as phonetically as possible.) This dish was usually made when bread baking was in progress, and the housewife was too busy to do much more than "throw somesing into a kettle." It was never considered a company dish and only a "schussely" (sloppy) housewife would have fed it to guests, but it has now become very popular.

Soak about 2 cups of sliced, sweet schnitz (dried apples) in water to cover for several hours or overnight. Put a ham bone which still has some meat on it, or two ham hocks, into a deep kettle with a tight lid, cover with water, and boil until meat falls off the bone. Remove meat and cut into bite-sized pieces. Put ham back into the broth, add apples, and the water in which they were soaked, together with two tablespoonfuls of brown sugar. Boil for about 30 minutes, or until apples are soft and mushy.

About twenty minutes before serving time, drop small balls of yeast dough on top of the meat mixture, cover tightly, and don't peek for 15 minutes! Serve immediately. (The frozen bread or rolls now on the market will make excellent knepp. Thaw them, let rise as directed, form into little balls, and use as directed above.)

Some people use baking powder dumplings, but they are not true knepp. Fresh sliced apples may be used instead of the schnitz, if desired, but then the dish will not be authentic.   *Serves 6 to 8*

Pawn Hase
(SCRAPPLE)

Scrapple was always made on the farm at butchering time, in the old iron kettles, and was cooked in great quantities. Pennsylvania Dutch names derive, apparently, from the familiar. Lobster, for example, is called "schellhase," in colloquial German, because it looks like a rabbit made of shell; so scrapple (made from scraps) was called Pawn Hase, because the flavor resembles that of panned rabbit. True scrapple is made from a hog's head, plus any other small scraps of meat not used at butchering time. However, it can be made in small quantities, and when it is, it is far better than most commercial scrapple.

1 large meaty pork bone	1 cup yellow corn meal
(may be the rack left over	1 teaspoon salt
from roast loin of pork)	⅛ teaspoon thyme
Water	⅛ teaspoon sage
2 teaspoons cracked pepper	

Boil pork until meat falls from bone. (The more meat, the richer the scrapple.) Remove meat, fat and all, and chop with fine blade of grinder. Set aside. Measure 3 cups of liquid in which pork was boiled, or add enough water to it to make 3 cups. Heat to boiling. Mix corn meal and salt with 1 cup of cold water. Pour slowly into boiling liquid, stirring constantly. Add chopped meat, thyme, sage, and pepper. Cook until thickened, stirring frequently. Cover; continue cooking over *very* low heat for 10 more minutes. Pour into well-greased loaf pan. When cold, cut into ½-inch slices; pan fry in lightly greased frying pan until brown on both sides.

Serves about 14

Puddings
(MEAT PUDDING)

Puddings, never referred to in the singular for some peculiar reason, is similar to scrapple, but is all meat, with no corn meal. All the scraps from butchering—ears, lungs, and everything imaginable—are cut up very fine, covered with water, and put on to boil with salt and pepper, thyme, and a little sage. The meat, when tender, is placed in crocks or molds, and the broth is boiled down and poured over the top. The fat rises and forms a protective shield. This keeps all winter, in a cool place.

Sometimes, when the larder is running low, scrapple is made from this meat pudding. Usually puddings is simply sliced and fried as a meat dish for breakfast or supper.

Spareribs and Sauerkraut

| 1 rack of spareribs | 1 quart of sauerkraut, |
| Salt and pepper to taste | canned or fresh |

Do not let the butcher crack the bones of the spareribs. Place them in roasting pan, and dust with salt and pepper. Cut off one piece (about 2 inches) of ribs at smaller end, put it into a two-quart saucepan, and add sauerkraut. Bring to boil, and cook at least 1 hour, preferably longer, until kraut is a golden yellow. You may have to add water to keep it from sticking, but add just a little at a time. (The Pennsylvania Dutch do not insult sauerkraut by adding caraway seeds, or any seasoning other than the pork, and perhaps a little salt.)

One hour before serving, preheat oven to 350°, and bake rack of ribs for 50 minutes, or until crisp and brown.

Spareribs and sauerkraut are always served with mashed potatoes. The juice from the sauerkraut serves as gravy.   *Serves 6 to 8*

Pork Sausage with Cabbage and Potatoes

1 head cabbage, shredded
Salted water
10 to 12 small new potatoes, scraped and cut in half

1 pound pork sausages (small links)
Salt and pepper to taste

Cook cabbage in salted boiling water for 8 minutes. Boil potatoes until just done, not soft. Brown sausages slowly in a large spider and pour off all grease. Cover sausages with alternate layers of potato and cabbage, salt, and pepper. Cook over low heat for 30 minutes, invert onto a serving platter, and serve at once.

Serves 4 to 6

Pork Tenderloin with Sour Cream Gravy

1 slice bacon
1 tenderloin of pork (about 3 pounds), or boned loin of pork
Salt and pepper to taste
Flour

½ cup water
½ cup sour cream
Paprika
1 can or package of fried onion rings (optional)

Fry bacon until crisp, taking care not to let fat smoke or bacon become too brown. Remove and save. Slice pork into ½-inch slices, season with salt and pepper, and dredge lightly with flour. Brown slowly in bacon fat, 15 or 20 minutes. Cover and continue cooking slowly for another 20 to 25 minutes until well done. Remove to hot platter and keep warm.

To brown bits in pan, add 1 tablespoon flour and stir to blend. Add water, and stir constantly to prevent lumps (it will be thick). Remove from heat and add sour cream, stirring until well blended. Then heat just to boiling. Taste for seasoning.

Arrange tenderloin in a circle on a hot platter or on a bed of cooked noodles. Pour thickened gravy in center of circle. Sprinkle with paprika, and crumble the piece of bacon over it.

This is delicious served with fried onion rings, which can be placed attractively around the sour cream gravy. I use the canned or frozen rings. *Serves 6 to 8*

Loin of Pork with Peaches

3 pounds boned pork loin
Flour, salt, and pepper
3 to 4 tablespoons butter or
    margarine
1 teaspoon whole cloves

1 can peach halves
1 cup wine (currant, vermouth, or any other light wine)
¾ cup half-and-half or light cream

Slice pork into ½-inch slices and remove as much fat as possible. Dredge with flour and season with pepper and salt. Brown pork in butter on both sides in an iron spider over a low fire. Cover and cook another 20 minutes, using enough butter to prevent meat from sticking.

Put a whole clove in each peach half, and pour wine over the fruit. Heat just to boiling and taste. If too sour, add a little sugar. Drain peaches but save juice.

Arrange pork on hot platter, surrounded by peach halves. Add peach juice to brown bits in the spider. Stir and boil down until quite thick and syrupy. Gradually add cream, but do not allow it to boil. Pour this gravy over peaches and pork, and serve immediately, with noodles or potato pancakes. *Serves 6 to 8*

Geschtuffte Sou's Maw
(FILLED PIG STOMACH)

1 pig stomach
2 pounds pork sausage (bulk)
4 medium-sized potatoes, finely diced

1 small onion, minced
¼ teaspoon marjoram
⅛ teaspoon poultry seasoning
½ cup water

Wash stomach carefully, being sure all membranes are removed. Mix rest of ingredients, except water, and stuff stomach loosely. Sew or skewer it closed. Put on rack in roasting pan, adding water to pan. Cover and bake 2 hours in slow oven, about 325°. Uncover for last ½ hour and baste until stomach is crisp and nicely browned. Remove threads, cut in thick slices with very sharp knife and serve at once. *Serves 4 to 6*

Kraut un' Chops

When we wanted to characterize anything as especially Pennsylvania Dutch, we'd say, "Ay, that's as Dutch as sauerkraut," since sauerkraut seems to be the epitome of Pennsylvania Dutch cuisine. (But we ate cabbage in many other ways— slaw, creamed, sweet and sour, fried, and boiled with beef. Red cabbage was also extremely popular, cooked in the old German way, redolent of cloves and vinegar.)

Brown desired number of pork chops in their own fat in a hot spider. Cover with 1 quart sauerkraut, add ¼ cup water, cover tightly, and steam for 50 minutes, or until chops are well done. This dish was always served with mashed potatoes, and the golden-brown pan juice was dribbled over the potatoes instead of gravy.

VEAL

Geschtuffte Kalb's Herz
(STUFFED CALF'S HEART)

Wash and dry the calf's heart thoroughly, stuff with the following dressing and sew up the opening, or use skewers to fasten securely.

Stuffing:

1 onion, chopped	1 egg
2 stalks celery, diced	Salt and pepper
2 tablespoons butter	½ teaspoon poultry seasoning
4 slices of bread dipped in water	Flour
1 teaspoon parsley	Oil for browning
	Water

Lightly brown onion and celery in butter. Add bread, parsley, and egg. Mix thoroughly. Season with salt, pepper, and poultry seasoning. Mixture should be quite spicy, as beef heart is bland. Sprinkle heart with salt and pepper, dredge with flour, and brown on all sides in a little hot oil or fat. Place in deep pan, half cover with water and bake for 2 hours, or until tender. Or use pressure cooker—45 minutes with stem at Cook position.

Remove from broth, slice and serve. *Serves 4 to 6*

Kalb Flaisch Bot Bei
(VEAL POT PIE)

All kinds of pot pies are known to the Pennsylvania Dutch. Veal, chicken, rabbit, and lamb are used in this delicious dish. It is really a stew, with noodle-like dumplings. It differs greatly from English meat pies, which are also made in Dutch country, because it contains no potatoes, nor does it have a crust.

2 pounds veal, cut in pieces (may be loin, ribs, or breast)
Flour
1 teaspoon salt
⅛ teaspoon pepper
2 tablespoons butter
1 small onion, sliced

2 stalks celery (with leaves), diced
2 small carrots, sliced
2 teaspoons parsley, dried or fresh
Dash of nutmeg
2 quarts water

Dredge meat with flour, salt, and pepper. Brown in butter on all sides in a 4-quart kettle. Add vegetables, parsley, and nutmeg and stir to brown. Cover meat and vegetables with water. Bring to boil, simmer uncovered until meat is tender—about 45 minutes. Taste and correct seasoning.

In the meantime, make the pot pie (as the noodle-dumplings are called).

Pot Pie:

2½ cups sifted flour
1 teaspoon salt

¼ scant cup shortening
⅔ cup *hot* stew stock or water

Mix flour, salt, and shortening until mixture resembles coarse meal. Add *hot* stock. Mix thoroughly. (The secret is in adding the liquid hot.) Roll very thin on floured surface and cut into squares. Drop squares into boiling stew and cook for 15 minutes. Serve at once.

You can buy pot-pie noodles now, but they are not as light or as thin as the homemade ones. *Serves 4 to 6*

Geschtuffte Kalb's Brust
(STUFFED BREAST OF VEAL)

Breast of veal (2 to 4 pounds)
1 onion, chopped
2 stalks celery, chopped
3 tablespoons lard or butter
2 chicken livers, or
   1 slice calf's liver, chopped
   fine

4 or 5 slices stale bread, dipped
   in warm water and wrung out
2 tablespoons chopped parsley
Salt and pepper
Pinch of nutmeg
1 egg

Have your butcher make a pocket in the breast of veal, or do it yourself—just cut into the thicker part, and lift up the top skin.

Fry onion and celery in fat until light brown, then add chopped liver. Cook just until liver turns brown, then remove from fire. Add bread, parsley, salt, and pepper to taste, and nutmeg. Break in egg and mix thoroughly.

Stuff filling in pocket of veal and sew or secure with skewers. Dust meat lightly with additional salt and pepper, and place in roasting pan. Bake at 325° for about 25 minutes to the pound.

This is usually served with apple sauce and noodles. *Serves 6 to 7*

Kalb's Chelly
(JELLIED VEAL)

1 envelope plain gelatine
½ cup cold water
2 cups soup stock, or canned
   chicken broth, or bouillon
2 cups cold veal, chopped fine
⅛ teaspoon vinegar

½ teaspoon Worcestershire sauce
¼ teaspoon sage
⅛ teaspoon nutmeg
Dash of Tabasco
Salt and pepper to taste
2 hardboiled eggs, chopped

1 teaspoon chopped parsley

Soak gelatin in cold water. Bring soup stock to boil and stir until gelatine is dissolved. Add cold veal and seasonings except parsley; cook about 5 minutes to blend flavors. Dip a 1-quart mold or loaf pan in cold water. Alternate layers of meat, chopped egg, and parsley. Pour any remaining liquid over mixture. Refrigerate at least 3 hours. *Serves 2*

Sweetbreads in Cream

1 pair calf's sweetbreads	¼ teaspoon paprika
Water, salted and plain	½ teaspoon chopped parsley,
1 tablespoon flour	fresh or dried
1 tablespoon butter	½ teaspoon sherry or currant
1 cup milk	wine
Salt and pepper to taste	2 or 3 slices of toast

Yolk of a hardboiled egg

Soak sweetbreads in cold, salted water for 15 minutes. Boil gently in salted water for 15 minutes. Place in cold water, and remove all membrane. Make thick white sauce (see Index) of flour, butter, and milk. Add salt, pepper, paprika, parsley, and sherry, then sweetbreads. Serve on toast, decorated with egg yolk put through a sieve.

Serves 2 to 3

Breaded Veal Schnitzel

1 veal steak (1 to 1½ pound)	½ teaspoon paprika
1 inch thick, or 4 veal chops	1 egg, beaten slightly
Dry bread crumbs	Lard or other shortening for
Salt and pepper to taste	browning

¼ cup sour cream

Wipe veal with damp cloth. Dip first into dry bread crumbs, to which seasonings have been added, then into beaten egg, then into crumbs again. Fry on both sides in lard for 15 to 20 minutes, depending upon thickness of veal, being careful not to let crumbs become too brown. Remove to warm platter. To brown bits left in frying pan, add sour cream and bring just to a boil. Pour over veal and serve at once.

Noodles "go good" with any veal dish, and usually accompany this one.

Serves 4

Veal Loaf

3 cups chopped cooked veal	Salt and pepper to taste
1 cup bread crumbs	⅛ teaspoon sage
1 egg	¼ teaspoon parsley

1 tablespoon butter

Mix all ingredients except butter, adding more bread crumbs, if needed, to make mixture stick together. Press mixture tightly into loaf pan and dot with butter. Bake at 350° for 45 minutes. May be served hot or cold. *Serves 3 to 4*

Geschtuffte Kalb's Leber
(STUFFED WHOLE CALF'S LIVER)

1 whole calf's liver
Bread stuffing (see Index)

Salt, pepper, and flour
3 slices bacon
½ cup water

Wash liver in cold water. Make pocket in thickest part, or ask your butcher to do it. Fill pocket with bread stuffing. Salt and pepper the liver and dredge with flour. Place bacon strips over liver, put it in roasting pan and add water. Bake at 400° for 15 minutes, or until nicely browned, then lower heat to 350° and bake for 45 minutes longer. Slice thinly and serve at once.

I like to make a cream gravy with this, which simply consists of adding 1 tablespoon flour mixed with ¼ cup of water to the pan drippings, stirring until all lumps are out, then adding ½ cup thin cream, and 1 teaspoon chopped parsley. *Serves 4 to 6*

LAMB

Lamb Schtew mit Spätzele
(LAMB STEW WITH EGG DUMPLINGS)

2 tablespoons lard or other shortening
3 to 4 pounds lamb shoulder or shank, cubed
2 small onions
1 clove garlic, minced
1 turnip, cubed (optional)

3 or 4 carrots, sliced
2 stalks celery, diced
1 tablespoon chopped parsley
1 bay leaf (optional)
¼ teaspoon pepper
1 teaspoon salt
3 cups water

Melt shortening, add lamb, onions, and garlic; brown in large, heavy kettle. Add turnip, carrots, celery, parsley, bay leaf, pepper, and salt. When meat is browned, add water and stir well, dissolving all brown bits in bottom of pan. Cover and cook 1 hour at low heat. (You may have to add a little more water to keep stew from sticking and to cover the dumplings so that they will cook. You need at least 3 cups broth.) Fish out bay leaf before putting in dumpling dough.

Dumplings:

1 egg
1 teaspoon baking powder
Pinch of salt

½ teaspoon minced parsley
Flour, enough to make a very
   stiff batter—about ½ cup

Beat egg and add to rest of ingredients. Drop by teaspoonfuls into boiling stew, cover and cook for 5 minutes. Serve immediately.

Serves about 6

Plain Lamb Stew

We also made lamb stew in the same way as the above recipe, except that we added potatoes, quartered, instead of dumplings. The potatoes should be added at the same time as the other vegetables.

The meat was piled in the center of the platter, surrounded by vegetables and bordered with the feathery egg dumplings called spätzele (see Index).

Roast Lamb

1 leg of lamb, or rack, or loin,
   or ribs (about 6 to 7 pounds)
1 clove garlic
1 teaspoon salt
1 teaspoon pepper

Flour
2 tablespoons lard or other
   shortening
1 medium-sized onion
1 cup cold water (approx.)

Make several small pockets in meat and insert a small piece of garlic in each. (Don't forget where you put them! I usually mark the place I've hidden them with a toothpick. It is unpleasant to bite into even part of a clove of garlic!) Rub roast all over with salt and pepper, and dust lightly with flour. Place in a roasting pan, together with lard, and whole onion. Bake at 400° for 15 minutes, then lower heat to 350° and continue roasting for 25 minutes to the pound. (If you are one of the people who like roast lamb pink, roast only 15 minutes to the pound.) Baste meat with melted fat every 15 minutes or so. If you want roasted potatoes with this, and we always served them with lamb, take the required number of peeled potatoes, and add them to the pan about 1 hour before the roast will be done. Place meat and potatoes on warm platter, remove garlic bits and serve.

To make gravy, pour off all but two tablespoonfuls of fat from pan, add 2 tablespoonfuls of flour, place over heat, and stir vigorously to get all browned bits off pan. Add water, stirring again to get gravy nice and brown. Taste and correct seasoning.

With roast lamb we usually served the following sauce:

1 small bunch of mint (leaves only), minced	1 jar of currant jelly

In a small saucepan, heat jelly until it begins to soften. Add mint and stir. Place in serving dish and keep cold until ready to serve. It will jell to a quiver and look and taste somesing vunderful!

Serves 8 to 10

Housewife's complaint: "Such a day I've had! It's enough to put a body in a fret! Here I am, vis market, and either the cat wanted in, or the dog wanted out, and then comes Pop vis two bushels of peaches! It's no vunder I'm verhuddled and verdutzed!" (*Verhuddled* means "mixed up," and the best translation I can think of for *verdutzed* is "frustrated.")

CHAPTER III

From the Smokehouse (Cured Meats)

Ham and bacon, as well as chicken, were the mainstay of a farm wife's larder. When unexpected company or hired help came, you could always send one of the children out to kill a chicken or two, or get out the saw and cut off a thick slab of ham.

At breakfast, the smell of home-smoked bacon fried slowly in a spider was enough to waken any sleepyhead. In most Pennsylvania Dutch homes, it is not sliced as thin as commercial bacon and is seldom cooked as crisp as I like it, but is left undercooked enough to be chewy. Crisp bacon was used for decoration only and wasn't considered fit eating—too done!

In the early days, hams and bacon were always cured in the smokehouse over long-burning, smoldering hickory fires. Other meats were smoked as well—sausage links, tongues, venison, beef; sometimes a loin or rack of pork; and perhaps a duck or a goose for a special treat. When "patent smoke," a mixture of saltpeter and other ingredients, was put on the market, most farmers welcomed it because it involved only "schmiering" the mixture over the meats at regular intervals and meant much less work. But the die-hards still kept to the old-fashioned methods, and even now some old smokehouses are still in use, and frequently neighbors will go together on the smoking.

Hams smoked by this method require long periods of soaking and cooking, but they have a wonderfully unique flavor, and although the modern methods result in less shrinking and tenderer meat, the flavor is only faintly reminiscent of the pungent goodness of the old smoke-cured delicacies.

When the meats were finally cured, they were usually hung from the rafters in the attic with a piece of twine which was run through a large guard plate of tin to keep rats and mice from reaching the meat.

In recent times, smoked turkey has become fashionable, but to my knowledge smoked goose is seldom available. And what a fabulous dish it was, slow roasted with a delicate chestnut stuffing! For the last hour of cooking, it was transferred to another pan, placed in a very hot oven, and basted until every bit of fat was melted. The goose emerged a dark, glowing brown, with skin as crisp as cracklings. Gravy made from the pan drippings accompanied it.

Baked Ham

Now that hams are precooked the long overnight soaking they used to need is no longer necessary. However, I find that a short period of moist heat keeps the ham from drying out, and constant basting during the glazing period keeps it succulent.

½ ham (butt or shank)	2 tablespoons whole cloves
Water	1 cup brown sugar
	½ cup orange juice

Place ham in roasting pan. Add enough water to fill ¾ of pan. Place in 350° oven and bake 1 hour. Take from oven, and with a sharp knife remove all rind. (Save liquid in which ham was cooked for flavoring string beans, limas, ham and cabbage, or ham and peas.) Score fat on meat into diamonds, and stick a clove in center of each diamond. Sprinkle with brown sugar, patting it in carefully. Add orange juice and return to a 400° oven. Bake 15 minutes, then begin basting with orange juice. Baste every 5 minutes, until all brown sugar is melted and ham is nicely glazed—about one hour.

Serves 8 to 10

Ham, Peas, and Potatoes

1 ham bone
Ham stock or water to cover
4 to 6 potatoes, pared and
cubed

1 package frozen peas, or
1 medium-sized can of peas
Salt and pepper to taste

Place ham bone in a large kettle. Add either ham juice, saved
from baked ham, or water enough to cover. Put in cubed potatoes
and boil until potatoes are done but not mushy. Add peas, and
cook until done. Taste for seasoning, and add pepper and salt if
needed. Remove bone, slice off shreds of ham, and serve with peas
and potatoes.   *Serves 4*

Ham and Cabbage

1 ham bone, with some meat left
on it, or
1 small piece of smoked
pork butt

Ham stock or water to cover
1 head cabbage

Place ham or smoked butt in a large kettle with stock or water.
Bring to boil, and cook slowly until tender, skimming off as much
fat as possible. Quarter cabbage and add to ham. Cook until cabbage
is tender. Serve with boiled potatoes and horseradish, if desired.
                                                          Serves 4

Ham and Potatoes

This is one way to use up leftover ham. Every bit of ham
was always trimmed from the bone and saved, before the bone
was put into the soup kettle.

Ham slices
Cold boiled potatoes, sliced
Salt and pepper
2 tablespoons parsley
⅛ teaspoon onion juice or
onion salt

½ cup sour or sweet cream
½ cup bread crumbs
3 tablespoons grated cheese
(optional)

Slice ham remnants and make alternate layers of ham and
potatoes, sprinkling each layer with salt, pepper, parsley, and

onion juice. Pour sour cream over mixture, being careful not to do more than moisten it. Top with bread crumbs (and cheese, if desired). Bake at 350° for 20 to 25 minutes, just enough to blend flavors and brown top.   *Serves 3 to 4*

Fried Ham

1 slice ham, at least ¾-inch thick   Dash of ground cloves
Brown sugar to cover
   (about ¼ cup)

Score fat of ham; sear ham quickly on both sides in hot iron spider. Cover, and cook for 15 minutes over medium heat. Spread top of ham with brown sugar and sprinkle with cloves. Cover again, and cook until brown sugar has melted. Serve with its own juice. (If you don't care for fried foods, you can use your broiler—just add the brown sugar and cloves at the end of the cooking.) Be sure to serve every smidgen of the sauce because it is delicious.
Serves 4

Ham Loaf

2 cups cold chopped ham   1 cup bread crumbs
⅛ teaspoon pepper   Dash of Tabasco or
½ chopped medium-sized onion   hot pepper sauce
1 egg   Catsup

Mix ingredients except catsup and put in a loaf pan. Bake at 350° for ¾ hour or until nicely browned. Invert on platter and decorate with catsup. This is good either hot or cold.   *Serves 4*

Hot Ham Loaf

1 pound lean fresh pork   ½ cup milk
½ pound smoked ham   1 cup dry bread crumbs
1 egg   1 slice onion, minced
            Salt and pepper to taste

Sauce:
¾ cup brown sugar   ½ cup vinegar
1 tablespoon prepared mustard   ½ cup water

Grind pork and ham together, add rest of ingredients, and mold into a loaf. Mix sauce ingredients and pour over meat. Bake at 300° for 1 hour, basting occasionally.   *Serves 4*

Schpeck un' Beans
(HAM AND BEANS)

Schpeck really means "fat." A piece of salt pork, rather than ham, is sometimes used when the beans are cooked alone without potatoes. This dish was originally made with dried stringbeans, which required long cooking to get tender. It still tastes best when made with dried beans, or string beans which are not as young as they used to be!

1 piece smoked ham (about 2 pounds), or ham bone with meat
Water to cover

2 pounds beans, strung but not cut up
6 to 8 medium-sized potatoes, quartered

Salt and pepper to taste

Cover ham with cold water and bring to a boil. Add beans and cook 1 hour or until ham is tender and beans thoroughly wilted, adding more water if necessary. Add quartered potatoes, and continue cooking until potatoes are tender. Taste, and season with pepper and salt if needed.

The beans should be completely wilted, and there should be very little water remaining in kettle. Not many vitamins left, but what succulence!   *Serves 4 to 6*

Schinken und Käse Pie
(HAM AND CHEESE PIE)

1 medium-sized onion, chopped
3 celery stalks, diced
2 tablespoons butter or margarine
2 cups ground ham
Pinch dry mustard

⅛ teaspoon horseradish
1 baked pie shell
2 ripe tomatoes, peeled and sliced thin
1 cup grated cheese (Cheddar or Swiss—or ½ cup of each)

¼ cup dry bread crumbs

Sauté onion and celery in butter until soft but not brown. Stir in ham, mustard, and horseradish. Put half of this into pie shell, add tomato slices, and cover with half of the cheese. Next put another layer of ham mixture, sprinkle with bread crumbs, and top with rest of cheese. Bake at 350° about 25 minutes, until cheese is melted and top is browned.

Serves 4 to 6

Macaronie und Schinken
(HAM AND MACARONI)

1½ cups elbow macaroni	Salt and pepper to taste
1 tablespoon flour	Pinch basil
1 tablespoon butter or	Pinch thyme
margarine	2 cups cooked ham, cubed
2 cups milk	¼ cup dry bread crumbs

Cook macaroni according to package directions, but keep it firm —cook about 10 minutes. Make a thin white sauce (see Index), using flour, butter, and milk. Add seasonings, taste and correct.

Grease baking dish or casserole. Put in a layer of macaroni, a layer of ham, a layer of cream sauce. Repeat until the ham is "all" (used up). Top with dry bread crumbs. Bake at 350° for 30 to 35 minutes, until top is nicely browned and mixture is bubbling.

Serves 4

Ham and Noodles

Substitute ½ package of noodles for the macaroni, and cook as directed for ham and macaroni.

Schinken un' Grumbere Pie
(HAM AND POTATO PIE)

3 cups ham, cubed	⅛ teaspoon pepper
1 tablespoon ham or bacon fat	½ teaspoon prepared mustard
½ slice onion, minced	1 tablespoon chopped parsley
1 tablespoon flour	1 cup mashed potatoes (may be
1 cup milk	leftover, or packaged mix)

Cut up ham, being sure to remove all fat and gristle. Heat fat in small frying pan, add onion, then flour. Stir until flour is well blended, then add milk, pepper, mustard, and parsley. Add ham and mix well. Taste for seasoning, as it may need a little salt, if ham is not too salty.

Pour mixture into greased, deep pie dish or shallow casserole. Spread mashed potatoes as a crust over meat. Bake at 350° for 10 to 15 minutes, until crust is golden brown. *Serves 4 to 6*

Smoked Pork with Sweet Potatoes

5 or 6 smoked pork chops
4 or 5 sweet potatoes
½ cup brown sugar
½ teaspoon salt

⅛ teaspoon pepper
2 sour apples, peeled, cored, and chopped
¼ cup water

Brown pork chops on both sides—about 20 minutes. Boil sweet potatoes about 20 minutes or until tender, cool, peel, and cut lengthwise into fairly thin slices.

Into greased pudding dish or casserole, put a layer of pork chops and a layer of potatoes. Sprinkle brown sugar over potatoes, add salt and pepper, then a layer of chopped apples. Repeat, ending with apples on top. Pour in water, being careful not to disturb layers. Cover and bake at 375° for 15 minutes. Remove cover and bake for 10 minutes longer, or until apples are soft and top is nicely browned. *Serves 4 or 5*

Smoked Sausage and Noodles

½ package noodles
1 pound smoked sausage
1 tablespoon flour
1 cup milk

Salt and pepper to taste
⅛ teaspoon paprika
½ cup grated cheese (optional)

Cook noodles according to package directions. Place in colander, rinse with boiling water, and let drain. Meanwhile, cut sausage into 1-inch pieces and brown slowly in heavy frying pan or spider. When done, remove sausage and pour off all fat except 1 tablespoonful. Add flour to fat, stir well, getting all browned bits of sausage into mixture. Slowly add milk, salt, pepper, and paprika and cook into a thin cream sauce. (You may have to add a little more milk, because the mixture should thin.) Sprinkle cheese into sauce and cook until just melted.

Add drained noodles to frying pan and stir until coated with cream sauce. Add sausage, stir to mix, and serve at once.   *Serves 4*

Smoked Turkey, Duck, or Chicken

Since you probably do not have access to smoked fowl, why not try smoking your own? It takes time, of course and it's not quite as good as the old-fashioned kind—slow-smoked over hickory fires—but I've tried smoking my own and it's very good indeed.

Get a bottle of patent smoke (or liquid smoke, as it's sometimes called) at a hardware store. I use a small turkey, about 8 to 12 pounds, for this method of smoking.

Turkey or Duck: Wash the fowl inside and out, and dry it thoroughly. Pour some of the patent smoke into a small bowl, and using a pastry brush, brush the liquid all over the fowl, inside and out. Cover with foil and let stand overnight, but do not refrigerate.

Put the fowl into a baking pan, brush again with the patent smoke, and roast in a slow oven, about 300°F., basting frequently. Do not stuff. If you like a very strong smoked taste, add a little of the patent smoke to the drippings.

Bake for 4½ to 5 hours, or until the drumstick moves easily. Remove to a warm platter, and make gravy by adding two tablespoons flour to the drippings, and enough water to make it the consistency you prefer. Wonderful sliced cold!

Smoked Chicken: Proceed as for turkey or duck, but allow it to stand for only an hour or so. Roast slowly, basting often.

Serves 6 to 8

Corned Beef

The process of pickling meat was a long one. First the meat was rubbed all over with a mixture of molasses, saltpeter, soda, and pepper, and allowed to stand for two days. It was then placed in a barrel or deep crock and covered with a brine made of salt and water "strong enough to float a egg." Then it was allowed to ripen for an indeterminate period. Every family had its own cherished recipe for pickling. Some added bay leaves and spices, others used brown sugar instead of molasses, and each family felt that theirs was the only method. You can buy beef already cured on the market, but if you ever corn it yourself you will never again be satisfied with the "boughten" kind.

5 to 10 pounds brisket of beef	6 to 8 bay leaves
1 cup salt	2 cloves garlic, chopped
½ cup brown sugar or unsulphured molasses	12 to 24 peppercorns
	1 tablespoon vinegar
6 to 8 whole cloves, with the little black buds removed	1 heaping teaspoon saltpeter (from the drugstore)

Water to cover

Remove as much fat as possible from brisket. Place in deep stone crock, or enameled kettle. Mix rest of ingredients except water and add to beef. (The amount of spice used depends upon whether you like it highly spiced or not—I do.) Add enough cold water to completely immerse beef. Put plate over meat and weigh it down with any non-metal weight, such as a jar or a clean, well-scrubbed stone. Leave meat in brine for 14 to 16 days in a cool, dark place. Remove from brine, wash thoroughly, and simmer in water to cover (after adding 1 cup of marinade, or fresh spices) for at least 4 hours or until tender.

You may cut off a portion of the meat for immediate use and leave the rest in the brine, if you want to—it will keep for several months. *Serves 6 to 8*

CHAPTER IV

From the Barnyard and Woods
(Poultry and Game)

Most farmers where I grew up raised ducks, geese, and turkeys, as well as chickens. Guinea hens were popular, and better than watchdogs, thanks to the fearful hue and cry they raised at the approach of any stranger. In the spring, squabs were available from the barn loft, and a "delicate dish they made." Pigeons, however, were seldom eaten, because there was such a wealth of other fowl, and they tend to be tough, even though "potted."

Although game isn't as abundant as it was in pioneer days, pheasant, quail, rabbits, squirrels, deer, and wild turkeys remain plentiful in the Pennsylvania Dutch region and the residents continue to be great hunters, but for sport now rather than for need. When I was young in the early 1900's, the only restriction on hunting—done in the late fall and early winter, when the farm work slackened off—was finding the time to go.

Roast Chicken with Sour Cream

1 roasting chicken	Bread stuffing (see Index)
(2½ to 3½ pounds)	Salt and pepper
	1 cup sour cream

Wash chicken, stuff with bread stuffing, dust with salt and pepper, and put in baking pan. Roast at 400° for 10 minutes, then lower

49

heat to 350° and continue roasting 2 hours, or until chicken leg moves easily at thigh. Remove chicken to warm platter. Add sour cream to juices in pan, heat, but do not boil, stirring to get all browned bits off bottom.   *Serves 3 to 4*

Housewife to husband: "Now come, and set vunst down. It gifs vaffles and they don't keep."

Hinkle mit Waffles
(CHICKEN AND WAFFLES)

This is an exceedingly popular company dish. Waffles go way back in culinary history. They used to be baked on the hearth in long-handled, fancy-shaped irons, few of which are to be found today outside of museums. At fairs in Germany waffles were sold in much the same way as popcorn and spun sugar are today. Apparently the Pennsylvania Dutch brought some of their irons with them. These old-fashioned ones which are used over a "ranche" (range) have varied shapes—heart, circular, and square. They have little iron legs and are set over the flame, with the stove lid removed. They must be watched carefully. Just before dinner was served, the housewife would begin baking the waffles, and as they were baked they were placed in the warming oven to give her a good start in making a quantity of waffles.

Chicken and Waffles

1 good-sized stewing chicken	2 teaspoons salt
Water to cover	½ teaspoon pepper
1 medium-sized onion, chopped	1 teaspoon garlic salt (optional)
2 celery stalks, including leaves	2 tablespoons flour
⅛ teaspoon saffron	½ cup water

1 cup chopped parsley

Wash chicken and cut into serving pieces. Put in deep kettle, giblets and all, and cover with water. Add onion, celery, saffron, salt, pepper, and garlic salt. Bring to boil, then gently simmer until chicken is well done—about 1 hour. Remove meat and keep warm on platter.

Cut up giblets, and return to kettle. Thicken stock with mixture of flour and water, just until it has consistency of gravy. Bring to a boil, return chicken, and add parsley. Taste and correct seasoning. Serve chicken on platter, with extra bowls of gravy to pour over the waffles.

Waffles:

2 eggs
1½ cups milk
½ cup melted butter, margarine, or lard

1 teaspoon sugar
2 cups flour
½ teaspoon salt
3 teaspoons baking powder

Beat eggs, add milk, then melted shortening. Sift sugar, flour, salt, and baking powder together. Pour egg mixture into dry ingredients, and mix thoroughly, beating just enough to mix, but not enough to "break down" the eggs.

Pour batter into waffle iron, and bake according to directions for your waffle iron. *Serves 4 to 6*

Hinkle Bot Bei
(CHICKEN POT PIE)

1 fowl (4 to 6 pounds)
Water to cover
1 small onion, sliced

4 stalks celery, including leaves
2 small carrots, sliced
2 teaspoons parsley, chopped
½ teaspoon saffron

Disjoint fowl and cover with water. Add rest of ingredients, bring to boil, then simmer until meat falls off bone—at least 1 hour. In the meantime, make the following—

Pot Pie Noodles:

2½ cups sifted flour
1 teaspoon salt
¼ scant cup shortening (lard or vegetable)

⅔ cup *hot* broth (from the chicken pot)

Mix flour, salt, and shortening until mixture resembles coarse meal. Add *hot* stock and mix thoroughly. Roll out very thin on a floured surface, and cut into squares or diamonds.

When chicken is done, drop noodle squares, one at a time, into boiling broth (there should be at least 2 quarts of broth—if not, add boiling water) and cook for 15 minutes. Serve at once. *Serves 6 to 8*

Hinkle mit Käse
(BAKED CHICKEN WITH CHEESE)

2 cups dry bread crumbs
½ cup grated cheese
    (Parmesan is best)
3 tablespoons parsley,
    chopped
Sprinkle of saffron
⅛ teaspoon garlic salt

1 teaspoon salt
⅛ teaspoon pepper
2 frying chickens (about 2½ to
    3 pounds each), cut into
    serving pieces
1 cup melted butter or
    margarine

Mix bread crumbs, cheese, parsley, saffron, garlic salt, salt, and pepper. Dip each piece of chicken into melted butter, then into crumb mixture, coating well. Put in roasting pan, pour over any remaining butter, and bake 1 hour at 350°. Do not turn.   *Serves 6*

Panned Chicken and Noodles

6 fryer thighs
Water to cover
1 12-ounce package medium-
    wide noodles
1 thin-sliced onion, minced

½ teaspoon paprika
1 teaspoon salt
Dash garlic salt
¼ teaspoon pepper
1 teaspoon parsley, chopped

In a large spider or electric frying pan, boil thighs in water for 45 minutes, or until meat falls off bone. Remove chicken. Add noodles, onion, salt, garlic salt, and pepper to water in pan and boil for 25 minutes, or until noodles are done. Remove meat from thighs, discarding skin and bones. Cut into small pieces. Add to noodles in skillet. (If gravy is too thin, thicken with a little flour and water, but this should not be necessary.) Let mixture cook a few minutes more to blend flavors. Sprinkle with parsley and serve at once.

Serves 4

Chicken Fricassee

1 fowl (about 4 or 5 pounds), cut in serving pieces
4 cups water (approx.)
1 small onion, minced
4 or 5 stalks celery, sliced
1 small garlic clove, or
½ teaspoon garlic powder
1 teaspoon chopped parsley
1 bay leaf

1 teaspoon salt
¼ teaspoon pepper
4 carrots, sliced into rounds
Pinch saffron
1 small potato, sliced very thin
2 tablespoons butter or margarine
2 tablespoons flour
2 egg yolks, beaten

Put chicken pieces in deep kettle and cover with water. Add rest of ingredients, except butter, flour, and eggs. Bring to a boil, then lower heat and simmer about 1 hour or until meat is fork tender. Remove bay leaf and garlic clove. Put chicken aside in warm place. Rub butter and flour together until smooth. Slowly add broth in which chicken was cooked. This should now be reduced to about a pint. Bring to boil. Strain if there are any lumps. Take from heat and add beaten egg yolks. Stir vigorously, but do not reheat. Pour thickened gravy over chicken.

We sometimes served this with toast but usually with rice or dumplings. *Serves 6 to 8*

Creamed Chicken

1 tablespoon butter or margarine
1 tablespoon flour
1 cup milk or half-and-half
1 teaspoon salt
¼ teaspoon pepper
⅛ teaspoon nutmeg
4 cups (or less) cold diced chicken

1 small can sliced mushrooms, or ½ pound fresh mushrooms, sliced
3 slices pimiento, or
4 stuffed olives, sliced
1 tablespoon sherry
Patty shells or toast

Melt butter, add flour, and stir until blended. Remove from heat and add milk. Stir to blend. Return to heat, add seasonings, then chicken, mushrooms (if fresh, first brown in butter), and pimiento or olives. Cook over low heat to thicken and blend flavors. Just before serving, stir in sherry. Serve in patty shells or on toast.

Serves 2 to 4

Chicken Salad

3 cups cold diced chicken
½ teaspoon grated onion
½ cup finely diced celery
1 teaspoonful capers (optional)
1 sliced pimiento, diced very
fine (optional)

Juice of ¼ lemon
½ teaspoon salt
⅛ teaspoon pepper, preferably
coarsely ground
½ cup good mayonnaise (about)
Hardboiled egg, sliced

Place diced chicken in large bowl. Add onion, celery, capers, and pimiento. Squeeze lemon quarter over salad and toss to mix. Salt and pepper, then add mayonnaise slowly—just enough to mix, not smother the flavor. Garnish with hardboiled egg, or more capers and pimiento in a ring. (If you don't have pimientos on hand, use a few slices of stuffed olives.) Chill for at least 1 hour. Serve on lettuce leaves, or in a bowl, surrounded by lettuce. *Serves 4*

Alice's Baked Chicken

1 broiler (2½ to 3 pounds)
Water
1 slice onion
1 stalk celery, sliced
1 teaspoon parsley

⅛ pound butter or margarine,
at room temperature
1 teaspoon salt
½ teaspoon pepper
⅛ teaspoon poultry seasoning

1 tablespoon flour

Wash chicken. Using sharp knife, cut out backbone and flatten chicken as you would for broiling. Cover giblets and backbone with water and bring to boil with onion, celery, and parsley. Let it simmer about 1 hour to make broth for gravy.

Place chicken in baking pan; dot all over with softened butter; and sprinkle salt, pepper, and poultry seasoning. Bake at 350° for 1 hour. Remove to platter, and make gravy. Add flour to pan juices and stir to get all browned bits up from bottom of pan. Add juice from giblets and stir until thickened. Delicious with rice or noodles!

Serves 3 to 4

Sweet and Sour Chicken

This is similar to barbecued chicken, although we didn't call it that. You could use the sauce to barbecue chicken or spareribs, if you like.

1 broiler or fryer (2½ to 3 pounds)

Sauce:

1 medium onion, minced	2 tablespoons brown sugar
1 small green pepper, minced (optional)	2 tablespoons prepared mustard
2 tablespoons butter or margarine	1 tablespoon hot sauce or Worcestershire sauce
	1 teaspoon salt

¾ cup catsup

Cook onion and pepper slowly for 2 minutes in butter. Add remaining ingredients; simmer 10 minutes.

Put chicken in roasting pan, and brush with sauce. Bake at 350° for 50 minutes, brushing frequently with sauce.   *Serves 3 to 4*

Chicken Pie

1 fowl (3 to 4 pounds)	⅛ teaspoon garlic salt
2 quarts water (about)	Pinch saffron
2 stalks celery, diced	2 tablespoons flour
½ onion, sliced	⅛ pound butter
1 tablespoon parsley	1 cup milk, if needed
2 teaspoons salt	1 recipe rich baking-powder crust (see below)
¼ teaspoon pepper	
⅛ teaspoon poultry seasoning	

Put washed chicken in water to boil with celery, onion, parsley, and seasonings. Let boil until chicken is tender enough to fall off bone—about 1 hour, depending upon toughness of fowl. Remove chicken from stock and refrigerate. Strain broth.

Mix flour with a little cold water and add to chicken broth. Bring to boil, and cook until thickened. Add butter, and taste to correct seasonings.

Cut chicken up into bite-sized pieces, discarding skin and bones. Put into a well-buttered baking dish, and pour the sauce over it.

If there isn't enough juice to cover, add a little milk, and stir. Meanwhile make the crust—

Pie Crust:

2 cups flour	6 tablespoons lard or vegetable
3 teaspoons baking powder	shortening
1 teaspoon salt	½ to ¾ cup milk

Mix dry ingredients and cut in the shortening, either with fingers or with two knives. Add enough milk to make a soft dough. On a floured cloth, roll dough out about ½ inch thick to the size of your baking dish. Place over chicken in baking dish, pinch edges to make a high crust. Cut wide slits to allow the steam to escape. Bake at 375° for 20 to 25 minutes, until crust is brown and flavors are blended.

Sometimes we extended this dish with slices of carrots or diced potatoes, especially if we were using leftover chicken. *Serves 6 to 8*

Quick Oven-Fried Chicken

While this is not an "echt Deitsch" (truly Dutch) recipe, it is one we use frequently for our church suppers—and it is just delicious.

1 2½ to 3 pound broiler,	¼ pound butter
cut up, or 6 chicken breasts	1 box Rice Krispie crumbs,
1 tablespoon salt	rolled fine with a rolling pin
½ teaspoon freshly ground	Dash poultry seasoning
pepper	

Cut up chicken into serving pieces, and salt and pepper them. Melt butter in fairly large frying pan. Dip pieces of chicken into butter, then into crumbs, and place in baking pan. Pour any leftover butter over chicken and sprinkle lightly with poultry seasoning. Bake at 350° for 1 hour, when chicken will be crisp and delicious. *Serves 3 to 4*

Baked Chicken with Rice and Walnut Dressing

1 roasting chicken,	1 teaspoon salt
3 to 5 pounds	⅛ teaspoon pepper

Wash chicken thoroughly, and salt and pepper the cavity and the outside. Stuff with the following dressing:

2 tablespoons butter or margarine	Dash nutmeg
1 slice onion, chopped	½ teaspoon salt
1 stalk celery, chopped	⅛ teaspoon pepper
2 cups cooked rice	Pinch saffron
1 tablespoon parsley, chopped	½ cup chopped walnuts (black or English)

Melt butter, add onion and celery, and cook until tender but not brown. Pour over rice, add other seasonings and walnuts. Toss together, and stuff cavity of chicken. Roast at 350° about 15 minutes per pound, or until thigh moves easily, basting every 15 minutes or so. *Serves 3 to 4*

Porcupine Chicken

1 fryer (2½ to 3 pounds), cut into serving pieces	¼ cup milk
	1 teaspoon salt
½ cup sour cream	½ teaspoon pepper
1½ cups pretzel crumbs	

Wash chicken. Mix sour cream, milk, salt, and pepper. Crush pretzels into coarse crumbs. Dip chicken in sour cream mixture, then in crumbs, coating it well. Place in baking dish and bake at 350° for 50 minutes or until done. *Serves 4*

Extra Crisp Chicken for Picnics

1 broiler (3 to 3½ pounds), cut into serving pieces	1 cup mayonnaise
	1 cup cold-cereal crumbs, such as corn flakes
1 teaspoon salt	
½ teaspoon pepper	

Place chicken on flat surface, and sprinkle with salt and pepper. Using spatula, coat all over with mayonnaise. Dip each piece into finely crushed cereal crumbs. Put in baking dish and bake at 350° about 1 hour or until done. Chill. Serve with fresh greens. *Serves 4*

"I was vunderful sick this after.
I guess I et too much hinkle."

Crispy Fried Chicken

To make this chicken you need giblet broth both for frying the chicken pieces and for the gravy. You could substitute a good commercial brand, but the homemade is better.

Broth:

Water to cover backs, giblets and necks from 2 frying chickens
1 stalk celery (leaves and stems), sliced
Dash garlic salt
¼ onion, diced
Few sprigs parsley
Salt and pepper

Put backs, giblets, and necks in water to boil with celery, garlic salt, onion, parsley, salt, and pepper to taste. Let cook while you are preparing chicken for frying. Save for gravy what you do not use for frying.

Chicken:

2 young fryers, cut up
½ cup and 2 tablespoons flour
1 tablespoon salt
1 teaspoon black pepper
½ teaspoon paprika
4 to 6 tablespoons butter and lard, mixed
½ cup giblet broth

Wash fryers, but do not dry. Put ½ cup flour, mixed with salt, pepper, and paprika in a flat soup bowl. Melt fat in two ovenproof spiders (it takes two if you want crusty chicken, as it cannot brown properly if pieces are crowded). Fry chicken until a golden brown on both sides. Turn off heat and add ¼ cup of giblet broth to each pan. Put in 350° oven, skin side *down*, and bake 50 minutes, when each piece of chicken should have a brown, crackling skin.

Gravy:

Remove chicken to a warm platter, and pour off all fat except 2 tablespoons. Add 2 tablespoons flour, and cook until flour is well blended. Then add rest of broth from giblets and stir vigorously, making sure to get all little brown pieces from bottom of pan. Strain, if you wish (we like it unstrained) and serve at once.

Serves 6 to 8

Hinkle Pudding
(CHICKEN PUDDING)

1 tablespoon butter	2 cups leftover chicken, ground
1 tablespoon flour	1 teaspoon salt
1 cup rich milk, or half-and-half	⅛ teaspoon pepper
	1 teaspoon onion juice
3 eggs, separated	1 tablespoon chopped parsley

Make a white sauce (see Index) with butter, flour, and milk. Beat egg yolks and pour a little of the hot sauce over them. Return to pan and bring just to boil. Mix together chicken, salt, pepper, onion juice, and parsley. Pour over white sauce and mix gently. Beat egg whites until stiff but not dry, and fold into first mixture. Bake at 350° for 15 minutes and serve at once. *Serves 3 to 4*

Roast Guinea Hen

1 guinea hen	1 tablespoon chopped onion
2 teaspoons salt	Dash of garlic powder or salt
½ teaspoon pepper	1 cup stock or water in which
Bread stuffing (see Index)	2 chicken bouillon cubes have
½ cup black walnuts	been dissolved
2 slices bacon	1 tablespoon flour
	½ cup water

Guinea hen is all dark meat and tends to dry out upon baking, so that it needs moist roasting.

Wash bird thoroughly, dry, and salt and pepper the cavity. Fill with bread stuffing, to which chopped black walnuts have been added. Tie bacon around breast.

Place in roasting pan with lid, add chopped onion, sprinkle with garlic powder and a little more salt and pepper, and put in the stock. Cover and roast until tender—about 1 hour at 350°.

Remove lid, turn heat up to 400° and baste frequently for 15 minutes, until nicely browned. Place hen on a warm platter; remove bacon slices and reserve.

Make gravy by dissolving flour in water and adding mix to juices in pan. Strain and serve. The crisp bacon slices may be crumbled into gravy, if desired. *Serves 4 to 6*

Squabs

In the early spring, when the boys were egg hunting, they used to keep an eye on the pigeons to see if they were nesting. I can still hear the girls squealing as the boys ran along the rafters of the high barn, hunting for the nests where the squabs would hatch out. Squabs were cooked in various ways, but our favorite method was to season them with salt and pepper, inside and out, fill them with a bread stuffing, and roast them in a hot oven. When they were almost done, after about 20 minutes, they were removed from the oven, rubbed all over with butter, and put back to roast for another five or six minutes, during which time they were basted two or three times. Pop would grumble, "They ain't enough *to* them to fill your hind teeth," and would never tuck away fewer than three.

Nowadays I usually broil squab, but I never forget to butter them just before they are done—it gives them a glowing brown coating which makes them doubly delicious! When I broil them I omit the stuffing and flatten the breastbone before cooking. You can cook Rock Cornish hen just as you do squab if you can't get squabs in your market.

Pigeon Pie

When the boys couldn't wait for squabs we had their tougher parents, the pigeons, in a pie.

6 to 8 pigeons
2 tablespoons butter
1 teaspoon salt
½ teaspoon pepper
1 pint of good stock (you can use chicken bouillon or canned soup)

1 medium-sized onion, sliced
1 tablespoon parsley
3 or 4 carrots, sliced
1 bay leaf (optional)
Dash Tabasco
¼ teaspoon Worcestershire or other hot sauce

Be sure pigeons are well singed, then quarter them. Rub pieces all over with butter; salt and pepper them; and brown them quickly over a hot fire. Mix stock, onion, parsley, carrots, bay leaf, Tabasco, and Worcestershire sauce, and bring to boil. Place pigeons in very deep casserole, or oven-proof kettle, and pour vegetables over them. Put over low flame, or in 350° oven, and cook for 45 minutes to 1 hour, or until birds are tender and vegetables are done.

Gravy:

1 tablespoon butter or margarine	1 tablespoon flour

Rub tablespoonful of butter and flour together, and add it to the casserole, being careful not to let it lump. (If it lumps, you'd have to take it all out and put it through a strainer, but you could still use it.) Bring to a boil again; let it cool a little while you make pie crust.

Pie Crust (see Index):

½ recipe, or ½ prepared pie-crust mix

Roll out pie crust to fit your kettle or casserole, place it over cooked pigeons, cut at least five good-sized slits to let steam escape, and bake at 450°, just until crust is nicely browned—about 7 minutes. Serve at once.

We usually had boiled rice or noodles with this.   *Serves 6 to 8*

Roast Welsch Hahn oder Hinkle
(WILD TURKEY)

I never could understand why, if wild tom turkeys were called Welsch Hahn and wild hen turkeys called Welsch Hinkle, corn was designated as Welsch Korn, but my sister unraveled the mystery for me. *Welsch* is colloquial German for "foreign," she explained, and the word "corn" in Europe is used to designate "wheat" or "barley." When the early settlers came over here and found maize, they dubbed it "Welsch Korn," or "that foreign kind of corn." Then when they found those big strange birds in the forests, they labeled them "strange roosters or chickens," hence Welsch Hahn oder Hinkle.

Clean and singe the turkey as you would a tame one. Place 1 stalk of celery and 1 apple (cut into quarters) in the cavity; truss or sew up. Rub the breast with butter, dust with pepper and salt, and place it in a hot oven to brown—about 400°. Do not add water, but you can make a tent of aluminum foil, if you wish, to keep the turkey from drying out. (We used to dip cheesecloth into a mixture of melted lard and butter and put it over the breast.) When the turkey is thoroughly browned, lower the heat to 350° and cook for 15 minutes per pound, or until the thigh moves freely. Let stand for at least 15 minutes before carving.

Most wild fowl taste better without stuffing. We usually made dressing to go with this, but cooked it in a separate pan.

Serves 8 to 10

Roast Wild Goose

After goose has been drawn and cleaned, let it soak overnight covered with milk. It looks awful, but it obviates the possibility of a fishy taste. Throw out the milk, wipe the goose inside and out, and put a stalk of celery, 1 apple, quartered, and a small peeled onion in the cavity. Truss or sew up. Dust the bird with pepper and salt rather thickly and roast in a 350° oven for 25 minutes to the pound. (If you prefer it rare, roast for only 15 minutes to the pound.) Put the goose into another baking pan, and pour all the fat except about 2 tablespoonfuls over it. Place in a very hot oven (500°) and baste constantly until the fat under the skin is all melted, and the skin is brown and crisp as cracklings. Make the gravy from the fat in the first pan by adding 2 tablespoonfuls of flour, a little paprika, a dash of garlic salt, and more pepper and salt if needed. Blend and stir, then add enough cold water to give it the proper consistency. Cook until thickened.   *Serves 6 to 8*

Roast Wild Duck

We cooked wild duck in exactly the same way as we did wild goose.

Duck mit Kraut
(DUCK AND SAUERKRAUT)

1 young duck
Salt and pepper to taste
Flour
2 tablespoons duck fat or
    other shortening

1 quart sauerkraut
½ cup water
1 teaspoon sugar

Wipe duck, inside and out. Sprinkle cavity with salt and pepper, and dust outside with flour, pepper, and salt. In a deep kettle, slowly brown duck on all sides in shortening. Remove from heat. Stuff cavity loosely with sauerkraut. Put duck back in kettle, cover with any remaining sauerkraut and its juice; add water and sugar. Simmer 1 hour, or until duck is tender, checking every so often to be sure there is liquid in bottom of kettle and adding water if necessary. Serve on large platter, surrounded by kraut. Mashed potatoes are a must with this. *Serves 4*

Quail with Rice

2 tablespoons chopped onion
1 stalk celery, chopped fine
5 tablespoons butter or
    margarine
2 cups boiled rice
1 teaspoon salt
¼ teaspoon black pepper
¼ teaspoon poultry seasoning

Pinch marjoram
Pinch thyme
¼ cup chopped parsley, minced
6 to 8 quail
1 jar currant jelly
4 tablespoons lemon juice
¼ cup currant wine, sherry, or
    vermouth

Lightly brown onion and celery in 2 tablespoons of the butter. Remove from heat and mix with rice. Add seasonings, parsley and taste. Mixture should be quite spicy.

Wash quail, and dry. Stuff loosely with rice mixture. Sew or close openings with a skewer. Melt remaining butter and brush birds well. Roast at 400°, uncovered, for 20 minutes, basting every 5 or 10 minutes. Use more butter if necessary.

Melt jelly with lemon juice over low heat, add wine, and use this mixture to baste quail frequently. Roast for 15 to 20 minutes longer, until they are well glazed and tender.

Serve on a bed of saffron rice (see below) if desired.

Serves 4 to 6

Baked Quail

After quail are cleaned and drawn, wipe with damp cloth, inside and out. Split down the back and place in baking pan, skin side up. Dot all over with butter; sprinkle with salt, pepper, and paprika. Brown in hot oven (450°) for 5 minutes, then reduce heat to 350° for 15 minutes more. After first 5 minutes, add 2 tablespoons of a sweet wine, such as sherry, and baste the quail often to keep them from drying out.

We always served saffron rice with quail.

Saffron Rice:

½ teaspoon saffron
2 teaspoons salt
2 quarts boiling water
1½ cups rice
1 tablespoon chopped parsley

Put saffron and salt in boiling water; add rice. Cook until just tender, then drain. Place in colander over boiling water, cover, and steam about 10 minutes. (We always used a clean white cloth to cover rice, because it absorbs any extra moisture.) Sprinkle with chopped parsley, and serve.

Short Cut:

Use instant rice, following package directions but also adding the saffron to the water.

Serves 4

Roast Pheasant

3 or 4 pheasants
3 cups sliced tart apples
Salt, pepper, paprika
3 tablespoons lard or butter
¼ onion, sliced very thin
2 cups cream—may be sweet or sour (I prefer the latter)

Stuff pheasants with sliced apples. Sew up or skewer, and dust with salt, pepper, and paprika. Brown birds lightly in fat, to which thin slices of onion have been added. Put in covered baking dish, pour over cream, cover, and bake at 350° for 50 minutes, basting once or twice during baking period. Serve hot, with noodles or mashed potatoes.

Serves 4 to 6

Pheasants with Chestnut Filling

Stuffing:

1 pint chestnuts	½ teaspoon salt
Water	1 teaspoon sugar
	2 tablespoons butter

Cut a small hole in the flat side of each chestnut; put nuts into pan of boiling water and boil for 10 minutes. Remove from fire, cover with cold water, and peel with sharp knife. (The inner skin will come off easily, and it must all be removed.) Cut chestnuts into very small pieces and put on to boil in water to cover. Add salt, sugar, and butter, and let simmer until nuts are tender—about a half hour. (All of this can be done the day before.)

Birds:

3 or 4 pheasants	2 tablespoons butter or
Salt and pepper to taste	2 slices bacon

Wipe pheasants inside and out with damp cloth; dust with salt and pepper. Fill with chestnuts, but don't pack tightly. (Any left-over chestnuts can be served separately.) Dot breasts with small pieces of butter, or cover with bacon. Put birds into roaster with cover. Roast, covered, at 350° for about 50 minutes. Remove cover, and if birds aren't nicely browned turn heat up to 450° and baste for 5 to 10 minutes more. Remove to warm platter.

Gravy:

½ jar currant or grape jelly	1 tablespoon flour mixed with water (optional)

Add jelly to juices in pan and scrape up all browned bits. If gravy is too thin, thicken with flour mixed with cold water, but this gravy should not be thick. Pour over birds, and serve with potato pancakes. *Serves 4 to 6*

Kraut un' Patrich
(PARTRIDGE WITH SAUERKRAUT)

After birds have been drawn and cleaned, wipe all over with a damp cloth. Sprinkle inside and out with salt and pepper. Place in deep baking dish, and cover tightly with 1 quart sauerkraut. Bake at 350° for 1 hour, checking every so often to be sure there is moisture in bottom of pot. If not, add a little hot water. Serve hot, garnished with parsley and a sprinkling of paprika. Count on *at least* ½ bird per serving.

Frogs' Legs

Farm children are always in action, it seems. After all the chores were done, sometimes the boys would take a bull's eye lantern and go hunting for frogs at night. Mom insisted that she'd cook the legs only if the boys cut them off for her, although she was never squeamish about chopping off chickens' heads! This is how we cooked them, and they much resembled chicken.

Only the hind legs are used in cooking frogs. Wash the legs, cover them with boiling water, let stand for 5 minutes. Drain, but don't dry. Dip into mixture of flour, salt, pepper, and paprika, pressing down to be sure they are well coated. Fry in deep oil or fat until well browned. Serve with catsup or mayonnaise mixed with a few chopped sweet pickles.

Hasen Pfeffer
(POTTED RABBIT)

1 rabbit (may be frozen), cut in serving pieces	1 teaspoon pepper
	8 whole cloves
Vinegar	2 bay leaves
Water	Butter or margarine for
1 medium-sized onion, sliced	browning
1 tablespoon salt	1 cup sour cream

Place rabbit pieces in glass or china bowl and cover with equal parts of vinegar and water. Add onion, salt, pepper, cloves, and bay leaves. Marinate for 2 days. Remove meat, dry it, and brown thoroughly in hot butter or margarine. Gradually add 2 cups of the marinade. Simmer at low heat 30 minutes, or until meat is tender. Turn off heat and add sour cream, stirring just to mix.

This is usually served either with noodles or grumbere kloess (see Index). *Serves 4*

Rabbit Stew

1 rabbit (2 to 2½ pounds), cut in serving pieces
Flour
Salt and pepper
½ teaspoon paprika

2 slices salt pork or bacon
1 teaspoon minced onion
1 jar currant jelly
1 tablespoon water
½ teaspoon parsley

Dredge rabbit pieces with flour which has been mixed with salt, pepper, and paprika. Let stand while you cook salt pork in frying pan with tight lid. Remove salt pork and set aside.

Brown rabbit in hot fat. Add onion and cover. Simmer until tender —about 30 minutes. (You may have to add a little water, but use as little as possible, letting the rabbit steam in its own juice.) Dissolve jelly in water. Remove rabbit from kettle, and pour dissolved jelly over it to glaze. Sprinkle with parsley and serve. *Serves 4*

Fried Rabbit

1 young rabbit, dressed for cooking
Salted water to cover
Flour
Salt and pepper to taste

2 tablespoons lard or butter
½ cup water
Dash of hot pepper sauce or Tabasco

Put dressed rabbit to soak in salted water for several hours or overnight. Remove from water, dry, then dredge with flour, salt, and pepper. Fry in lard until golden brown. Cover skillet and cook until tender, at a lowered temperature. Or place in oven to complete cooking, at 350° for about 20 minutes. Remove rabbit to warmed platter, and make gravy by adding 1 tablespoon flour dissolved in ½ cup of water to juices in pan. Add a dash of hot pepper sauce and serve. *Serves 4*

Venison Stew

2 or 3 pounds venison
  shoulder and neck
2 slices bacon
1 tablespoon flour
1 teaspoon salt
⅛ teaspoon pepper
1 tablespoon chopped onion

½ teaspoon garlic salt or
1 clove garlic, minced
2 cups water
4 tablespoons vinegar, or
  4 tablespoons dry wine
⅛ teaspoon saffron
1 tablespoon flour mixed
  with water (optional)

Cut meat into cubes; dust with flour, salt, and pepper. Try out bacon—remove crackly pieces and reserve. Add meat to kettle and brown on all sides. Add onion and garlic and brown a little more. Add water and stir to loosen all brown bits from bottom of pan. Add vinegar and saffron. Cook about 40 minutes, or until meat is tender but not mushy. Taste for seasoning. If gravy is too thin, thicken with flour mixed with a little cold water. Serve with noodles. Sprinkle the saved crisp bacon over the top. *Serves 4 to 6*

Squirrel Stew

Since squirrels are hard to bring down, the younger boys learned to become hunters by shooting at them. When they brought them home we always had squirrel stew.

3 or 4 squirrels
1 quart water
3 stalks celery, sliced

½ small onion, chopped
1 teaspoon salt
⅛ teaspoon pepper

Split squirrels down the center. Disjoint hind legs, take off back, then forelegs. Peel off skin.

Put pieces on to boil in cold water, add rest of ingredients, bring to boil, then simmer gently for about 30 minutes, or until meat is tender. By this time, broth should be reduced by almost half. Remove meat to platter.

Gravy:

2 tablespoons butter or
  margarine

2 tablespoons flour

Blend butter and flour together over low heat, add some of the broth to it, then return to rest of broth, and stir until thickened. Pour over squirrel and serve.

We usually added dumplings or boiled rice to this.   *Serves 3 to 4*

CHAPTER V

From the Market (Fish and Shellfish)

Land for the market was set apart in 1730 in the city of Lancaster, where the original central market house is still in use. Because the stalls in the market house were rented annually by the city to the highest bidders at a public auction, many farmers who attended market only when they had produce to sell began to set up stalls on the streets, where the rent was less expensive. Street markets were later discontinued because they were unsanitary, and also because they became an automobile hazard.

Nowadays there are three market houses—the southern, the old central, and the northern. All three hold market on Friday and Tuesday, but only the southern market is open on Saturdays. Street markets were only held on Fridays.

The two new market houses differ little from the old historical central market, which appears just as it must have in the eighteenth century—it has high, barnlike rafters, a cold stone floor, and is crowded with homemade stalls with wooden counters. In the new markets, the aisles are a little wider, and there are more commercial stands.

Most families used to "tend market" not only to acquire cash and sell surplus food but also for the pleasure of visiting, especially after a housebound winter.

Everything grown or made on the farm—eggs, poultry, vegetables, cakes, pies, bread, cheese, jams and jellies, and even homemade soap—was loaded into the market wagon before dawn, and father, mother and oldest children crowded into it to make the trip to the nearest city. Market began early, and lasted until after noon. Each farmer had a chosen location on the market street, and he had to be there early to be sure of keeping it. Once in the city, the wagon was backed into the allotted space, the tailgate was let down and a stand made of planks placed on sawhorses was set up.

The women began to put out the wares, while the men took the horse to the livery stable. Everything was arranged to look as attractive as possible, and the variety of foods offered was astonishing. Plants and flowers in the spring and summer added to the color.

About one o'clock, when trade was slack, the women started going up and down the street, looking critically at the baked goods of other women, trading to replenish their stocks of herbs and spices, cautiously fingering yard goods that took hard cash that was seldom plentiful, or just gossiping with friends, relatives, and acquaintances.

At this point, Pop would put some of his unsold items in a basket, and go see what he could swap for them. Depending upon the condition of the larder, he visited the grocery stand or the fruit man, and then the fish stall. This arrangement suited everyone; the fish and fruit dealers were as anxious to get rid of perishables as were the farmers. The children could hardly wait to see what was in the "tutts" (paper bags) that Pop brought back. Perhaps there were lemons, oranges, even bananas—and oysters or clams, salt mackerel or cod. Seafood was especially popular among the Pennsylvania Dutch, and it was a genuine triumph when Pop could swap for it.

As a great treat at the end of the day we children were sometimes taken to the local cafe (pronounced to rhyme with "safe") for oyster stew or fried oysters. The oysters were brought to town by train from Baltimore in small wooden barrels—these were the plump Chesapeake Bay oysters. In those days there was no nonsense about washing the oysters, so that they had the salty tang of the sea, which none of us had seen but which we could imagine from the taste and smell of the oysters.

To me, market day somehow always seemed climaxed by the pleasure of that scarcity, seafood, and so I associate my recipes for the sea's bounty with that special day.

Oyster Fritters

1 egg	Salt and pepper
4 tablespoons flour	1 pint whole oysters
¼ teaspoon baking powder	Bread crumbs
	Lard

Make batter of first 4 ingredients. Dry oysters, dip in bread crumbs, and then put in batter. Drop by tablespoonfuls into hot lard about ½ inch deep. Turn once. Be careful! They "spritz!" (spatter). (If batter runs too much, add a little more flour. Oysters vary in their moisture content.) *Serves 4 to 6*

Clam Fritters

About 25 clams (may be canned)	Salt and pepper
1 egg	½ teaspoon parsley
4 tablespoons flour	Dash of cayenne
¼ teaspoon baking powder	Lard

Grind clams. Make batter from remaining ingredients and stir in clams. Drop by tablespoonfuls into hot lard about ½ inch deep. Turn once to brown on both sides. *Serves 6 to 8*

Clams and Potatoes

3 tablespoons butter or margarine	6 to 8 potatoes, sliced thin
2 tablespoons flour	2½ teaspoons salt (about)
3 cups milk, or mixture of equal amount of clam juice and milk	Dash of pepper
	2 tablespoons chopped onion
1 teaspoon chopped parsley	1 dozen chopped clams (may be canned)

Make a white sauce (see Index) with butter, flour, milk, clam juice, and parsley. Grease 2-quart casserole. Alternate potatoes, salt, pepper, onion, clams, and white sauce. Make no more than 2 layers. Bake uncovered at 350° for 50 to 55 minutes until potatoes are soft. *Serves 4 to 6*

Deviled Crab

2 tablespoons butter	½ teaspoon salt
2 tablespoons flour	Dash of pepper
1 cup milk	1 pound fresh or canned
2 tablespoons sherry	crab meat
2 tablespoons chopped parsley	½ cup dry bread crumbs

Make a thick white sauce with butter, flour, and milk (see Index). Remove from heat, add sherry, chopped parsley, salt and pepper. Then add white sauce slowly to crab which has been picked over, keeping mixture very thick. Fill shells or ramikins to brim. Sprinkle lightly with bread crumbs. Bake at 400° for 15 minutes.

Serves 8 to 10

Baked Shad

In the spring when the Susquehanna River shad began to run, we feasted on it. The roe was particularly prized.

Stuffed Baked Shad

1 cup bread crumbs	1 onion, sliced
3 tablespoons butter	1 bay leaf
Salt and pepper to taste	1 cup water
1 good-sized shad	Lemon quarters
	Watercress

Make filling of bread crumbs, 2 tablespoons *melted* butter, salt, and pepper. Stuff shad, and sew up. Place in baking pan. Dot shad with remaining butter. Put onion and bay leaf in pan, and add water. Bake at 350°, basting frequently, about 45 minutes. Garnish with lemon wedges and watercress. *Serves 4 to 6*

Shad Roe with Bacon

1 or 2 shad roes
Water to cover
Bread crumbs

1 egg, beaten
Butter for frying
Lemon wedges
3 to 5 slices crisp bacon

Soak roe for ½ hour in cold water. Dip into bread crumbs, then into beaten egg, and again into bread crumbs. Fry slowly in butter. Garnish with lemon and a few slices of crisp, hot bacon.　*Serves 2*

Fried Salt Mackerel or Herring

2 or 3 salt mackerel or herring
1 to 2 tablespoons butter
Pepper to taste

2 teaspoons parsley, chopped
¼ teaspoon lemon juice, or
lemon (optional)

Remove head and tail of mackerel. Soak fish overnight in cold water. Drain and wipe dry. Place in spider in which butter has been melted, and brown lightly. Add 2 tablespoonfuls of water and let simmer until liquid is absorbed. Add pepper and parsley, and lemon juice, if desired.

This was usually served with hot boiled new potatoes, or with scrambled eggs and fried potatoes.　*Serves 2*

Baked Salt Herring

2 salt herring
6 or 7 medium-sized cold
　boiled potatoes
1 small onion, chopped

⅛ teaspoon pepper
2 or 3 tablespoons bread
　crumbs
2 tablespoons butter or
　margarine

This was a supper dish. Frequently it was made from any herring left over from breakfast. The herring was skinned and boned, and cut into ½-inch pieces. (If you start from scratch, you must soak the herring in cold water overnight.) Put alternate layers of herring, potatoes, and onion in baking dish, sprinkling each layer with pepper. Top with bread crumbs, and dot with butter. Bake at 400° for 30 minutes.　*Serves 4 to 6*

Herring Salad

2 salt herring
Water to cover
1 cup diced cold chicken or veal
2 cups diced boiled potatoes
½ cup pickled beets, diced
1 small tart apple, peeled and
  diced
1 small onion, chopped fine

¼ cup vinegar
⅛ teaspoon pepper
½ tablespoon sugar
2 or 3 tablespoons mayonnaise
¼ cup chopped parsley
1 hardboiled egg
2 to 3 dill pickles, chopped
  (optional)

Soak herring in cold water overnight. Skin, remove bone, and cube. Mix together with diced meat, vegetables, and apple and toss. Combine vinegar, pepper, and sugar, and pour over mixture. Refrigerate for several hours to blend flavors. Then add mayonnaise and parsley. Decorate with hardboiled egg. Sometimes we add a few chopped dill pickles for "extra good."

Short Cut:

Buy 2 jars of Bismarck herring. Drain it and then mix as above.
Serves 6 to 10

Pickled Herring

2 salt herring
Water to cover
1 cup vinegar
½ cup sugar
2 bay leaves

½ teaspoon ginger
½ teaspoon yellow mustard seed
1 teaspoon horseradish
  (optional)
2 cups sliced onion

Cover herring with cold water and soak overnight. Clean herring, cut off heads, remove all bones, and cut into ½-inch slices.

Combine rest of ingredients except onion and cook, stirring until sugar is dissolved. Boil 5 minutes. Let cool.

In wide-mouth jar, or glass bowl, layer herring pieces and onion slices; pour pickling mixture over them. Cover, and refrigerate 3 or 4 days.
Serves 4 to 6

Anderes Oyster Pie
(ANOTHER OYSTER PIE)

4 cups dry bread crumbs
2 tablespoons minced onion
½ teaspoon celery salt
1 teaspoon salt
¼ teaspoon sage
⅛ teaspoon pepper

1 cup melted butter or
bacon fat
2 cups thick white sauce
(see Index)
1 pint oysters
1 cup buttered bread crumbs

Combine bread crumbs, minced onion, and seasonings with melted butter or fat. Press into well-greased baking dish, to form a shell. Bake at 350° for 5 minutes, or just until light brown.

Make 2 cups white sauce, add oysters, and pour into browned crust. Sprinkle with buttered bread crumbs. Bake at 350° until crumbs are browned—about 10 minutes.   *Serves 4*

Fried Clam Puffs

1 pint clams, or 1 can
minced clams
1 egg
1 teaspoon salt
¼ cup milk
1 onion slice, minced

Dash Tabasco or pepper sauce
1 cup flour
1 teaspoon baking powder
Lard, with a small piece of
salt pork melted in it

Put clams through grinder, saving juice. (If juice is less than ¼ cup, add a little water.) Beat egg, add clam juice, clams, salt, milk, onion, and Tabasco. Sift flour and baking powder together and add to clam mixture. Mix thoroughly. Drop by tablespoonfuls into hot fat, and fry until brown—about 5 minutes. Drain on paper towels and serve at once.   *Serves 4*

Codfish Puff

1 cup shredded salt codfish
Water to cover
5 large potatoes, mashed with
butter and milk
Pepper to taste

½ teaspoon grated onion
3 eggs, separated
1 slice bacon, partly fried and
cut in small pieces

Soak shredded codfish in cold water overnight. Mash potatoes, using plenty of butter and hot milk. Squeeze all water from shredded fish and add to potatoes. Season with pepper and grated onion. Add 3 well-beaten egg yolks and stir well. Beat whites until stiff but not dry, and fold into first mixture. Put into well-greased baking dish or casserole and sprinkle with bacon. Bake at 250° 20 to 25 minutes, or until it puffs up and is a golden brown. *Serves 4*

Codfish Balls

1 cup shredded salt codfish	⅛ teaspoon pepper
Water to cover	1 egg, beaten slightly
2½ cups potatoes	Flour if needed
1 tablespoon butter, melted	Shortening for frying

Soak fish overnight. Rinse and squeeze dry with fingers.

Pare potatoes and dice into large pieces. Add fish, and boil with water to cover until potatoes are soft. Drain very dry—put fish and potatoes in strainer and press with back of tablespoon. Mix thoroughly, add 1 tablespoon butter, pepper, and egg. Beat with spoon. Shape into little cakes. If mixture doesn't hold its shape, add a little flour. Fry in shortening until brown on all sides. Be careful, they "spritz!" (spatter). Just wrap a towel around your arm and approach with caution. *Serves 4*

Eyster Botts
(OYSTER BOATS)

6 slices bread	2 dozen oysters (fresh or
6 slices ham (boiled or baked;	defrosted frozen)
cut thin)	Butter
	Salt and pepper

Toast bread on one side. Top untoasted side with 1 slice of ham and 3 or 4 oysters, depending on size. Dot with butter, dust with salt and pepper. Bake in hot oven until oysters just begin to curl at edges—about 5 minutes. *Serves 4 to 6*

Fish Salad

2 cups leftover fish or shellfish, such as crab, tuna, or lobster
1 teaspoon lemon juice
1 tablespoon mayonnaise (about)
1 tablespoon minced celery

Salt and pepper
Lettuce
Chopped parsley, hardboiled egg, or paprika to use as garnish

Use any leftover fish or shellfish. Add lemon juice, enough mayonnaise to moisten, and minced celery. Season to taste with salt and pepper. Serve on lettuce leaves, with parsley, hardboiled egg, or paprika garnish. Quick and easy. *Serves 4*

Shrimp Salad

1 pound shrimp
Water to cover
1 tablespoon vinegar
1 tablespoon seafood seasoning (optional)
1 teaspoon lemon juice

2 stalks celery, diced
2 to 3 tablespoons mayonnaise
Salt (optional)
Lettuce or whole tomatoes
Hardboiled eggs, parsley, or lemon slices for garnish

Wash shrimp, and put in pan with cold water, vinegar (to mask odor) and seafood seasoning. Bring to a boil, then turn off heat and let stand for 5 minutes—no more, or they will be tough. Drain, shell, and take out black vein.

If the shrimp are large, halve them. (We never had the jumbo shrimp in the old days, and I still prefer the flavor of the little sweet ones.) Sprinkle with lemon juice, add celery and just enough mayonnaise to moisten. Taste for seasoning, add salt if needed. Toss together and refrigerate. Line a bowl with lettuce leaves, or fill hollowed-out tomatoes and serve cold, garnished with lemon slices, hardboiled egg, or parsley. (We sometimes extended this dish with hardboiled eggs, cut up in eighths.) *Serves 4 to 6*

Oyster Omelet

6 eggs
½ cup cream
Salt and pepper to taste

1 tablespoon butter, melted
1 dozen oysters, cut in half
1 teaspoon chopped parsley

Beat eggs until very light, add cream, salt, and pepper. Melt butter in large spider and pour in eggs. Lower heat, stir as you would for scrambled eggs once or twice, then keep rotating the pan, letting the soft part of egg run to outside. When it begins to set, place oysters around evenly. Sprinkle with parsley and cook until eggs are set. (I like to put the pan under the broiler for a few seconds.) Fold over and serve immediately.　　　*Serves 3 or 4*

Fried Oysters

The secret of good fried oysters is to use butter for frying and to use bread crumbs, not cracker crumbs. Oysters should be cooked quickly so that they don't shrink.

1 to 2 dozen large oysters	1 cup bread crumbs
Salt and pepper	4 to 5 tablespoons butter or
3 tablespoons flour	other shortening
1 egg, well beaten	Catsup or chili sauce

Pick over and drain oysters. Salt and pepper them, and dredge with flour. Dip in crumbs, then in eggs and again in crumbs. (I use soup plates for this—one for the flour, one for the eggs, and one for the crumbs—and this makes a sort of assembly-line operation.) Let oysters stand for about 15 minutes. Then melt butter and fry oysters quickly, browning them on both sides and not crowding them. (You may have to wash out the frying pan and start again, because bread crumbs burn quickly.) Serve at once with catsup or chili sauce.

Serves 2 or 3

Panned Oysters

25 oysters	2 tablespoons butter
	Salt and pepper

Drain oysters in colander. Heat spider hissing hot, toss in oysters, and shake and stir until they just come to a boil. Then add salt, pepper, and butter. Serve immediately.　　　*Serves 3 or 4*

Cold Salmon Pudding

1 1-pound can red salmon	1½ tablespoons melted butter
¾ tablespoon gelatine	or margarine
2 tablespoons cold water	2 egg yolks, beaten
¾ cup milk	¼ cup vinegar
½ teaspoon salt	Lettuce and hardboiled egg to
1½ teaspoons sugar	garnish
1 teaspoon dry mustard	Mayonnaise

Chili sauce (optional)

Rinse salmon with hot water; drain thoroughly. Pick over the salmon, removing skin and bones. Soak gelatine in cold water. Scald milk, and pour over salt, sugar, and mustard which have been mixed together. Put in double boiler, and cook 5 minutes, stirring constantly. Add melted butter, then beaten egg yolks, and finally hot vinegar. Stir and cook until mixture thickens slightly. Add softened gelatine and stir until it dissolves. Remove from fire, add salmon. Turn into mold which has been rinsed out with cold water. Refrigerate until stiff.

Turn out onto platter garnished with lettuce and hardboiled eggs, and serve with plain mayonnaise, or mayonnaise combined with 3 or 4 tablespoons of chili sauce.   *Serves 4*

Creamed Seafood

2 tablespoons butter or	2 or 3 small potatoes, boiled and
margarine	cubed (may be leftover)
2 tablespoons flour	1 pound scallops
1 cup milk	1 can shrimp, or ½ pound
1 teaspoon salt	cooked shrimp
⅛ teaspoon pepper	½ pound crabmeat, or 1 can crab
2 tablespoons sherry or any	(optional)
other sweet wine	Buttered crumbs

Make white sauce (see Index) with butter, flour and milk, seasoned with pepper and salt. Let cool, then add wine.

Cut potatoes quite small, and cut scallops in small pieces. Add shrimp and crabmeat (if desired). Place in baking dish or casserole, pour over it the white sauce, top with buttered crumbs, and bake at 350° for 30 minutes.

Short Cut:

Thaw 1 can frozen shrimp soup and 1 can frozen potato soup. Add fish, sherry, 1 tablespoon butter, and seasonings. Put in casserole, and bake at 350° for 30 minutes.

Serve with rice or in patty shells, which we sometimes made out of very rich pie crust.   *Serves 4 to 6*

CHAPTER VI

From the Springhouse and Hen Houses (Eggs and Cheese)

The springhouse was usually located near the kitchen, and sometimes adjacent to it and the pump, so that one spring served a dual purpose. It was built right over a spring, and the water ran continuously through a handmade wooden trough. Milk cans were placed in this trough to keep cool until the early morning trip to the creamery. Shelves were built right in the shallow part of the water, and cheeses, butter, and other perishables were kept there.

The springhouse smelled very much like a damp cave, which it really was, since the floor of earth was below the level of the outside ground. You stepped down into coolness on a hot summer's day. Deep pans of milk were stored here for the cream to rise, to be skimmed off for making butter, and the skimmed milk was used for cheese making. In the early days on the farms there was no other source of refrigeration, but later there were iceboxes which were kept filled by an itinerant ice man. Every bit of milk and cream was precious and used in some way.

The clabbered (souring) milk was made into cheese—schmierkäse (cottage cheese), kochkäse (cup cheese), and handkäse (hand cheese). You can still find kochkäse and handkäse at market. There are three varieties of cup cheese—mild, sharp, and extra sharp. It is a semi-liquid cheese, light yellow and faintly reminiscent of Camembert in flavor. It is made by cooking well-drained cottage cheese with butter and a little soda. Making cup cheese is almost a lost art now, but we often made it when I was a child. It had to be stirred constantly with a wooden spoon because it stuck easily. Handkäse has a center of hard schmierkäse and an outer covering of hardened cup cheese. When well ripened the blend of the two textures is an experience to the tastebuds, but frequently it is bland and insipid. It can still be found at Dutch markets, usually at the cup cheese stand.

The hen house was considered to be the women's province in the days before poultry and eggs became big business. The women fed the chickens, and the children usually gathered the eggs and put them down in the springhouse. Mom almost always got the egg money, which was carefully hoarded for special treats or for emergencies. Usually only the cracked eggs were used for cooking and eating—the whole eggs were kept for market. Eggs were always served for breakfast, and were used lavishly in baking and cooking. They also frequently appeared in one guise or other on the supper table, either deviled, creamed, or made into an omelet, or as red beet eggs, and they were almost as indispensable as parsley for garnishing.

When eggs were abundant, in the old days, they were put down in a preparation called "water glass," against the time when the chickens would be molting and eggs would be scarce, and kept in that solution for several months. Water glass is a preparation that is still available in any hardware store. It is sold as a powder or in liquid form and consists of sodium silicate, or potassium silicate, or a combination of both, in which case it is known as double water glass. To use it, you dissolve 1 pint of water glass powder in 16 to 18 pints of cooled, boiled water, which makes a viscous, syrupy liquid. Then you put it in a large crock or container, and "drop the eggs in."

There was a constant changeover in the poultry population, and any hen that didn't cooperate and lay well usually wound up in the stew pot.

F U N E X?

S V F X.

F U N E M?

S V F M.

O K, L F M N X.

Phonetic rendition:

Have you any eggs?

Yes, we have eggs.

Have you any ham?

Yes, we have ham.

O.K., I'll have ham and eggs.

Schmierkäse
(COTTAGE CHEESE)

Pour 2 quarts boiling water into 2 quarts thick, sour milk. Let mixture stand a few minutes until it separates, then pour it all into a cheesecloth bag. Hang over the sink, or over a bowl, and let drain overnight. (Do not squeeze although the temptation may be strong!) Empty bag into a bowl, beat cheese with a wooden spoon, season with salt and pepper and just enough sweet cream for the consistency you prefer.   *Serves 4*

Schmierkäse mit Schnittlach
(COTTAGE CHEESE WITH CHIVES)

Prepare cottage cheese as above. Chop 1 tablespoonful of chives, fresh or frozen, add to cheese and stir well. This is simply luscious with little new potatoes, boiled and served in their jackets.

Cream Cheese

We made our own cream cheese on the farm, before the days when it was widely available, and this is how we made it:

To each pint of drained curd, we added 2 tablespoonfuls of melted butter, salt and pepper to taste, and enough thick, sweet cream to achieve the proper consistency. The cheese was stirred with a wooden spoon until smooth, and then shaped, and placed in a cool place. We used to make it into the shape of a ball, but you could make it into squares. It doesn't keep very well, but it is delicious.

Kochkäse
(CUP CHEESE)

Few people make cup cheese any more, but it is still very popular at market, and it comes in three styles—mild, medium, and strong (and the strong is just that!). Many farmers' wives still make it, if only to use up the clabbered (soured) milk.

2 quarts boiling water	1 to 2 tablespoons butter
2 quarts thick sour milk	⅛ teaspoon baking soda
1 cup skim milk (approx.)	

Pour boiling water into sour milk and let stand a few minutes to separate. Place in cheesecloth bag and hang at least 2 days, or until thoroughly dry. Squeeze bag to be sure all moisture is removed. (You squeeze cup cheese, you don't squeeze schmierkäse!)

Put dry curds into frying pan together with butter, place over low flame, and stir constantly with wooden spoon. As soon as curds begin to melt, add baking soda and continue stirring. Gradually add enough skim milk until mixture has consistency of a thick custard, smooth and yellow. Be careful to stir constantly because it "schticks so easy." Pour into buttered baking cups, and cool. It will keep for a week.

The strength of the mixture depends upon how long cheese is allowed to age. If you like a strong cheese, let it hang for a few more days, but stir it with a fork every so often—about once a day. At its best, cup cheese is faintly reminiscent of good Camembert.

Serves 4 to 6

Gekochte Käse
(COOKED CHEESE)

This is another version of cup cheese, but it has quite a different flavor. It is strong but delicious, especially on rye bread.

1 quart homemade or packaged (small curd) cottage cheese	1½ cups water
1 teaspoon salt	1 tablespoon butter or margarine
1 teaspoon caraway seed	1 egg yolk, beaten

Put cottage cheese into bag, and squeeze until dry, or drain for an hour or so in colander. Put into covered glass bowl or casserole, add salt and caraway seed, cover tightly, and leave in warm place to ripen. Stir every day for a week, until cheese becomes slightly runny and yellow. Heat water together with butter in frying pan, add cheese, and boil slowly for 20 minutes, stirring constantly. Take from fire, add slightly beaten egg yolk, and beat mixture until thoroughly mixed and shiny. Pour into custard cups, or small bowls, and refrigerate. It hardens upon refrigeration but never gets truly hard.

Handkäse or Schtinkäse
(HAND CHEESE)

Although we used to make this frequently, it is becoming harder and harder to find, and the last I bought at market didn't even resemble the real thing. In my childhood the cheese was formed by hand, hence the name, and was sometimes called "schtinkäse" for obvious reasons. Cottage cheese was placed in a cheesecloth bag and hung to drip, as for cup cheese, until it was completely dry. (We used the bags salt came in—does *anyone* recall when salt came in little bags?) Then it was formed into balls about 2 or 3 inches in diameter. Each ball was then wrapped in cheesecloth and set in a warm place to "make." When the outside turned clear and yellow, and the center was still white, it was ready to eat. The combination of the pungent yellow exterior with the crunchy center is a taste sensation. It really does schtink, but tastes somesing wonderful good!

Basic White Sauce

2 tablespoons butter or margarine	½ teaspoon salt
2 tablespoons flour	⅛ teaspoon pepper
	1 cup milk

Melt butter in saucepan. Stir in flour and seasonings gradually, being sure to get out all lumps. (I like to use a wooden spoon for this.) Remove from fire, and add milk very, very slowly. Return to fire, and stirring constantly cook until desired thickness. Use as described in various recipes. *Makes about 1⅓ cups sauce*

At market: "What are your eggs?"
"Oh, they're dear today—20¢ a dozen!"

Red Beet Eggs

Bring eggs to a boil, simmer for 20 minutes. Immediately plunge them into cold water (to avoid a ring around the yolk). In the meantime, boil one or two beets until tender, peel and dice, and cover with 2 tablespoons vinegar, 2 tablespoons sugar (or to taste), and a dash of salt. Peel eggs, put them into a jar with the beets, and cool. They will turn a rosy red, and are not only beautiful but delicious. The longer they stand the redder they become. They should be in the solution for at least 1 hour.

Deviled Eggs

5 or 6 eggs
Water to cover
¼ lemon, juiced
¼ teaspoon prepared mustard

Salt and pepper
1 or 2 teaspoons mayonnaise or
    salad dressing
Dash of paprika

Bring eggs to a boil and let simmer for 20 minutes. Immediately plunge into cold water. When cold, cut in half lengthwise. Put yolks through a sieve, keeping whites separate from filling. Add to yolks the lemon juice, mustard, salt, and pepper to taste, and just enough mayonnaise so that mixture will spread nicely. Fill whites, rounding the top. Sprinkle with paprika and refrigerate until ready to serve.

Serves 5 or 6

Chellied Eier
(EGGS IN ASPIC)

2 envelopes plain gelatine
½ cup cold water
1 18-ounce can tomato juice
½ teaspoon horseradish
½ teaspoon Worcestershire
    sauce
½ lemon, juiced
½ teaspoon sugar

Dash Tabasco or hot pepper
    sauce
2 tablespoons catsup
Deviled eggs (see above)
Red and green pepper, diced for
    garnish
½ cup mayonnaise, mixed with
    3 tablespoons chili sauce

Soak gelatine in cold water to soften. Heat tomato juice to boiling, add to gelatine, and stir until gelatine is dissolved. Add horseradish, Worcestershire sauce, lemon juice, sugar, and Tabasco. Taste and correct for seasoning.

Make deviled eggs and put halves back together to form whole egg. Pour ½ cup of aspic into ring mold. If you want a square mold, use a bread pan. Chill until gelatine begins to hold its shape. Place eggs carefully into chilled gelatine, at equal intervals, and cover with remaining aspic. Chill until firm. Unmold on platter and garnish with diced pepper. Serve with mayonnaise mixed with chili sauce.

Serves 4 to 6

Egg and Cheese Chelly

Jelly:

2 envelopes unflavored gelatine	1 slice onion, minced
1 18-ounce can tomato juice	½ teaspoon salt
2 stalks celery, diced	1 teaspoon sugar
	¼ teaspoon pepper

Soak gelatine in ½ cup of the tomato juice. Combine rest of ingredients in saucepan, bring to a boil, then simmer 10 minutes. Strain tomato mixture, add to gelatine and stir until dissolved.

Eggs:

6 hardboiled eggs	1 tablespoon lemon juice
3 tablespoons mayonnaise	Dash of Worcestershire sauce
3 tablespoons sharp cheese, crumbled or grated (I use blue cheese)	1 can salmon or tuna fish
	Lemon slices, lettuce, or cress for garnish

Slice eggs lengthwise and remove yolks. Mash them, add rest of ingredients, except fish, and mix well. Stuff whites just level with this mixture. Refrigerate.

Pour about ½ cup aspic into ring mold. (You can use another shape if you prefer.) When aspic begins to thicken, space the eggs, cut side down, around ring. Pour about 1½ cups of remaining aspic around eggs, carefully keeping them in place.

To remaining gelatine, add fish, drained. Mix gently and refrigerate. Chill until firm. Unmold eggs on platter and spoon fish mixture into center. Decorate with lemon and lettuce or cress.

Serves 8 to 10

Egg Patties

5 or 6 hardboiled eggs	1 teaspoon salt
About 1 cup cooked rice (may be instant, or leftover)	⅛ teaspoon pepper
	½ cup mayonnaise (about)
1 teaspoon onion, chopped fine	Bread crumbs

Catsup or chili sauce

Chop eggs, add to rice. Add onion, salt and pepper, and just enough mayonnaise to make mixture hold together. Shape into patties. Pour some bread crumbs on shallow plate, and press in patties, coating on both sides.

Bake on greased cookie sheet at 400° just until nicely browned, about 15 minutes. Serve hot with catsup or chili sauce.

Makes 6 patties

Egg and Potato Pie

3 medium-sized white potatoes	1 teaspoon salt
Water to cover	1 teaspoon parsley
1 recipe pie crust (packaged mix may be used)	Dash of paprika
	2 tablespoons butter or margarine
4 hardboiled eggs, sliced	
⅛ cup chopped onion	2 tablespoons flour
⅛ teaspoon pepper	1 cup milk (about)

Dice potatoes in fairly large cubes, and boil until almost soft. Now make pastry for two-crust pie. Drain potatoes; spread them and the sliced eggs on bottom crust. Sprinkle with onion, pepper, salt, parsley, and paprika. Make a white sauce (see Index) with butter, flour, and milk, keeping it about as thin as thick cream. Pour over potatoes and eggs. Roll out top crust, and cover pie. Wet your hand with cold water and rub the top, for a nice brown crust. Make slits to let steam escape. Bake at 350° for about 30 minutes, or until crust is browned and contents bubble.

We sometimes added bits of ham to this dish. *Serves 4 to 6*

Egg and Corn Pie

Pastry for a 2-crust pie (see Index)   1 teaspoon salt
  —packaged mix may be used   ⅛ teaspoon pepper
4 or 5 hardboiled eggs, sliced   1 teaspoon parsley
1 can whole kernel corn, or   1 teaspoon sugar
   1 cup fresh corn, cut from   4 tablespoons butter
   the cob   2 tablespoons flour
1 cup chopped leftover chicken   1 cup milk (about)
   or pork (optional)

Prepare two-crust pie. Fill bottom crust with alternate layers of sliced eggs and corn. If you are using leftover meat, make a layer of that, too. Sprinkle with salt, pepper, parsley, sugar, and 2 tablespoons of melted butter. Make white sauce (see Index) with remaining butter, flour and milk, keeping it fairly thin. Pour over the whole, place second crust, moisten lightly with cold water, cut vents, and bake at 350° for about 30 minutes or until nicely browned.

Serves 4 to 6

Egg and Ham Casserole

4 hardboiled eggs, sliced   1 cup white sauce (see Index)
2 cups bread crumbs   ⅛ teaspoon minced onion
2 cups ham, chopped   2 tablespoons milk

   Place sliced eggs in greased baking dish or casserole. Cover with ⅓ bread crumbs, then some of white sauce, then another ⅓ bread crumbs, then ham, white sauce and rest of bread crumbs. Sprinkle the onion over each layer. Sprinkle milk over the top and bake at 350° for 20 minutes, until top is nicely browned.   *Serves 4 to 6*

Farmer's Omelet

2 tablespoons butter or   ¼ teaspoon minced onion
   margarine   (optional)
2 or 3 cooked potatoes, diced   3 eggs
   into very small cubes   1 tablespoon cream
¼ cup diced ham (leftover)   Salt and pepper

   Melt butter in frying pan, add potatoes and fry until they begin to brown. Add diced ham, and onion (if desired). Lower heat.

Beat eggs with cream, add salt and pepper, and pour over ham-potato mixture in pan. Cook very slowly, rotating so that egg mixture runs out to sides of pan. When omelet is almost dry on top, turn over with spatula, and cook a few seconds longer. Serve at once.

Serves 2 or 3

Filled Omelet

This omelet was baked like a jelly roll, and various types of fillings were used. One time it might be well-seasoned and sweetened schmierkäse; another time ground meat, mixed with a little white sauce (see Index) or salad dressing; and when it was served as a dessert, it was filled with jam or jelly. It is especially delicious with a ham filling.

¼ cup butter or margarine	¾ teaspoon salt
½ cup flour	Dash of pepper
2 cups milk	Pinch of dried thyme
	4 eggs, separated

Make white sauce (see Index) with all ingredients except eggs. Beat egg yolks, gradually beat in white sauce. Beat egg whites until they form stiff peaks. Fold sauce into egg whites until no white streaks show. Turn into greased jelly-roll pan, 15½ by 10½ inches. Bake at 325° for 40 to 45 minutes, or until top springs back when touched. Loosen edge with knife, and "up-dump" the omelet onto clean towel. Quickly spread any desired filling over it and roll up. Cut in slices and serve immediately. *Serves 4 to 6*

Cheese, Corn, and Tomato Custard

1 tablespoon butter or margarine	Dash of dried basil (optional)
1 tablespoon flour	1 cup corn, fresh or canned
½ cup tomato juice	2 eggs, separated
Salt and pepper	1 cup grated cheese
	1 cup bread crumbs

Melt butter, add flour, then tomato juice and seasonings. Cook until mixture thickens, stirring constantly. Add to corn and mix thoroughly. Add egg yolks. Beat whites until stiff, but not dry, and fold into other ingredients. Pour into baking dish, sprinkle with cheesed crumbs and bake in moderate oven (350°) for 30 to 40 minutes or until firm. *Serves 4*

Cheese Biscuits

Although we made these cheese biscuits for supper, I use the same recipe for making tiny cheese canapés.

¼ pound butter, softened   2 cups flour
½ pound sharp cheese, grated   ½ teaspoon salt
Dash of red pepper

Combine softened butter and cheese. Add rest of ingredients. Roll out on floured board and cut into biscuits. Bake on greased cookie sheet at 400° for about 10 minutes, just until nicely browned.

Makes 12 to 14 biscuits

Cheese Pudding

4 slices white bread
1½ tablespoons butter or margarine, at room temperature
¼ pound (1 cup) sharp cheese,
   grated
2 eggs

1¼ cups milk
1 tablespoon prepared mustard
½ teaspoon Worcestershire
   sauce
¼ teaspoon salt
Dash of paprika

Spread bread with butter, then cut into large squares. Put about one third of them in 1-quart baking dish or casserole. Sprinkle with one third of cheese; repeat with remaining bread and cheese to make 2 more layers of each. (You don't have to be too fussy about exact thirds—just make layers of the bread and cheese.)

Beat eggs with milk, add seasonings, and pour over bread and cheese. Cover and refrigerate at least 3 hours or overnight.

Bake, uncovered, at 350° for 1 hour, when pudding will have puffed up and will be a golden color. Unlike most soufflés this can stand a little waiting, but it should be served fairly soon after it is taken from the oven. *Serves 4 to 6*

Cheese with Wine

This is a good way to use up those little tads of cheese which seem to accumulate.

2 tablespoons butter
½ pound grated Cheddar cheese
¼ to ½ cup Madeira, sherry, or homemade wine

1 egg yolk, slightly beaten
Several tablespoons of cream
Dash of red pepper
Salt, if needed

Melt butter, add grated cheese, and cook over low flame until cheese has melted. Add wine and beaten egg yolk, and continue to cook until thick and smooth. Add just enough cream, a tablespoonful at a time, to thin. Add pepper, taste, and add salt if needed—it depends upon the cheese. Pour into little crocks, cups, or small jars, and refrigerate.

This recipe may be halved, but it freezes well and I often use it for a dip, so I usually make the whole amount. We used to serve it at supper with crackers, to "spread out the table."   *Serves 6 to 10*

Cheese Straws

Whenever there was just a little pie dough left, the housewife would say, "I belief I'll make myself some cheese straws," and she added some grated cheese, rolled the dough out, cut it into strips, sprinkled it with paprika, and baked it in a hot oven. I like them so much that I make up a whole batch, like this:

To ½ recipe pie dough (see Index)—packaged mix is acceptable —add ½ cup grated sharp Cheddar cheese and 1 egg yolk. Mix thoroughly, roll about ⅛ inch thick and cut into strips. (Sometimes I use a doughnut cutter, and after the strips are baked slip a few of them through the ring "for pretty.") Bake at 425° for 8 to 10 minutes. May be frozen.   *Makes about 2 dozen*

Zwievelkuche
(ONION CAKE)

Sudden company? If you have a baked pie shell in your freezer, you can make this very quickly. If you don't have cottage cheese on hand, try it with cream cheese, mixed with cream and beaten slightly. It goes wonderfully with drinks, especially with beer.

2 cups cottage cheese
1 to 2 tablespoons cream
⅛ teaspoon salt

⅛ teaspoon pepper
1 baked pie shell (see Index)
2 medium-sized onions, diced

1 to 2 tablespoons butter

Mix cottage cheese with cream—not too runny, please—and salt and pepper to taste. Place in baked pie shell. Fry onions in butter until just golden brown, and sprinkle over cheese. Bake 10 minutes at 350°. *Serves 6 to 8*

Schmierkäse Kuchen
(COTTAGE CHEESE PIE)

1 unbaked pie crust (see Index)
1¼ cups cottage cheese
2 eggs, separated
⅓ cup sugar
2 tablespoons flour or cornstarch
¼ teaspoon salt

⅔ cup sour cream
½ teaspoon nutmeg
3 tablespoons melted butter or melted vegetable shortening
1 teaspoon lemon juice
1 teaspoon grated lemon rind

Put cottage cheese through sieve. Beat egg yolks until thoroughly mixed; add sugar, flour, and salt, and then sour cream. Beat until mixture is entirely free of lumps. Slowly blend in cheese and nutmeg. Add melted shortening, lemon juice, and rind.

Beat egg whites until stiff, but not dry, and fold into cheese mixture. Pour into unbaked pie crust. Bake at 450° for 10 minutes, then lower heat to 325°, and continue baking for 50 minutes, or until a silver knife inserted near center comes out clean. Cool, but don't refrigerate. *Makes 1 9-inch pie*

"Mary, go vunst and comb yourself. Your hairs are too strubbly." (*Strubblepeter* is a Pfalz folk tale about a boy with unruly hair. Hair is usually referred to in the plural, as in French.)

CHAPTER VII

From the Patch
(Vegetables and Salads)

In the early spring, Pop spread manure on the vegetable patch, plowed it and disked it, and from then on it was up to the women. If he wasn't too busy, he might be talked into putting up posts, with wire between them, for the tall peas, and perhaps plant a few rows of potatoes, but the weeding, sowing, and picking were left to the women and children. The rows had to be completely straight, or what would the neighbors think? The vegetable gardens of the Pennsylvania Dutch are a joy to behold, colorful and neat as the pictures in the seed catalogues. From the earliest radishes and leaf lettuce to the last cabbages and turnips, weeds are never permitted to raise their heads, or the family would have shame. The older children sometimes ran the cultivator over the garden, but most of the work was done by hand.

In the old days vegetables were salted down or dried, or placed in a layer of dirt and sand in the root cellar, but in later years canning came into its own. The cellar shelves of a Pennsylvania Dutch farm wife burgeon with jars of preserved fruits and vegetables, and few women visitors escape without being shown this evidence of the hostess's providence.

The vegetables, for the most part, are the usual ones, but

there are some, such as sugar peas, which are novelties to out-siders. These are called "edible podded peas" in the catalogues and are known to the Chinese as "snow peas." How they ever came from China to the Pennsylvania Dutch country is un-known. I remember finding a note from a visitor to my present home in Delaware: "I wasn't sure I had the right house, but when I saw the sugar peas in the patch, I knew it must be!" These delicate, delicious peas are picked before the pods fill out, the strings are removed, as in preparing stringbeans, and then they are cooked either sweet and sour, or with butter and cream. They can be found at market in most Pennsylvania Dutch areas, but only in the spring.

Sweet and Sour Sugar Peas

Wash and string the peas, and put in boiling salted water. They do not require long cooking. When they are tender, remove from the heat. Do not drain. In a small bowl, blend 1 tablespoon of butter with 2 tablespoons of flour until all lumps are removed. Add 2 tablespoons of vinegar and 2 tablespoons of granulated sugar, and stir well. Add this mixture to the peas and heat just to a boil. Since vinegars differ in strength, taste the peas before serving. If too sour, add more sugar; add salt, if needed.

Dandelion Hot Salad

Dandelion didn't come from the patch, Heaven forbid, but it was nevertheless considered to be the first fresh vegetable in the spring. The children went out to hunt for it as soon as the snow had melted. Armed with a big kettle and a sharp knife, they went searching in the fields and roadsides. The younger the dandelion, the more tender. It was considered a fine spring tonic, good for "the *insides*." After it was dug, the roots were carefully cut off, and it was washed and washed again—mixed with a hot sauce it was served as "hot salad." Young leaf lettuce is dressed in the same way.

Dice two slices of bacon, fry in deep kettle until not quite crisp. Add 2 tablespoons granulated sugar, and 2 tablespoons vinegar, and stir until sugar is melted. Add dash of salt, and 1 raw egg. Stir rapidly until egg curdles. (It looks awful, but tastes sublime!) Remove from fire. Add dandelion (or young lettuce) and toss quickly until all leaves are covered and slightly wilted. Serve hot. (It is necessary to taste for seasoning, as vinegars differ. If too sour, add more sugar; if too sweet, more vinegar.)   *Serves 2 to 4*

Peas with Spätzele
(PEAS WITH DUMPLINGS)

1 quart peas (or 2 packages frozen peas)	1 teaspoon sugar
	1 tablespoon butter
Salted water to cover	1 teaspoon chopped parsley
Pepper	(fresh or dried)

Cook peas in salted water with pepper, sugar, butter, and parsley until just tender. (Follow package directions for frozen peas.) Do not drain. While peas are cooking, mix dumpling batter.

Dumplings:

1 egg, well beaten	4 teaspoons baking powder
¼ cup milk	½ teaspoon salt
2 cups flour	Dash of nutmeg
⅛ teaspoon parsley	

Combine egg and milk. Sift flour, baking powder, salt, and nutmeg together. Add them with parsley to egg mixture. Stir. Drop by scant teaspoonfuls onto top of peas, which have been brought to a boil. Cover closely, and cook for 10 minutes, without peeking.

Serves 4 to 6

Creamed Spinach

Many people seem to abhor spinach, but when it is cooked the Dutch way, it is a delicacy.

1 pound fresh spinach, or 1 package frozen chopped spinach	1 tablespoon butter
	1 tablespoon flour
	Pepper, salt, nutmeg
1 hardboiled egg as garnish	

If spinach is fresh, wash thoroughly. Put on to cook without adding water, or cook according to frozen package directions. Cook just until tender, remove from fire, drain, and save juice. Chop spinach (if fresh) and set aside. Melt butter, add flour, and cook until brown. Remove from heat, add spinach juice slowly, stirring constantly. Season to taste with salt, pepper, and nutmeg, and pour over spinach. Heat again. Serve, decorated with hardboiled egg.

Serves 4

Frauen Kraut
(LADIES' CABBAGE)

1 head cabbage	Pepper and salt
2 eggs, beaten	3 tablespoons cream or
1 tablespoon butter	rich milk

Boil firm cabbage for 15 minutes. When tender, drain and set aside until perfectly cold. (You can use leftover cabbage—about 3 cups—for this dish.) Chop fine; add beaten eggs, butter, pepper, and salt to taste, and cream. Stir well, and bake uncovered in buttered casserole until brown—about 20 minutes.   *Serves 6 to 8*

Hot Sweet Cabbage

The Pennsylvania Dutch call green cabbage "sweet cabbage" to differentiate it from sauerkraut.

2 slices lean bacon	1 stalk celery, diced
1 small head cabbage, sliced very thin, as for slaw	

Cut bacon into small pieces and fry, but do not let it get too brown. Add cabbage and celery and turn them frequently—just enough to absorb the fat, not to brown. Then pour over it the following dressing:

1 egg, well beaten	¼ cup vinegar
1 tablespoon cornstarch	1 cup water
½ cup sugar	½ teaspoon salt

Beat egg. Mix cornstarch and sugar. Add egg very slowly to avoid lumps. Beat again, then add vinegar and water. Bring to boil, then cook over low heat until it coats a spoon.

Pour over cabbage, taste and correct seasoning. Serve warm.

Serves 4 to 6

Sauerkraut mit Spätzele
(SAUERKRAUT WITH DUMPLINGS)

1 quart sauerkraut,
  fresh or canned
1 small piece pork

½ teaspoon salt
  (omit, if salt pork is used)
½ cup water

Put sauerkraut on to boil with pork, salt, and water. Boil at least 50 minutes, until kraut is golden yellow. In the meantime, make the dumplings:

1 cup flour
Pinch baking powder

2 eggs, slightly beaten
Water

Mix flour and baking powder, add slightly beaten eggs. Add just enough water to make dough drop easily from a spoon—not too thin.

Bring kraut to a good rolling boil, adding a little water if necessary for cooking dumplings. There should be at least 2 cupfuls broth. Drop dumplings into sauerkraut, cover and let cook 3 to 5 minutes until dumplings are done. (Test by taking out one dumpling, and cutting it open—it should be dry in the center.) Remove dumplings with slotted spoon. Put kraut in deep dish or platter and surround with dumplings.   *Serves 4 to 6*

Cabbage and Noodles

1 small head cabbage, or
  4 cups leftover cabbage
Salted water
4 tablespoons butter

½ package medium-wide
  noodles, boiled as package
  directs

Shred cabbage as for slaw, and boil in salted water for 15 minutes. (If using leftover cabbage omit this step.) Drain and fry light brown in 1 tablespoon butter. Boil noodles for 20 minutes. Alternate layers of fried cabbage and noodles and top with remaining butter, which has been melted and allowed to brown lightly.   *Serves 4 to 6*

Sweet and Sour Beans

½ pound dried navy beans
Water
2 pounds string beans—fresh,
  canned, or frozen

2 tablespoons butter
2 tablespoons flour
1 tablespoon vinegar
1 tablespoon sugar

Salt and pepper to taste

Soak dried beans overnight. Bring to boil, and simmer until soft—about one hour. Drain, but save water used for boiling. Slice fresh beans on a diagonal (French style), and cook in salted water until tender, or follow package directions for frozen beans. Combine the two kinds of beans. In saucepan, melt butter and add flour, but do not allow to brown. Slowly add enough bean water, stirring constantly, to make smooth sauce. Add vinegar, sugar, salt, and pepper. Pour over beans and correct seasoning. Heat to blend flavors. This is not only unusual, but also delicious and pretty. *Serves 6 to 8*

Rotkraut
(RED CABBAGE)

1 head red cabbage	3 to 4 tablespoons vinegar
Water	3 to 4 tablespoons sugar
6 whole cloves	Dash of salt

Shred cabbage as for slaw. Put on to boil in as little water as possible. Add cloves and boil gently for 25 minutes, or until cabbage is done. Add vinegar, sugar, and salt, and boil at least 10 minutes longer. (Some people put a piece of pork in this, but it makes it a little greasy, and it is excellent "so.") Taste before serving, and correct seasoning. *Serves 6 to 8*

Fried Cabbage

Left-over cooked cabbage was drained and fried lightly in brown butter. It was so good that we sometimes cooked a few quarters, just so we could fry it. After the cabbage has been removed from the pan, brown about a half cup of dry bread crumbs in butter, and sprinkle them over the top.

Sweet and Sour Cabbage

1 small head cabbage	4 slices bacon
6 tablespoons sugar	1 tablespoon flour
Water	3 to 4 tablespoons vinegar

Salt and pepper to taste

Shred cabbage. Add sugar, barely cover with water and cook just until cabbage is tender—about 15 minutes. Fry 4 slices of bacon until crisp. Remove bacon, add flour to fat and stir until it browns. Add liquid from cabbage, stirring constantly until sauce thickens. Add vinegar, salt, and pepper, and taste. Mix sauce with cabbage and serve hot. *Serves 4 to 6*

Fried Tomatoes

4 large tomatoes, not quite ripe
1 tablespoon water
1 teaspoon salt
2 teaspoons sugar
⅛ teaspoon pepper

1 egg, slightly beaten
Fine bread crumbs—
  about ½ cup
Shortening
¼ cup milk

Core tomatoes and slice about 1 inch thick. Mix water, seasonings, and beaten egg. Dip tomatoes in egg batter, then in crumbs. Fry quickly in hot fat, turning once. You must watch tomatoes carefully, or they will stick. Remove to warm platter and pour off any fat remaining in pan. Add milk, and stir rapidly to get up all the luscious brown bits in the pan. Pour this over tomatoes and serve at once.

If you like an extra "bite," you can fry completely green tomatoes, but we preferred fruit that had just begun to turn red. *Serves 6 to 8*

Welsch Korn Eysters
(CORN FRITTERS)

These were called "corn oysters," probably because they look like fried oysters when they are cooked. Made from fresh-picked corn, they are wonderful, but they're also good made with canned whole-kernel corn. We even served the fritters for breakfast, if there was time and we had leftover corn.

3 eggs, separated
½ teaspoon salt
⅛ teaspoon pepper
2 tablespoons flour

2 cups grated fresh or canned
  whole-kernel corn
2 teaspoons sugar
Lard or other shortening

Beat egg whites until stiff but not dry. Mix rest of ingredients except lard and fold into beaten whites. Drop by tablespoonfuls into hot lard or other fat and cook on both sides until brown. Serve at once. *Serves 4 to 6*

Tomato Fritters

There is no end to the resourcefulness of a Pennsylvania Dutch cook trying to find something different for her family, and this dish is one evidence of her ingenuity.

1 pint canned or stewed fresh tomatoes

1 tablespoon sugar

1 tablespoon melted butter

1 cup or more bread crumbs or cracker crumbs

Salt and pepper to taste

Flour

Butter

Mix first 6 ingredients, adding more crumbs if needed to hold together. Divide into small oblong rolls, dip in flour and fry in butter. Serve hot. *Serves 4*

Baked Tomato Rice

1 can tomatoes, or
   3 cups tomato juice

1 cup water

1 teaspoon salt

1 teaspoon sugar

1 bay leaf (optional)

Sprinkle of basil

2 teaspoons butter

1½ cups white rice, uncooked

Combine all ingredients except rice and boil 5 minutes. Remove bay leaf. Butter a baking dish or casserole with a tight lid. (You may use foil if you haven't a tight cover.) Wash rice and put in bottom of dish. Pour tomato sauce over rice and cover tightly. Bake 1 hour at 350°. *Serves 4*

Fried Carrots

5 or 6 small carrots

Salted water

½ teaspoon salt

3 tablespoons butter or margarine

1 teaspoon sugar

1 teaspoon chopped parsley

½ teaspoon vinegar (optional)

Scrape carrots and slice crosswise. Boil in salted water until just tender. Drain. Melt butter in frying pan, add drained carrots, sprinkle with sugar and parsley, and brown quickly, turning once. (Some Dutch families added vinegar—and you might try it to see if you like it that way.) *Serves 4*

Peas and Carrots

6 or 8 small carrots
Salted water
4 cups peas (fresh, frozen, or canned)
1 tablespoon butter

1 tablespoon flour
1 teaspoon salt
⅛ teaspoon pepper
1 tablespoon sugar
1 teaspoon chopped parsley

Scrape carrots and cut into ⅛-inch slices. Cook in salted water until tender. Do not drain. Cook peas (unless they are canned) and add them, together with their juice, to carrots.

Put butter in small bowl, blend in flour thoroughly. Add 2 tablespoons of the juice from vegetables and stir to a smooth paste. Add salt, pepper, and sugar. Bring vegetables to boil, add paste slowly, stirring constantly. Remove from fire as soon as thickened, taste and correct seasoning. Sprinkle with parsley and serve. *Serves 4 to 6*

Welsch Korn Pudding

6 ears fresh corn, or
1 can creamed-style corn
2 eggs, separated

2 cups milk
1 tablespoon sugar
½ teaspoon salt
1 tablespoon flour

Cut corn off cob, and scrape ears to get all the milk; or use canned corn. Beat egg whites until stiff but not dry. Then beat yolks. Add corn, milk, sugar, salt, and flour to yolks and mix well. Fold in beaten egg whites, and turn into well-buttered pudding dish. Bake at 350° until firm—about 25 minutes. (Use the silver knife test—if the knife comes out clean, the pudding is done.)

Overcooking will cause pudding to become watery. *Serves 3 or 4*

Anderes Korn Pudding
(ANOTHER CORN PUDDING)

This pudding is a little richer than the first. "Bose is good."

2 eggs	2 tablespoons butter,
2 cups corn	melted
2 cups milk	1 teaspoon salt
1 tablespoon sugar	⅛ teaspoon pepper

Beat whole eggs, add rest of ingredients. Bake at 350° in buttered pudding dish for 25 minutes to ½ hour, until a silver knife inserted in pudding comes out clean. Do not overcook.   *Serves 5 or 6*

Baked Corn with Ham or Sausage

3 tablespoons ham fat or butter	⅛ teaspoon pepper
½ cup bread crumbs	1 cup cooked ham, chopped, or
1 can creamed-style corn	1 cup cooked pork sausage,
1 cup milk	crumbled

Line casserole with mixture of fat and ¼ cup bread crumbs. Mix together corn, milk, pepper, ham or sausage, and top with remaining bread crumbs. Bake at 400° for 45 minutes.   *Serves 4*

Fried Corn

Leftover corn, or	3 tablespoons butter
1 can whole-kernel corn	1 teaspoon sugar
well drained	Pepper and salt

This is such a delicacy that we sometimes boiled corn just to make it. Boil corn for just 5 minutes, cut it from cob, and scrape ears to get all the milk out. Melt butter in frying pan, add corn, sprinkle with sugar, pepper, and salt, and fry slowly. Turn once so that corn is nicely browned. You have to watch this, as it tends to stick.
Serves 4

Baked Squash

You can use any kind of squash for this dish, but acorn is exceptionally nice made this way.

Wash squash, remove stem and end, and split lengthwise. Remove seeds. Put in shallow baking pan. Fill each half with 1 tablespoonful of maple syrup or molasses, and fill to top with cream. (If you don't happen to have cream, use milk with a little butter in it.) Sprinkle with salt, pepper, and nutmeg. Bake at 350° for about 30 minutes, or until tender.

Summer Squash

3 or 4 young squash
Boiling water
1 slice onion, minced

2 tablespoons butter, or
    bacon fat
⅛ teaspoon nutmeg

Do not peel squash. Cut off ends, and dice into fairly large cubes. Add boiling water to fill saucepan about half way up; add onion. Boil slowly at least 45 minutes, until squash is very soft and water considerably reduced. You may have to add a little water, but keep mixture as dry as you can without scorching it. Season with butter, pepper, and salt. Serve hot.

This may be frozen, and it is a delicious change in the wintertime when these delicate yellow squashes are not available.

Serves 4

Baked Eggplant

1 eggplant
Boiling water to cover
2 tablespoons butter or
    margarine
1 tablespoon flour
1 cup milk
2 tablespoons grated Cheddar
    cheese

1 teaspoon salt
⅛ teaspoon pepper
1 cup dry bread crumbs
2 tablespoons minced onion
1 tablespoon chopped fresh or
    dried parsley

Peel eggplant and cut into 1-inch slices. Then dice. Cover with boiling water and boil about 15 minutes. Drain. Make white sauce (see Index) with butter, flour, milk, half the cheese, salt, and pepper —keeping it thin. Butter a baking dish or casserole; make layers of eggplant, crumbs, half the sauce, half the onion, then another layer of each. Cover with rest of sauce, add remaining onion, and sprinkle

with remaining grated cheese and parsley. Bake in hot oven, 400°
about 25 to 30 minutes, or until nicely browned.   *Serves 6*

Baked Eggplant and Tomato

1 eggplant	1 tablespoon brown sugar
Boiling water to cover	1 teaspoon salt
¼ cup chopped onion	⅛ teaspoon pepper
1 clove garlic, minced	Sprinkle of basil (optional)
3 tablespoons corn or olive oil	1 cup mushrooms, sliced
3 stalks celery, sliced thin	(optional)
1 can tomatoes, or	2 tablespoons grated cheese—
1 quart stewed tomatoes	Cheddar, Parmesan, or any
	other cheese

Peel eggplant, slice about ½ inch thick, then cut each slice in
half. Boil in salted water about 10 minutes, or until just tender.
Lightly brown onion and garlic in oil. Add celery, tomatoes, sugar,
salt and pepper, and basil (if you like). I always feel that every
tomato dish is better for a touch of basil.

Butter baking dish or casserole, put in eggplant, and cover with
sauce. If you use mushrooms, layer them with the eggplant. Sprinkle
with grated cheese and bake at 350° for 30 minutes, until brown
and bubbling.

We sometimes added a little pork sausage, if any was left over—
we just crumbled it into the mixture.   *Serves 4 to 6*

Dried Lima Beans mit Schpeck

1 pint dried lima beans	2 tablespoons molasses
Water	1 teaspoon prepared mustard
¼ pound salt pork, diced	Salt and pepper

Soak beans overnight. Drain, cover with fresh water, cook slowly
1 hour or until beans are soft but not mushy. Put diced salt pork in
kettle and fry until crisp. Add beans with their juice, the molasses,
mustard, salt, and pepper to taste. Mix well. Simmer 10 minutes
until nicely thickened.

Short Cut:

Use canned lima beans, and cook as above. Serve with catsup.
          Serves 4

Hot Sweet and Sour Red Beets

We cooked many things sweet and sour, and I've always thought that it was because so much pork was served, which was usually fairly greasy. "A body needs something sour to cut the grease, not?"

3 or 4 beets	1 tablespoon vinegar
Water to cover	1 tablespoon sugar
1 tablespoon butter or margarine	1 teaspoon salt

Wash beets, cover with boiling water, and cook until tender—about 25 minutes. (Do not drain.) Pare and cube and return to water in which they were cooked. Blend butter and flour in small bowl, add vinegar, sugar and salt, and stir to a smooth paste. Add a little hot beet juice to flour mixture, then return all the thickening to beets. Cook just until thick. Taste and correct seasonings. *Serves 4*

Cold Sweet and Sour Red Beets

3 or 4 beets	1 tablespoon sugar
Salted water to cover	1 teaspoon salt
1 tablespoon vinegar	¼ teaspoon pepper

Wash beets and cook in boiling salted water until tender. Drain, and when cool enough to handle, peel—the skin slips right off—and slice into ⅛-inch slices. Mix vinegar, sugar, salt, and pepper together and pour over beets. Taste to correct seasoning and refrigerate.

Serves 4 to 6

Stuffed Onions

6 large onions	1 cup milk
Boiling salted water to cover	1 cup leftover meat (chicken, lamb, veal, or beef)
1 tablespoon butter	
1 tablespoon flour	Salt and pepper
2 tablespoons grated cheese	

Skin onions and cook in boiling, salted water about 20 minutes, or until almost tender. Cool just until you can handle them. Cut off about 1 inch from top, and scoop out center.

Make a white sauce (see Index) from butter, flour, and milk. Mix with leftover meat and add salt and pepper. Stuff into onions. Put tops back on onions, pour over any remaining sauce, and sprinkle with cheese.

Bake in greased shallow pan or casserole at 400° for about 20 minutes, or until onions are tender but not mushy.　　*Serves 6*

Gekochte Gurken un' Zwievel
(COOKED CUCUMBERS AND ONIONS)

4 or 5 medium-sized cucumbers	1 tablespoon sugar (or to taste)
2 medium-sized onions	Salt and pepper to taste
2 or 3 tablespoons mayonnaise	

Slice cucumbers in ⅛-inch slices—not too thin. Slice onions, combine with cucumbers and put on to boil in a little salted water. Boil 5 minutes, until vegetables are tender but not mushy. Put in colander, and let drain 1 hour. Add sugar, salt, and pepper, and just enough mayonnaise to mix thoroughly but not to be runny. Serve very cold.　　*Serves 4 to 6*

Kohlrabi

We used to raise many root vegetables, because they kept so well in the cellar, bedded down in dirt. One of the most delicious, to my fancy, is kohlrabi, although it is not strictly a root vegetable, since the bulbous section grows above the ground. It is often called turnip cabbage, probably because both the root and the tops are edible.

4 or 5 kohlrabi	1 tablespoon butter
Salted water to cover	1 tablespoon flour
Dash nutmeg	

Peel kohlrabi thinly and slice. Chop green tops finely and save. Boil roots in salted water just to cover until fork tender, about 25 to 30 minutes. Don't drain. Mix butter and flour and stir with a wooden spoon until smooth. Add a little kohlrabi juice to mixture, then add this to the vegetable. Sprinkle chopped tops into mixture, add dash of nutmeg, stir and serve.　　*Serves 2 to 4*

Baked Salsify or Oyster Plant

Salsify is an edible root resembling a parsnip, only it is smaller. You may have passed it by, thinking "Ugh, parsnips," but if you did you've missed a treat. Some people think the flavor resembles that of oysters, hence its second name. Ask for it by both names in your market.

6 to 8 salsify	⅛ teaspoonful celery seed
Salted water to cover	Sprinkle of chopped parsley
2 cups white sauce (see Index)	Bread crumbs

Scrape salsify and slice thin. Boil in salted water until tender—about ½ hour. Drain. Make white sauce. In buttered baking dish put layer of salsify, sprinkled with a few celery seeds and parsley, then a layer of white sauce. Alternate layers until the salsify is "all" (used up). Top with bread crumbs and bake at 400° for 20 minutes.

Serves 4 to 6

Mock Oysters

1 dozen salsify	3 eggs, beaten
Salted water to cover	2 or 3 tablespoons lard or other
1 teaspoon salt	shortening
⅛ teaspoon pepper	

Scrape salsify and place in salted water. Bring to boil, then cook slowly until mushy. Drain, and press through a sieve or food mill. Mix in salt, pepper, and well-beaten eggs. Drop into hot lard by rounded spoonfuls to make them look like oysters. Brown on both sides and serve hot with catsup.

Serves 4 to 6

POTATOES

A probably apocryphal story about the happily plump singer, Madame Schumann-Heink, always reminds me of a Pennsylvania Dutch meal. She was sitting in a restaurant with an enormous steak on the table before her, and someone said to her, "Ernestine, you're not going to eat that steak all alone, are you?"—whereupon she smiled beatifically and said, "Oh no, vis potatoes." Every Dutch meal is "vis potatoes"—breakfast, lunch, and dinner—and I still feel that a meal isn't complete without them, although I have now learned to forgo them for breakfast and lunch.

The Dutch outdo themselves in the variety of ways they cook potatoes—from the earliest tiny ones which Pop "steals," without disturbing the roots, and which are boiled in their jackets and served with schmierkäse and schnittlach (cottage cheese with chives mixed into it) to potato pancakes, dumplings, soup, and even potato stuffing for fowl. Leftover mashed potatoes find their way into many dishes—pancakes, kloess, or pudding; boiled ones are fried, or schnitzed (hash-browned), or end up as potato salad or in a farmer's omelet. Potatoes are boiled, baked, fried, stewed, creamed, or roasted, and all of these variations are delicious.

Raw Fried Potatoes

This is a contradiction in terms, but that's what we call them. They are a quick dish in case of unexpected company.

3 tablespoons lard or other shortening	1 teaspoon salt
	½ teaspoon pepper
4 or 5 large potatoes, peeled and sliced thin	Sprinkle of paprika (optional)

Melt fat in a large spider. Add sliced potatoes and brown on both sides. Cover pan and cook 10 to 15 minutes, until potatoes are soft. Take off lid and turn slices once more, adding seasonings. Taste to be sure they have enough salt. You may have to add a little more shortening to prevent sticking. Potatoes should be crisp on outside and soft in middle. Sprinkle with a little chopped parsley, if you wish, "for pretty."   *Serves 4 to 6*

Roasted Potatoes

These are usually thought of as an accompaniment to roast beef, but we often served them with other meat, not necessarily a roast. If you are cooking them with beef, you simply wait until the roast has been seared, with an onion in the pan for flavor, and then add the potatoes, whole if small, or quartered if they are large, at least an hour before the roast is to be removed from the oven. They are equally delicious cooked as follows:

2 tablespoons lard or other shortening

4 or 5 peeled potatoes, or as many as you need

1 small onion, peeled

Melt lard in small pan on top of stove, then add potatoes and onion. Bake at 350° turning potatoes to be sure all parts are browned—for 45 minutes or until soft. Serve at once.

More Potatoes

Potatoes in Pennsylvania Dutch are called *grumbere,* or *grumberre,* which are probably corruptions of the German *grundbeere,* which literally means "ground berries." After all, potatoes grow underground, and the name is more apt than the High German *kartoffel.*

Grumbere Balls
(POTATO BALLS)

¼ pound Cheddar cheese
1 cup mashed potatoes
  (can be from a packaged mix)
1 cup flour

1 teaspoon baking powder
1 teaspoon salt
1 egg, well beaten
5 tablespoons milk (about)

Fat for deep frying

Cut cheese into cubes, about ¼ inch square. Mix rest of ingredients, except shortening, keeping mixture thick enough to hold its shape. Form into balls around cubes of cheese and fry in deep fat. Drain on paper towels and serve at once.   *Serves 2 to 4*

Potato Filling

8 to 10 potatoes
1 egg, beaten
½ teaspoon onion, chopped
3 stalks celery, diced
4 or 5 tablespoons butter or
  margarine

2 cups dry bread crumbs
2 teaspoons chopped parsley
1 to 2 teaspoons salt
¼ teaspoon pepper
⅛ teaspoon saffron (optional)
⅛ teaspoon poultry seasoning

Boil potatoes in jackets, peel and mash. Add well-beaten egg. Lightly brown onion and celery in butter, then add bread crumbs. Stir into potato mixture, with rest of ingredients. Taste and correct seasoning. Stuffing should just hold its shape, but not be crumbly. If too dry, add a little milk.

This is used to stuff fowl, or is sometimes baked in a well-buttered casserole at 350°, or is browned in a spider on top of the stove.

Serves 4 to 6

Filled Potato Surprise

1 onion, minced and browned in butter	1 egg, beaten
1½ cups mashed potatoes, seasoned to taste	⅛ teaspoon nutmeg (optional)
1 cup flour (approx.)	Boiling salted water
	Butter

Filling: Stir browned onion into potatoes and set aside to cool.
Dough: Add enough flour to beaten egg to make a very stiff dough. Add nutmeg. Roll it out very thin, as for noodles, and cut into 3-inch squares.

Put a teaspoonful of potato mixture on each square and fold over in a triangle, completely covering potato. Moisten your fingers with cold water, wet edge of dough and press edges tightly together. Cook triangles in rapidly boiling salted water for 10 minutes. Drain. When ready to serve, brown triangles in a little butter.

Cottage cheese, jam, or finely minced meat may be used as a filling, as a change from the potato. *Serves 4 to 6*

Baked Fried Potatoes

3 or 4 large potatoes, peeled and thinly sliced	4 tablespoons butter, melted
Salt and pepper	Parsley, chopped (optional)

You must use an iron spider for this. Arrange sliced potatoes in a well-buttered spider. Season each layer with salt and pepper and pour a little melted butter over each. Bake in moderate oven 350° about 40 minutes, until soft and well browned. "Up-dump" (invert) onto a round plate or platter. They will be deliciously browned on the bottom and soft in the middle. Sprinkle with chopped parsley and serve at once. *Serves 4 to 6*

Gelb un' Silwa
(GOLD AND SILVER)

Fresh, hot applesauce
(or canned sauce, heated)

3 or 4 large potatoes,
quartered and boiled

The potatoes are served quartered, and each person mashes them on his plate and pours the hot applesauce over them. A terrific combination! *Serves 2 to 4*

Fried Sweet Potatoes

Leftover boiled sweet potatoes
2 or 3 tablespoons lard or
other shortening

Salt and pepper
1 tablespoon sugar

Cut cold, boiled sweet potatoes into slices. Melt fat in large spider, add potatoes, salt and pepper them, and fry quickly on both sides. Sprinkle with sugar, then turn over and cook half a minute more to caramelize the sugar. Serve at once. *Serves 4*

Candied Sweet Potatoes

3 tablespoons butter or
vegetable shortening
¾ cup dark brown sugar
1 tablespoon corn syrup

1 tablespoon orange juice or
vinegar
5 or 6 large sweet potatoes,
boiled, peeled, and sliced
lengthwise—not too thin

Mix butter, sugar, corn syrup, and orange juice together in large spider or frying pan. Bring to boil, then add potatoes, being careful not to crowd. Cook slowly, basting every so often, and turning once, so that they are evenly coated. These are pretty sticky, but they are really candied! I often make this with small whole potatoes as well as with sliced ones. *Serves 4 to 6*

Baked Sweet Potato Pie

4 cups mashed sweet potatoes
5 tablespoons flour
1 teaspoon salt
1 cup crushed pineapple
1 teaspoon cinnamon

½ cup nuts, chopped
(walnuts or pecans)
½ cup seedless raisins (optional)
3 tablespoons butter, softened
½ cup boiling water

Mix mashed potatoes with flour. Add rest of ingredients, and mix again. Pour into buttered baking dish, and bake at 350° well covered, then uncover and bake 10 minutes more to brown.   *Serves 4 to 6*

Sweet Potato Fluff

5 or 6 large sweet potatoes
½ cup dark brown sugar
½ teaspoon salt
1 egg
2 tablespoons butter or margarine, melted

¼ cup walnuts or pecans, chopped
2 tablespoons sherry or any sweet table wine
½ small box marshmallows (optional)

Boil sweet potatoes, peel, and mash while hot. Add sugar and salt and stir until it melts. Add egg, melted butter, nuts, and finally wine. Put in greased baking dish or casserole, and top with whole marshmallows, if desired. (In the days before marshmallows were readily available we made a meringue with white of egg and added it at the last minute to brown. Using marshmallows is easier!) Bake at 350° for 50 minutes to 1 hour, until marshmallows are completely melted.   *Serves 4 to 6*

During a drought, farmers' wives are hard put to find things to eat besides the everlasting "red beets" which don't mind a dry spell. Some of the alternatives are noodles and potatoes; potato pie; corn pies made with dried corn; home-grown dried soup beans, served hot and cold; and dried chick peas, also served both hot and cold. Even today, many farmers who have suffered from the droughts of recent years, haven't the cash to buy vegetables, especially those who have huge families to feed. With no vegetables to sell at market, they have even less available cash. One woman told my sister, "In last year's drought my mother said 'I nefer before had to cook noodles in August,' and now, this year we're cooking noodles in Chuly!" The Dutch "make do" with fish soup made with a can of salmon and lots of skim milk and crackers; they eat skim milk puddings at least once a day, for dinner or for supper (they use the cream to make butter, which is sold at market). They make one duck do the work of three or four by cutting it up very fine and floating it in gravy, with lots of mashed potatoes. This scarcity is very unusual, but so has the weather been unusual in recent summers. "If'n we had to eat out of our own garden, ve'd absolutely starve," one of the wives told me.

Baked Beans

This is always thought of as a New England dish, but it was a stand-by in Pennsylvania Dutch homes as well. We made ours a little sweeter than the New England beans. They were eaten both hot and cold.

1 quart dried beans	⅛ teaspoon pepper
Water to cover	3 tablespoons molasses
½ pound fat salt pork, or	4 tablespoons brown sugar
1 pound smoked shoulder	½ tablespoon prepared mustard,
1 onion, stuck with 6 cloves	or 1 teaspoon dry mustard
1 tablespoon salt	4 tablespoons vinegar

1 cup catsup (optional)

Pick over beans, discarding any that are dark or broken. Soak overnight or bring to a boil, let stand 2 hours, and drain. Cover with fresh water, bring to a boil, then lower heat and simmer until skins burst. (Take a spoonful of beans, blow over them—if they're done, the skins will burst.) Drain, saving 1 cup of the broth.

Cut salt pork or shoulder into 2 large pieces. Put one piece in bottom of large casserole or bean pot, pour on layer of beans, then onion, stuck with cloves, then rest of beans. Mix rest of ingredients and pour over beans, adding bean broth and enough boiling water to cover. Put remaining piece of meat on top. Cover and bake at 300° for 4 or 5 hours, removing cover during the last hour to get a nice crisp crust. *Serves 6 to 8*

Dried Chick Peas

1 pint chick peas	1 tablespoon butter
Water	1 tablespoon flour
¼ pound salt pork, or	1 tablespoon onion, minced
leftover ham, or	Salt and pepper
2 tablespoons ham fat	

Soak chick peas overnight in cold water. Drain, place in deep kettle and cover with boiling water. Add salt pork, ham, or ham fat. Boil gently until peas are perfectly tender—about 1 hour. Remove pork, drain, but save water.

Blend butter and flour, add pea broth, onion, salt, and pepper to taste. Bring to a boil, add beans and cook for 15 or 20 minutes more. Dry the salt pork or ham, and dice. Fry a few minutes until crisp and sprinkle over peas. Serve hot.   *Serves 4 to 6*

Corn and Noodles

This is one of the ways we used leftover noodles. It is unusually good.

2 cups cooked noodles (approx.)	4 tablespoons grated cheese
	Salt and pepper to taste
2 cups corn (approx.)—fresh, canned, or frozen	1 cup of milk

Make layers of noodles, corn, and cheese until they are used up, having at the last a layer of grated cheese. Salt and pepper each layer of noodles and corn. Test seasoning and pour milk over all. Bake at 350° until cheese is melted—about 20 to 25 minutes

Serves 4 to 6

Polite Housewife to Guest: "Ess, Ess, die Schweine griechen es doch." (Translation: "Eat, eat, else the pigs will get it.")

SALADS AND SLAWS

There was always an abundance of sour cream to use up, especially during muggy summer days. If this was not made into cheese, it was used in salads, since olive oil was unknown. Salad dressing was homemade, but if it was "all" (used up), sour cream could always be substituted.

Bohne Salat
(BEAN SALAD)

1 quart string beans (may be frozen or canned, but buy French-style beans)
Boiling water
Salt to taste

2 tablespoons sour cream
1 tablespoon vinegar
1 tablespoon chopped parsley, fresh or dried

Cut beans on a slant in very thin slices. Place in kettle, add salt, and enough boiling water to partially cover. Cook until tender and drain. While hot, add sour cream, vinegar, parsley, and more salt, if needed. Correct seasoning because vinegars differ in strength. Sauce should be quite sour, as the beans are bland and absorb some of the acidity. Refrigerate at least 1 hour.   *Serves 4*

Gurken Salat
(CUCUMBER SALAD)

3 or 4 young cucumbers (all green, with no yellow spots)
1 medium-sized onion, thinly sliced
1 tablespoon salt

2 tablespoons sour cream
1 tablespoon vinegar
1 tablespoon chopped parsley, fresh or dried
Dash of pepper

Peel cucumbers and slice very thin. Add sliced onion and salt. Place in a bowl, cover with a saucer and weigh down (I use anything handy—the vinegar bottle, or another kettle). Let stand at least ½ hour. Drain by pushing down on saucer to gently press out juice. Add sour cream, vinegar, and parsley. Taste and correct seasoning, adding pepper. You may need a little salt, but probably not. Do not refrigerate, but serve at once. The aroma of this is wonderful!

Serves 4

Lettuce, Egg, and Sour Cream Salad

This is best made from the early leaf lettuce, such as Black Seeded Simpson, although I have used Boston lettuce with delicious results.

1 bunch of leaf lettuce, or
1 head Boston lettuce
2 young spring onions, or
½ small onion, sliced thin
4 hardboiled eggs

1 teaspoon chopped borage
(optional)
2 tablespoons sour cream
1 tablespoon vinegar
½ teaspoon salt

Wash lettuce and place in serving bowl. Quarter hardboiled eggs and add to lettuce, along with onions and borage. Mix sour cream, vinegar, and salt, and add to lettuce. Toss until every leaf is covered with dressing. Serve at once. *Serves 4*

Tomato Salad

2 or 3 fresh ripe tomatoes
1 large slice of green or red
sweet pepper
1 teaspoon salt

1 tablespoon vinegar
Dash of Tabasco, or hot
pepper sauce

Peel and cut tomatoes into eighths. Dice pepper and add to tomatoes. Salt the mixture and let stand at least 5 minutes. Pour vinegar and Tabasco over tomatoes. Correct seasoning and serve at once. *Serves 3 or 4*

Pepper Slaw

1 small head young green
cabbage, shredded (about
2 cups)
1 red or green sweet pepper,
diced
1 teaspoon salt

1 tablespoon sugar
1 tablespoon vinegar
½ teaspoon pepper, cracked or
freshly ground
⅛ teaspoon celery seed
(optional)

Shred cabbage very fine, add diced pepper, then other ingredients. Taste, adding more sugar if too sour or more vinegar if too sweet. Slaw should be quite peppery and is unusually good! *Serves 4 to 6*

Cole Slaw

1 head cabbage
2 tablespoons sugar
1 teaspoon salt
⅛ teaspoon cracked pepper

1 tablespoon lemon juice
2 or 3 tablespoons salad
dressing

Shred cabbage fine and spread in pan. Sprinkle with sugar, salt, pepper, and lemon juice, and let stand at least 15 minutes. Stir in salad dressing—homemade (see below) or "boughten." You may have to add more dressing because the size of cabbages differs, but don't let slaw become drippy. This may be refrigerated until ready to use, but not longer than 4 or 5 hours. *Serves 6 to 8*

Boiled Salad Dressing
(FOR POTATO SALAD OR COLE SLAW)

1 cup water
½ cup vinegar
½ teaspoon dry mustard
1 tablespoon butter
Pinch of sugar

⅛ teaspoon salt
⅛ teaspoon pepper
3 eggs
1 tablespoon flour or
cornstarch

Bring first 7 ingredients to boil. Beat eggs well, then add flour. Pour a little of the vinegar dressing into eggs to prevent curdling, then add eggs to dressing and return to low heat. Cook just until it coats a metal spoon. Refrigerate. This keeps several weeks.

About 1 pint dressing

Onion Salad

4 or 5 large onions
2 teaspoons salt
⅛ teaspoon pepper

1 tablespoon olive oil, or
2 tablespoons sour cream
2 tablespoons vinegar

Peel onions and slice very thin. Add salt. Place in bowl, cover with plate and weigh down. Let stand at least 20 minutes. Drain. Add pepper to oil or sour cream, then vinegar, and beat until thoroughly mixed. Pour over onions. Cover tightly and chill half an hour or longer. *Serves 4*

Mixed Vegetable Salad

1 cup cooked carrots
1 cup cooked stringbeans
1 cup cooked peas
1 cup cooked lima beans
   (optional)
½ cup cooked cauliflower
   (optional)
½ cup raw celery
1 teaspoon chopped parsley

½ teaspoon salt
⅛ teaspoon pepper
1 tablespoon cream
   (sweet or sour)
1 tablespoon vinegar
1 tablespoon mayonnaise
Pinch of sugar
Lettuce or pepper cups for
   garnish

Drain vegetables, adding whatever other leftover vegetables you may have. Mix rest of ingredients except garnish, pour over vegetables and chill at least ½ hour. Taste and correct seasoning. Serve in bowl lined with lettuce, or in pepper cups, made by removing all seeds and pith from peppers (pretty, and different).   *Serves 4 to 6*

Potato Salad

4 or 5 large potatoes
Water to cover
1 teaspoon parsley, chopped
½ teaspoon finely chopped
   onion
2 celery stalks, diced

1 tablespoon vinegar
Salt and pepper to taste
2 to 4 tablespoons boiled salad
   dressing (see Index)
1 hardboiled egg
   (optional)
Slice of crisp bacon

Boil potatoes in their jackets. Peel, and while hot, add parsley, onion, celery, vinegar, pepper, and salt. Let stand to marinate. Add two tablespoons of boiled dressing and toss. You may need to add more dressing, but add just enough to coat the potatoes, not drown them!

This may be served hot or cold. If served hot or warm, crumble a slice of fried crisp bacon over top. If cold, decorate with hardboiled egg, cut into slices or eighths.   *Serves 4 to 6*

CHAPTER VIII

From the Bake Oven
(Breads, Pies, and Cakes)

Few people use the old limestone ovens any more, which is regrettable. They were separately housed, near the back door, and they were wide enough to hold as many as a dozen loaves of bread. On the night before baking day, a roaring fire was built in the oven. The bread was set to rise in a dough tray near the kitchen stove. In the morning, when the fire had burned low and the coals were white hot, the fire was raked out and the oven was ready for baking. Once the loaves were in the oven, the air began to take on a yeasty, penetrating, luscious aroma, which brought anyone within smelling distance on the run. When the loaves were removed on a flat wooden shovel and hurried into the kitchen, droplets of butter oozed from them. We all waited eagerly for a taste. It was sacrilege to use more butter, but we did and with greasy faces munched away. The crunchy, buttery taste of the crust encasing the hot, elastic goodness of the middle was an unforgettable experience. That stone oven gave baked goods an indefinable something, just as charcoal imparts a special quality to meats. We made rye, white, and pumpernickel breads; rolls, when the oven had cooled somewhat; and finally, perhaps, a pot of beans mit schpeck (bacon) was put in to use up the last of the heat.

Even with the multitude of quick breads available today, most Pennsylvania Dutch housewives still bake "from scratch."

Homemade bread, rolls, and especially sticky buns are still thought to be the final test of the homemaker's art.

BREADS

In the early days, yeast was homemade with potatoes, water, and hops. Enough was made to last for five or six months, and a cupful was always saved as a starter for the next batch. It was a long-drawn-out process, and when the yeast we now know came on the market, it was called Magic Yeast, which indeed it must have seemed to the early settlers. The recipe for homemade yeast will be found in the section called Wine, Mush, and Miscellaneous, for those with a pioneer spirit. Homemade yeast takes much longer to rise, which is why dough was set the night before.

We often used sour milk in our baking. For those recipes that call for sour milk, which you may not have on hand, you can add a half teaspoon of vinegar to 1 cup sweet milk and let stand for a few minutes—or you can simply use buttermilk.

White Bread

¾ cup milk or ¾ cup potato water	1 egg
¼ cup and 1 teaspoon sugar	2 cakes or 2 envelopes yeast
2¼ teaspoons salt	¼ cup lukewarm water
4½ tablespoons shortening	4½ cups all-purpose flour (approx.)

Scald milk, or use potato water—made by boiling a potato in 3 cups water for 20 minutes. (I prefer the more yeasty taste given by the potato water.) Stir in ¼ cup sugar, salt, shortening, and egg. Cool to lukewarm. In another bowl, sprinkle yeast into water, adding ¼ teaspoon sugar. Let yeast stand until dissolved; stir. Add to milk or potato-water mixture. Then add and stir in 2¼ cups flour. Beat until smooth (you can use a mixer for this). Add and stir in rest of flour, or enough so that dough leaves the bowl easily.

Turn dough out on lightly floured board. Knead gently until smooth and elastic. Place in greased bowl, then invert dough so that top is greased.

Cover with clean towel. Let rise in warm place, free from drafts. (A good place is the oven. Before placing dough in oven turn on heat for 5 minutes at its lowest. Then turn off oven, and put covered dough in.) Let rise until doubled in bulk—about 50 minutes.

Punch dough down—just push it down gently with your fist—and turn out onto lightly floured board. Shape into two loaves, or one loaf and rolls, if you prefer. Let rise again, for about 40 to 50 minutes. Bake at 400° for 5 minutes, then lower heat to 350° and bake ¾ hour longer. A good test for doneness is to rap bread with your knuckles; if it sounds hollow, it is done. *Makes 2 large loaves*

Sweet Potato Biscuits

3 cups sifted flour
2 teaspoons baking powder
1 teaspoon salt
2 cups mashed sweet potatoes

¾ cup sugar
½ cup lard or other
   shortening

Sift flour, baking powder, and salt together. Mix *warm* sweet potatoes with sugar and lard. Add flour to potato mixture and mix thoroughly. Roll out on lightly floured surface to about ½-inch thickness. Cut with biscuit cutter and place on baking sheet. Bake at 425° for 12 to 15 minutes, or until well browned.

Makes 15 to 20 biscuits

Pumpernickel

½ cake yeast, either compressed
   or dry
2 cups lukewarm water
4 cups rye flour, sifted

1 teaspoon salt
1 teaspoon sugar (optional)
2 cups white flour
1 tablespoon melted butter

The night before, dissolve yeast in water. Add 2 cups rye flour and beat well. Cover and set in warm place to sour—this means letting it rise, and then fall.

In the morning, beat yeast mix, add salt, sugar, 1 cup rye flour and 1 cup white flour. Beat again at least 3 minutes. Cover and let rise in warm place. Punch down, and turn out onto a board sprinkled with almost 1 cup each of rye and wheat flour. Knead, working in as much flour as is necessary to make a stiff dough.

Shape into two small loaves, place in greased pans, and cover with dry cloth. Let rise until double in size.

In a slow oven, about 300°, bake about 1¼ hours, or until loaves sound hollow when tapped. Brush with melted butter while still warm. If you don't like a hard crust, place a pan of warm water on the bottom of the oven while baking. (The surface may crack a little, but it's supposed to.) *Makes 2 small loaves*

Rye Bread

5 cups rye flour	Salt to taste (about 1 teaspoon)
5 cups white flour	2 tablespoons caraway seeds
½ cake yeast, compressed	(optional)
or dry	1 tablespoon melted butter

The above is my mother's recipe in its entirety and this is as far as she went, assuming that any of her children would know enough to go on from there!

Follow the above recipe for pumpernickel until you come to the shaping. While you are kneading bread for the last time, sprinkle the caraway seeds together with the flour (white and rye) on the board, and turn and roll the dough in them, until they are well distributed throughout. Grease your hands and divide the dough into 3 or 4 portions—depending on how large you want them to be. Shape into an oval, brush with melted butter, and place on greased cookie sheets. Bake at 300° for about 1¼ hours, or until they sound hollow when tapped. These are very crusty, and the odor when they are baking is heavenly—they taste as good as they smell! *Makes 2 loaves*

Whole Wheat Bread

½ yeast cake	1 teaspoon sugar
2 cups warm water	1 teaspoon salt
5 cups whole wheat flour	2 tablespoons butter, melted

Dissolve yeast in warm water, then add 2 cups flour and beat well. Add sugar, salt, and 1 tablespoon melted butter, and beat again. Cover and let rise for 1 hour—it will not come to top of bowl but will form what is called "a sponge." Punch down, and add white flour and rest of flour, stirring and mixing until all the flour is absorbed. Dough will be stiff. Place in greased bowl, cover with dry cloth, and let rise again until double in bulk, or until two fingers applied gently leave a mark which stays. Punch down, turn onto floured board, and knead until little bubbles form, or until you feel that dough is thoroughly mixed. (Those little bubbles don't always form for me, nor can I always hear the little crackle or pop you're supposed to hear, but my breads are always nice and light, so don't worry if none of these things happen.)

Form into round loaves or place in greased bread pans, and cover again, letting rise in a warm place until doubled in size. Bake at 350° for about 50 minutes to 1 hour. Brush with remaining melted butter while still warm. *Makes 2 large loaves*

Frühlings Zwievelkuche
(SPRING ONION CAKE)

There is a Pfalz poem about Swievelkuch-Pälzer Wei(n) or Onion Cake and Wine which says "Oh, what a wonderful combination!" Here is how we made the onion cake:

2 cups onions or scallions, sliced thin	Salt and pepper
Vinegar to cover	½ cup coffee cream
4 tablespoons bread dough, or rich biscuit dough (you can use frozen)	1 egg
	2 slices diced bacon, cooked crisp

This is best when made from new spring onions or scallions, with stem and leaves sliced on a diagonal. Put onions in vinegar to marinate about 15 minutes. Grease fingers and spread dough in a 9-inch pie pan, making a high rim. Do not spread too thin. Remove onions from marinade, and spread over dough. Season with salt and pepper. Beat egg and cream together, pour over onions, and crumble bacon over top. Bake at 400° for 15 to 20 minutes, or until browned. This is marvelous with beer, as well as with wine.

Makes 1 9-inch cake

Corn Bread

1 cup flour	½ cup sugar
2 cups yellow corn meal	1 tablespoon baking powder
1 teaspoon salt	2 cups milk
4 eggs, beaten	

Sift together flour, corn meal, salt, sugar, and baking powder. Slowly add milk, and stir until all lumps are removed. Add beaten eggs.

Pour into a greased 9-inch square pan. Bake in 425° oven approximately 30 minutes, or until a straw inserted in the middle comes out clean. *Serves 6 to 8*

Buttermilk Biscuits

½ cup sour milk or buttermilk
⅛ teaspoon baking soda
1 cup flour

½ teaspoon baking powder
½ teaspoon salt
2½ teaspoons lard or other shortening

Mix buttermilk and baking soda and stir until it foams. Set aside. Sift dry ingredients together, add shortening, and mix until fine as meal. Add buttermilk mixture and stir thoroughly. Turn out on floured board. Knead gently, just until thoroughly mixed. (Pat until it is ½ inch thick, and cut out with biscuit cutter.) Place on cookie sheet, and bake at 400° for 15 minutes, or until nicely browned.

Makes 10 to 15 biscuits

Yeast Muffins

1 cup milk
2 tablespoons sugar
1 teaspoon salt
2 tablespoons shortening
2½ cups flour (approx.)

1 yeast cake or 1 envelope granular yeast
¼ cup lukewarm water
1 egg

Scald milk; add sugar, salt, and shortening; cool to lukewarm. Dissolve yeast in water, add to milk mixture. Add egg and enough flour to make a stiff batter. Beat until smooth. Cover and let rise in warm place until doubled—about 1 hour. Fill well-greased muffin tins half full. Cover and let rise again until doubled, about ½ hour. Bake at 375° about 30 minutes. *Makes about 24 muffins*

Semmel Rolls
(BUTTER ROLLS)

Semmel in German means "made of wheat flour," and any rolls made of white flour are so designated. The usual semmel rolls, made for special dinners, are very rich. This is how we made them:

1 package yeast	½ teaspoon salt
¼ cup lukewarm water	3 cups flour
1 teaspoon sugar	Poppy or sesame seeds
½ cup milk	(optional)
1 cup butter (at room temperature)	

Dissolve yeast in lukewarm water, to which you have added ½ teaspoon sugar. (This makes it dissolve more quickly, and it bubbles up wonderfully. "To feed the yeast," we used to say.)

Scald milk, add ½ cup butter, ½ teaspoon salt, and remaining ½ teaspoon sugar. Let cool to lukewarm, then stir in flour, and stirred yeast mixture. When all the flour has been absorbed, and dough comes away from sides of bowl, turn out onto lightly floured board and knead about 5 minutes, or until dough is smooth. Put in greased bowl, cover and let rise in a warm place, free of drafts, until it has doubled.

Punch dough down, and roll out to about ½-inch thickness. Spread rest of butter all over the dough, as you would butter a slice of bread. Fold dough over in half, then again in quarters, and chill until spread butter has become stiff. Roll and fold again, chilling after each rolling. Put back in bowl and let rise again for ½ hour. Divide dough in half. Roll out about ¼ inch thick.

Form into any shape you like—I roll it into a circle, cut pie wedges from each circle, and roll them up as for crescents, starting at the wider end. Put on ungreased baking pans, cover and let rise again until doubled in size. Bake at 375° for 15 to 20 minutes until golden brown. You can sprinkle with poppy or sesame seeds "for fancy," if you like.

These are sometimes rolled up like a jelly roll, cut in slices, and baked in a pie pan; or little pieces of dough are rolled with the hands into a ball, and the balls are put in a pie or baking dish, rather close together, to make "old-fashioned rolls."

Makes about 24 rolls

Popovers

2 eggs   1 cup flour
1 cup milk

Grease deep muffin tins (the old-fashioned iron ones are best)
and place in oven while it is heating to 425°.

Beat eggs slightly, add milk, pour slowly into flour. If there are
any lumps, strain dough. Pour into heated muffin tins, filling only
half full, and bake in hot oven (425°) for 35 to 45 minutes, or until
puffed up and golden brown.   *Makes 8 to 10 popovers*

Cholly Poys
(JOLLY BOYS)

So called because they make little boys jolly, I should presume!

3½ tablespoons corn meal   ¾ teaspoon baking powder
2½ tablespoons flour   1 egg
1 heaping tablespoon sugar   ⅓ cup milk (approx.)
¼ teaspoon salt   ½ teaspoon melted butter

Sift together corn meal, flour, sugar, salt, and baking powder.
Beat egg until thoroughly mixed, add to dry ingredients, and then
add just enough milk so that batter drops easily from spoon. Stir in
melted butter and drop by small spoonfuls into hot fat. Brown on
both sides. These are delicious for breakfast. *Makes 6 to 10 pancakes*

Funnel Cakes or Plowlines

The name "plowlines" is purely local and is undoubtedly
due to the fact that these delicious, little, hot cakes look like
reins. They are a breakfast dish and are usually served with
syrup or table molasses or dusted with cinnamon and sugar.

3 eggs   ½ teaspoon salt
2 cups milk   1 tablespoon baking powder
4 cups flour   Lard or vegetable shortening
⅓ cup sugar   for frying

Beat eggs and add milk. Sift dry ingredients together, and add
egg-milk mixture, beating as you pour. Continue beating until

smooth. Let stand for a few minutes while you heat the fat to 375°
to a depth of at least 3 or 4 inches.

Pour batter into small pitcher for easier handling. Take an ordinary
household funnel and put your finger over the end of it. Pour some
batter into the mouth of the funnel, take off your finger, and let
batter drop into hot fat, swirling it around and around, until it is
about 3 inches in diameter. This forms concentric circles which are
most attractive. Fry until they are a light golden brown, drain on
paper towels, and serve hot. (This sounds harder than it actually is,
but you might want to practice a little before serving funnel cakes
to guests!) *Makes about 12 cakes*

Blotch Kucha
(FLAT CAKE)

The name probably comes from the German *Blach*, which
means "flat." It is similar to blitzkuchen but not quite as rich
and delicate.

⅓ cup butter
⅓ cup lard or vegetable
  shortening
1½ cups brown sugar
  (preferably light brown)

2 eggs
½ teaspoon baking soda,
  dissolved in a little water
3 cups flour
1 teaspoon baking powder

1 cup coarsely chopped nuts

Cream butter and shortening together, add brown sugar, eggs,
and baking soda. Gradually add flour, to which baking powder has
been added. Stir until thoroughly blended. Turn into a greased
shallow baking pan, 15½ by 10½ inches. Sprinkle chopped nuts over
top and bake at 350° for 20 to 25 minutes, or until top springs back
at a touch. *Serves 8 to 10*

Topsy Turvy Cherry Nut Bread

Batter:

2½ cups flour
1 teaspoon salt
4½ teaspoons baking powder
¾ cup sugar
1¼ cup milk

2 tablespoons melted shortening
1 egg, beaten
1 cup bran cereal
⅓ cup chopped candied or
  maraschino cherries

¼ cup chopped nuts

Sift first 4 ingredients together, add milk and melted shortening to beaten egg, and blend with dry ingredients. Mix in bran, cherries, and nut meats. Now make the topping.

Topping:

1 tablespoon butter	⅓ cup chopped cherries
¼ cup brown sugar	¼ cup chopped walnuts

Melt butter in a loaf pan 4¾ by 8¾ inches. Sprinkle brown sugar, cherries, and nuts evenly in bottom of the pan. Top with batter. Bake at 350° for 1 hour. Remove from oven and turn upside down at once.   *Serves 4 to 6*

Schticky Buns
(STICKY BUNS)

Few Dutch dishes are more popular or better known than schticky buns. They are almost always served at company meals, but we also served them for breakfast, especially on baking days. They were "up-dumped" by the panful and disappeared so rapidly that it was amazing! The secret is in the syrup, since almost any light, sweet dough—even the frozen kind—will make good buns, although I prefer to make mine "from scratch." They are extremely popular for morning get-togethers and are always served with coffee.

Dough:

¾ cup milk	2 packages yeast, dry or
¼ cup sugar	compressed
2¼ teaspoons salt	5 cups all-purpose flour
4½ tablespoons shortening	2 tablespoons butter, melted
1 egg	½ cup brown sugar (approx.)
¾ cup lukewarm water	Cinnamon

Scald milk, add and stir in sugar, salt, and shortening, and when slightly cooled, add egg. Let cool until lukewarm.

Place water, yeast, and pinch of sugar in bowl. Let stand until yeast dissolves. Add to milk mixture. Add and stir in 2¼ cups flour and beat until smooth. Add and stir in another additional 2¼ cups flour. Go slowly on remaining ¼ cup flour—when the dough sticks together and leaves the side of bowl, you have used enough. Hold butter, brown sugar, and cinnamon in reserve.

Turn dough onto a lightly floured surface, and knead gently until well mixed. This dough needs gentle handling and as little additional flour as possible. Place in greased bowl, and turn dough once, so that top is greased. Cover with clean towel, let rise in warm place, free from drafts, until doubled in bulk—about 50 minutes. Meanwhile make the schticky part:

½ cup brown sugar 2 tablespoons corn syrup
1 tablespoon butter ¼ teaspoon cinnamon

Mix all ingredients and bring to a boil. Pour into 3 or 4 pie plates, covering bottoms to a depth of ⅛ inch. Let cool. The corn syrup prevents the syrup from granulating. (I sometimes put pecan halves at alternate intervals with the rounded side down on the syrup, and then I have pecan rolls.)

Punch dough down, and taking about ¼ of it at a time, roll gently into an oblong, about 14 by 8 inches, and about ¼ inch thick. Spread dough with the 2 tablespoons melted butter, and brown sugar held in reserve, and sprinkle with cinnamon. Roll up tightly like a jelly roll. Cut into two-inch slices, and place, cut side down, in pie plate, using all the syrup. Don't crowd slices because they are going to rise. Cover with clean cloth, and allow to rise again, until doubled, about 50 minutes. Bake at 350° for 15 to 20 minutes, or until they are brown and bubbling. Immediately "up-dump" (invert) pan into a serving plate, and serve hot.

These freeze unusually well, but if you intend to freeze them, don't "updump," just cool and wrap securely in freezer paper. When ready to serve, reheat and invert, so that the sticky part runs over the buns. Sometimes currants or raisins are added before rolling the buns, but they are delicious "so."   *Makes about 4 dozen rolls*

"Chennie, don't be so dopplich (clumsy).
You almost made my cake to fall."

WINTER PIES AND CAKES

In the winter, fruit for pies was scarce, even though a good Pennsylvania Dutch housewife canned or dried bushels of available fruits, nuts, and berries. The resourceful cook made do with substitutes she could find in the larder. Among these creations was the concoction which is now called "Shoofly Pie," and so good it is served summer and winter. We always called it simply "molasses pie." Some people think the new name might be a corruption of the French *chou-fleur* (cauliflower) since the finished product somewhat resembles cooked cauliflower. Others feel that it was called shoofly simply because it was so attractive to flies that someone constantly had to shoo them away. I can remember, as a young child, being designated to swish the fly chaser—a long wand with colored streamers— whenever we served this dish.

Shoofly Pie

Dough for 9-inch pie crust   4 tablespoons butter
  (see Index)   ½ cup boiling water
1 cup flour   ½ cup molasses
½ cup sugar   ½ teaspoon baking soda

Pinch of cinnamon

Line a deep 9-inch pie plate with pie crust, making a high rim. Mix flour, sugar, and butter together with hands until crumbly. Add water to molasses, cinnamon, and baking soda, and beat with a spoon until foamy. Pour molasses mixture into pie shell. Add crumb mixture, pressing it down into the molasses filling but leaving some on top. Bake at 350° for 35 to 40 minutes, until bubbly and brown. (For a drier pie, use 1½ cups flour.)

Amish Vanilla Pies

This is very similar to shoofly pie but has a vanilla flavor rather than spiciness.

Dough for 2 9-inch pie crusts (see Index).

Filling:

1 cup sugar   2 cups water
1 egg, well beaten   4 tablespoons flour
1 cup table molasses   1 teaspoon vanilla

Crumbs:

2 cups flour
1 teaspoon baking soda
1 cup brown sugar
1 teaspoon cream of tartar

¼ cup butter or margarine
¼ cup shortening—lard or
   vegetable

Line 2 pie plates with dough. Combine ingredients for filling in saucepan, and bring to a full boil. Set aside to cool. Make crumbs. Mix dry ingredients, then add butter and shortening, mixing well until good and crumbly.

Pour half of the cooked mixture into each pie shell, and top with crumb mixture. Bake at 350° for 40 to 45 minutes, or until nicely browned.   *Makes 2 9-inch pies*

Funny Cake

Another winter dessert is Funny Cake, so called because of the way in which the ingredients seek their own level. It makes a delicious breakfast cake and can be served at any time, always with coffee.

Sauce:

1 square unsweetened
   chocolate
½ cup water

⅔ cup sugar
¼ cup butter or margarine
1 teaspoon vanilla

Put chocolate and water in saucepan over low heat (my recipe says "on the back of the stove"). Stir until chocolate is melted, then add sugar, stirring constantly. Bring just to a boil, remove from heat and add butter and vanilla. Stir until blended, and allow to cool while mixing cake.

Cake:

Dough for 9-inch pie crust
   (see Index)
1¼ cups flour
1 teaspoon baking powder
½ teaspoon salt
¾ cup sugar

¼ cup lard or other
   shortening
½ cup milk
1 teaspoon vanilla
1 unbeaten egg
½ cup chopped nuts

Line a deep 9-inch pie plate with pie crust, making a high rim. Sift dry ingredients into lard. Add milk and vanilla, mix until all flour is dampened. Beat two minutes at low speed on electric mixer (or 150 strokes by hand). Add egg and beat 1 minute more. Pour batter into pie crust. Pour lukewarm sauce gently over batter. Sprinkle with chopped nuts. Bake at 350° for 50 to 55 minutes. Serve warm. *Serves 4 to 6*

Schnitz Pie

"Schnitz" (cut) always refers to dried apples, even though a prudent housewife also dried pears, plums, cherries, and even raspberries and grapes. Schnitzing went on all through the apple season. Apples were peeled, cored, quartered, and tossed into a tub of vinegar and water, to keep them from discoloring. They were then drained, placed on homemade screens, covered with a clean cloth, and placed either in a very cool oven, or in the sun, or at the back of the wood cookstove. They were turned frequently until a toasty brown and dried through. Then they were placed in string bags, labeled "sweet" or "sour," and hung from the attic rafters, away from marauding mice or rats. They were eaten "so" (as is) or made into pies, and sometimes into Schnitz un' Knepp (see Index). They can be found at specialty food stores or at market, or you could dry your own.

2 cups dried, sour apple slices	1 teaspoon cinnamon
3 cups water	Dough for 2-crust 9-inch pie
1 orange (juice and grated rind)	(see Index)

Cook apples and water in saucepan until soft as applesauce; add orange juice, grated rind, cinnamon, and sugar. Mix well, let cool. Pour into pastry-lined pie plate. Cover with second crust and bake until brown—about 50 minutes. *Makes 1 9-inch pie*

Fassnachts
(FAST NIGHT CRULLERS)

Fassnachts are a form of cruller. On Fassnacht (Fast Night), or Shrove Tuesday, the day before the beginning of Lent, they are made in abundance so that everyone can fill up before the fasting begins. Nowadays Fassnachts are made at any time, but the true Fassnachts were made only once a year.

1 cup granulated sugar
2 tablespoons lard
1 egg
1 cup mashed white potato
1 cup milk
5 teaspoons baking powder

Dash salt
⅛ teaspoon nutmeg
2 to 3 cups flour—enough to
   stiffen dough
Lard for frying
Confectioners' sugar

Cream sugar and lard, add egg and beat. Carefully mix with unseasoned mashed potato, then beat in the milk. Mix baking powder, salt, nutmeg, and 2 cups of flour and add to mixture. Add more flour if necessary to make a stiff dough. Pat mixture on floured board to ½-inch thickness. Cut with doughnut cutter and fry until brown in hot lard, turning once. Drain and dip in confectioners' sugar.

Makes about 3 dozen

Apple Sauce Cake

Apple sauce cake was another winter dish and was usually made for the Christmas holidays. Since candied peels were "dear" or unavailable, this was a substitute for fruit cake.

½ cup butter or margarine
1 cup light brown sugar
1 cup applesauce (may be
   canned)
2¼ cups sifted flour
3 teaspoons baking soda
Pinch of salt
1 teaspoon cinnamon

¼ teaspoon nutmeg (my recipe
   says "1 grated nutmeg")
⅓ cup chopped nuts
½ cup each raisins and currants
   (if currants are unavailable,
   use 1 cup raisins)
Confectioners' sugar
¼ cup sweet wine

Cream butter and sugar until light; add applesauce. Sift flour, baking soda, salt, cinnamon, and nutmeg and gradually add to first mixture, beating until smooth. Add nuts and fruits. Bake at 325° about 1 hour. Turn out on rack to cool. Frosting may be added, if desired, but we just sprinkled the cake with confectioners' sugar, wrapped it in a cloth soaked in wine, and stored it for several weeks to allow the flavors to mingle. *Makes 2 large loaves*

Grossmutter's Brodtorte
(GRANDMOTHER'S BREAD TORTE)

9 eggs, separated
1¼ cups sugar
¾ cup grated chocolate
(my recipe says "1 saucerful")
¾ cup almonds, ground with the skin (walnuts may be substituted)
¾ cup fine, dry rye-bread crumbs, wetted with a little cold coffee
Rind of 1 lemon
Juice of ½ lemon
1 teaspoon cinnamon
½ teaspoon cloves

Beat egg yolks with sugar until light. Add rest of ingredients, except whites of eggs. Beat whites until very stiff but not dry. Gently fold into first mixture. Bake in 2 greased and floured 9-inch layer cake pans, at 325° for 40 minutes.

Filling:

2 egg yolks
1 cup sugar
Juice of 1 lemon
½ cup chopped walnuts or almonds
1 egg white, beaten stiff but not dry
Confectioners' sugar

Beat egg yolks with sugar, add lemon juice and nuts, then fold in beaten egg white. Spread between layers, and dust top of cake with confectioners' sugar.

Bread Pudding with Wine Sauce

6 to 8 slices stale bread
½ cup raisins (optional)
2 eggs
2 cups milk
½ teaspoon salt
2 tablespoons sugar
1 teaspoon vanilla
¼ teaspoon cinnamon

Butter a 1-quart pudding dish or casserole. Fill to top with slices of bread, torn into small pieces. Sprinkle in raisins, if desired. Beat together eggs, milk, salt, sugar, vanilla, and cinnamon. Pour over bread. Put dish in pan of hot water. Bake at 350° about ½ hour. Test with a knife; if it comes out clean, pudding is done.

Wine Sauce:

2 eggs
¾ cup sugar
1 cup wine (sherry, Madeira, or currant)

Beat eggs and sugar until light. Heat wine to boiling, and pour slowly into egg mixture. Cook over very low heat, or in a double boiler until it thickens. Serve hot over pudding.   *Serves 4 to 6*

Blitzkuchen

Another of my grandmother's recipes is for blitzkuchen, so named because it is made quick as lightning or "in a blitz." It is a delicious, thin coffee cake.

1 cup butter or other shortening	1 teaspoon vanilla
1 cup granulated sugar	2 cups flour, sifted
2 eggs	½ cup sugar mixed with 1 teaspoon cinnamon

½ cup chopped nuts

Cream butter, add sugar, beat until light. Beat in eggs, vanilla, and sifted flour. Spread on cookie sheet, keeping it quite thin, sprinkle thickly with sugar, cinnamon, and nuts. Bake at 375° about 15 minutes, until the top springs back when touched. Cut into squares while hot.   *Makes about 36 squares*

Streisel Kuchen
(CRUMB CAKE)

This is a quick breakfast cake, very good with coffee.

2 cups flour	1 teaspoon baking powder
⅓ cup shortening	Dash of nutmeg
⅔ cup sugar	1 egg
½ teaspoon baking soda	¼ cup milk
Dash of salt	Chopped nuts (optional)

Mix dry ingredients, except nuts, with shortening, until thoroughly mixed and crumbly. Take out about ¼ cup. Add egg and milk to rest of ingredients. Mix and pour into greased 9-inch square baking pan or 9-inch pie plate. Sprinkle with crumb mixture. Chopped nuts may be added to crumbs, if desired. Bake at 350° about 20 minutes, or until top springs back at a touch.   *Serves 4 to 6*

Sour Cream Pie

Dough for 1 9-inch pie
(see Index)
⅔ cup sugar
2 eggs, separated
1 cup sour cream
½ cup seeded raisins

2 tablespoons flour
¼ teaspoon lemon extract
¼ teaspoon cinnamon
¼ teaspoon cloves
4 tablespoons sugar
(for meringue)

Line a pie plate with crust. Beat ⅓ cup sugar into egg yolks, and other ⅓ cup into sour cream. Then mix them together. Combine raisins, flour, lemon extract, cinnamon, and cloves. Add to sugar mixture. Pour into unbaked pie shell. Bake at 350° until firm in center—about 25 minutes. Meantime, beat egg whites, gradually adding 4 tablespoons of sugar. Spread meringue over pie, and return to oven for a minute or two, just enough to brown meringue.

Dutch Coconut Custard Pie

Pennsylvania Dutch cooks welcomed a chance to show off their prowess in cooking and baking by using foods that weren't indigenous to the farm. Coconuts, one of the exotic delights to be had at market, were highly esteemed. Pop usually "busted" them for us, and then we grated them, saving every smidgen of the milk. One of the by-products was "coconut custart" pie, which we made a little differently from any I've ever seen, with a sprinkling of browned coconut and brown sugar on top. Ach, but it tasted us good!

1 cup grated coconut, either
fresh or canned
Dough for 1 9-inch pie crust
(see Index)
3 whole eggs
3 tablespoons sugar

1½ cups coconut milk (if you
don't have this, just use half-
and-half)
1 teaspoon vanilla
½ teaspoon nutmeg
Sprinkle of brown sugar—
about ⅓ cup

Heat oven to 450°. Spread 2 tablespoons of coconut in pan. Brown lightly in oven. Be careful, it browns quickly! Line a 9-inch pie plate with dough, keeping edges high.

Beat eggs, add sugar, then coconut milk, vanilla, and nutmeg. Put untoasted coconut in bottom of pie dish and pour custard over it. Bake at 450° for 10 minutes, then lower heat to 350° and bake for 25 to 30 minutes more, or until a silver knife inserted in custard comes out clean. Remove from oven and sprinkle with toasted coconut and brown sugar. Return to oven for a minute or so, just until lightly browned, or run under broiler. Let cool, but don't chill —custard pies taste best when lukewarm.

Makes 1 deep-dish 9-inch pie

Montgomery Pie

No one seems to know why this was called Montgomery, but it probably came from Montgomery County, which is on the fringe of the Pennsylvania Dutch country. There are many different recipes for the pie, but this is the one we used. It has a rich lemony taste with almost a cake-like texture.

Dough for 2 9-inch pie crusts (see Index)
1 cup brown sugar
1⅓ cups flour
Dash of salt
1 teaspoon baking powder
2 eggs

5 tablespoons butter or margarine, melted
1 lemon—juice and grated rind
½ cup milk
½ cup table molasses
½ cup sugar
⅔ cup water

Line two 9-inch pie plates with dough. Mix together brown sugar, flour, salt, and baking powder. Beat eggs, add melted butter, lemon, and milk. Pour into dry ingredients, mix and then pour into pie shells. Combine molasses, sugar, and water and pour on top. Bake 45 minutes at 350°.

Makes 2 9-inch pies

Karupss Pie
(PUMPKIN PIE)

1½ cups cooked pumpkin
¾ cup brown sugar
2 eggs, beaten
1½ cups milk
½ teaspoon vanilla
½ teaspoon salt

1 teaspoon cinnamon
½ teaspoon ginger
¼ teaspoon mace
½ teaspoon nutmeg
Dough for 1 9-inch pie crust (see Index)

To cook pumpkin, remove seeds and pith, cut into strips and peel. Cover with water, and boil until completely tender—about 30 minutes.

Mix sugar with pumpkin. Add eggs, then milk, then vanilla and seasonings. Line pie plate with dough and pour in pumpkin mixture. Bake 10 minutes at 450°, then reduce heat to 350° and bake until filling is firm, or a knife inserted in center comes out clean—about 40 minutes. *Makes 1 deep-dish 9-inch pie*

Süsse Grumbere Pie
(SWEET POTATO PIE)

1 cup mashed sweet potatoes
2 cups milk
1 cup sugar
4 eggs
½ teaspoon salt

½ teaspoon cinnamon
¼ teaspoon nutmeg
1 unbaked 9-inch pie crust
   (see Index)

Mix well, in order named. Pour into pie shell and bake at 400° for 10 minutes, then lower heat to 350° and bake about 25 minutes more, or until a knife inserted in center comes out clean.

Makes 1 9-inch pie

Banana Cream Pie

2 cups milk
¼ cup cornstarch
⅔ cup sugar
¼ teaspoon salt
3 egg yolks, slightly beaten

2 tablespoons butter
½ teaspoon vanilla
1 baked 9-inch pie crust
   (see Index)
2 or 3 bananas

Scald milk and let cool slightly. Mix cornstarch, sugar, and salt, and add milk gradually. Cook over very low heat, or in double boiler until thick, about 10 minutes, stirring constantly. Add a small amount of this to egg yolks, then stir yolks into hot mixture and cook 5 minutes more. Add butter and vanilla and cool.

Slice bananas into cooled pie shell and pour filling over it. Bake at 350° for 12 or 15 minutes. Cool and serve. *Makes 1 9-inch pie*

Fried Pies

We made fried pies out of any available dried fruit, but the echt deitsch (truly Dutch) fried pies were made from schnitz.

2 cups dried apples or other
    fruits
1½ cups warm water
½ cup sugar

2 tablespoons butter
½ teaspoon cinnamon
Dough for 2-crust 9-inch pie
    (see Index)
Confectioners' sugar

Soak fruit in water overnight. Cook until tender. Drain off most of juice, and season with sugar, butter, and cinnamon. (Berries need only be brought to a boil; they should not be mushy.) Roll out pastry and cut into 4- to 5-inch squares or circles. Place several tea-spoonfuls of fruit on one half of square. Moisten edges and fold over other half, completely covering fruit. Press together securely so that no fruit can leak out. Fry in deep fat, at 375° for about 4 minutes, or until brown on both sides. Sprinkle with confectioners' sugar, and serve at once. These may be baked, if preferred, in a 375° oven about 20 minutes, or until nicely browned. *Makes 6 to 8 pies*

Snicker Doodles

Goodness only knows where the name for this came from, but it probably started as one of those family jokes. It always makes me think of a little crossroads near my home which was named Noodle Doosey, to our great amusement.

2 cups sugar
1 scant cup butter
3 eggs

3 cups flour
2 teaspoons baking powder
1 cup milk
Cinnamon and sugar

Beat sugar and butter together. Add eggs and continue beating. Mix baking powder and flour, and add alternately with the milk to eggs. Mix well. Spread in baking dish about 1 inch thick. Sprinkle with cinnamon and sugar. Bake at 350° for 25 to 30 minutes, or until nicely browned, and the top springs back when touched.

Serves 6 to 8

Mock Lemon Angel Food Cake

1 cup sugar
1¼ cups flour
3 teaspoons baking powder
½ teaspoon cream of tartar

⅔ cup scalded milk
1 teaspoon lemon extract
1 teaspoon lemon rind, grated
   (optional)

3 egg whites

Sift dry ingredients together 4 times. Gently add first milk, then lemon extract. (I like to add a little grated lemon rind, as it adds to the flavor.) Beat egg whites until stiff, but not dry, and fold into batter. Bake in greased shallow pan, 12 by 8 inches, at 325° for 45 minutes. Allow to cool, then turn upside down on a platter until cake drops from the pan.

Lemon Icing:

1 tablespoon butter or
   margarine
3 tablespoons lemon juice

1 tablespoon grated lemon rind
1 box confectioners' sugar
4 or 5 tablespoons hot water

Melt butter, but do not allow it to brown. Add, together with lemon juice and rind, to confectioners' sugar, stirring well. Continue adding hot water until icing has right consistency to spread.

Serves 6 to 8

Brown-Eyed Susan Cake

½ cup shortening
1 cup sugar
3 eggs, separated
2¼ cups flour
¼ teaspoon salt
2½ teaspoons baking powder

1 cup plus 1 tablespoon milk
½ teaspoon baking soda
2 squares unsweetened chocolate, melted
1½ teaspoons grated orange rind
Yellow vegetable coloring

Cream shortening, add sugar, and beat thoroughly. Add egg yolks, beat a little longer. Sift flour, salt, and baking powder together and add to creamed mixture alternately with 1 cup milk. Beat egg whites until stiff, and fold gently into batter.

Divide batter into 2 bowls. To 1 bowl add 1 tablespoon milk (in which you have dissolved baking soda) and melted chocolate. Stir gently until no white streaks show. To second bowl add orange rind and a few drops of yellow coloring to make a nice pale yellow.

Drop the chocolate and the yellow batters by alternate spoonfuls into 2 greased 8-inch layer pans. Bake 30 minutes at 350°.

Icing:

6 tablespoons light cream	3 cups confectioners' sugar
4 tablespoons melted butter or	1 tablespoon orange juice
margarine	1 tablespoon orange rind

2 squares chocolate, melted

Add 3 tablespoons cream to melted butter and pour hot into confectioners' sugar. Blend thoroughly. Divide icing into unequal halves. To smaller amount add orange juice and rind, and stir. To larger portion add chocolate and just enough of remaining cream—about 3 tablespoons—to make mixture smooth and glossy.

Spread chocolate icing between layers and around sides of cake. Spread orange icing on top. If you wish, sprinkle a little shaved chocolate (use your vegetable peeler) and a little grated orange rind around the top of the cake, making a petal design. *Serves 8 to 10*

Cocoa Pudding Cake

This nice gooey pudding is similar to Funny Cake but is more of a dessert. We always used Holland Dutch cocoa which is processed with potash. It has a rich taste.

1 cup flour	2 tablespoons melted shortening
2 teaspoons baking powder	¾ cup chopped walnuts or
½ teaspoon salt	shellbarks
¾ cup granulated sugar	¾ cup brown sugar
¼ cup plus 2 tablespoons cocoa	1¾ cups hot water
½ cup milk	Whipped cream or vanilla
1 teaspoon vanilla	ice cream

Sift together flour, baking powder, salt, sugar, and 2 tablespoons cocoa. Add milk, vanilla, shortening, and chopped nuts. Mix and pour in greased pan, 8 by 8 inches. Mix brown sugar with rest of cocoa and sprinkle over mixture in pan. Finally pour hot water gently over top. Bake at 350° for 45 minutes. Serve with whipped cream or vanilla ice cream. *Serves 6 to 8*

Eins, Zwei, Drei Kucha
(ONE, TWO, THREE CAKE)

½ cup butter or
  margarine
2 cups sugar
4 eggs, separated
3 cups flour

2 teaspoons baking powder
1 cup milk
1 teaspoon vanilla
½ cup brown sugar (optional)
½ teaspoon cinnamon (optional)

½ cup chopped nuts (optional)

Cream butter and sugar, add egg yolks, and beat until light and fluffy. Mix flour and baking powder and add alternately with milk. Mix well. Beat egg whites until stiff, and fold into first mixture, adding vanilla last.

Pour into jelly-roll pan, 13½ by 15 inches, and bake at 350° for 40 to 45 minutes, or until the top springs back when touched and is nicely browned.

Sometimes we iced this, but often we just mixed brown sugar with cinnamon and chopped nuts, spread it over the still warm cake, and returned it to the oven for a few minutes to melt the sugar.

Serves 6 to 8

Molasses Layer Cake

2 cups flour
1 teaspoon cinnamon
1 teaspoon cloves
1 teaspoon baking soda

1 cup buttermilk, or sour milk
2 tablespoons butter
1 cup sugar
2 eggs

1 cup New Orleans molasses

Mix flour and spices. Dissolve baking soda in milk. Cream butter and sugar. Stir in eggs and molasses. Then add flour and milk alternately. Grease and flour 2 9-inch layer pans. Bake at 350° about 35 minutes, or until the top springs back at a touch. Frost with butter cream icing.

Butter Cream Icing:

¼ cup butter or margarine
1 pound confectioners' sugar
Pinch salt

½ teaspoon vanilla, or
  ¼ teaspoon vanilla and
  ¼ teaspoon almond extract
4 to 6 tablespoons hot milk
Raisins (optional)

Cut butter into sugar, add salt, and flavoring. Then slowly add hot milk until icing is of desired consistency. After spreading icing on cake you may dot with raisins "for pretty."   *Serves 6 to 10*

Yum Yum Cake

¾ cup butter or margarine
2 cups brown sugar
2 eggs
1 cup sour milk or buttermilk
1 teaspoon baking soda
2½ cups flour

2 teaspoons cinnamon
1 teaspoon nutmeg
2 teaspoons baking powder
1 cup raisins
1 cup walnuts, coarsely
chopped

Cream butter and sugar, add eggs, then sour milk or buttermilk in which baking soda has been dissolved. Sift flour, cinnamon, nutmeg, and baking powder together, and blend with egg batter. Lastly fold in raisins and walnuts. Bake in greased tube pan at 350° for 50 minutes, or until top springs back lightly when touched. (This may also be baked in layers and iced.)   *Serves 6 to 10*

Chocolate Coconut Dessert Cake

2 cups sifted flour
¾ teaspoon baking soda
¼ teaspoon salt
½ cup butter or other shortening
1¼ cups sugar

3 eggs
3 squares unsweetened
chocolate, melted
¾ cup sour milk or buttermilk
1 teaspoon vanilla

Sift flour, measure, add baking soda, and salt, and sift together 3 times. Cream butter thoroughly, add sugar and cream until fluffy. Add eggs, one at a time, beating between additions. Add chocolate and blend. Then add flour alternately with milk, beating after each addition until smooth. Add vanilla.

Bake in 2 greased and floured 9-inch layer-cake pans at 350° for 30 minutes, or until top springs back at a touch. Spread with chocolate seven-minute frosting.

Chocolate Seven-Minute Frosting:

2 unbeaten eggs whites
1½ cups sugar
1½ teaspoons light corn syrup
5 tablespoons water

3 squares unsweetened
chocolate, melted
1 teaspoon vanilla
1 4-ounce can moist coconut

Combine egg whites, sugar, corn syrup, and water in double boiler. Beat with rotary beater until thoroughly mixed. Place over rapidly boiling water and beat constantly for 7 minutes, or until frosting stands in peaks which hold their shape. Remove from fire, stir in chocolate and vanilla, and stir gently, just enough to mix. Do not beat.

Spread over chocolate cake and sprinkle coconut over top and sides. *Serves 8 to 10*

Chocolate Sheet Cake

1 cup boiling water
1 cup cocoa
1 cup shortening—lard and
butter
4 cups brown sugar, or
3 cups white sugar
5 eggs, separated
2 teaspoons baking soda,
dissolved in a little vinegar

1 cup sour milk or
buttermilk
4½ cups flour
2 teaspoons baking powder
1 teaspoon vanilla
10 to 12 marshmallows,
quartered

Pour boiling water slowly over cocoa and stir to dissolve. Set aside.

Cream shortening and mix in sugar, then egg yolks. Stir baking soda into sour milk or buttermilk until it fizzes, then add to creamed mixture. Sift flour and baking powder together, and stir into mixture. Add vanilla and cooled cocoa. Blend until no white streaks show.

Pour into greased and floured baking pan. Bake at 350° for 25 to 30 minutes, or until top springs back at a touch. While still hot, cover top with marshmallows. Ice with Fudge Icing.

Fudge Icing:

4 cups sugar
1 cup milk

1 cup cocoa
1 tablespoon butter

1 teaspoon vanilla

Mix all ingredients in saucepan and cook until mixture forms a soft ball in water (236° on a candy thermometer). Cool and beat until it begins to thicken. Pour over marshmallows covering top of cake. *Serves 10 to 15*

Pfund Kucha
(POUND CAKE)

The amounts for this recipe were originally all in pounds, hence pound cake, but I've converted a few into cups.

9 large eggs, separated, or	4 cups flour
11 medium-sized eggs	½ teaspoon salt
2 cups sugar	1 teaspoon baking powder
1 pound butter	1 teaspoon lemon extract

Beat egg yolks, add sugar and beat until fluffy. In another bowl, cream butter, then add flour which has been sifted with salt and baking powder. Cream again. Add yolk mixture to this; beat well. Add lemon extract. Beat egg whites until they stand in peaks. Fold batter into egg whites and keep folding until no white streaks show. Pour into a tube pan, which has been greased and floured. Bake at 300° for 1½ hours. Cool. Wrap in a clean cloth which has been wrung out in wine or brandy, and store in a cool, dark place. Will keep for weeks. *Serves 10 to 12*

Burnt Sugar Cake

½ cup sugar	2 eggs, separated
½ cup boiling water	3 cups sifted flour
⅔ cup shortening	3 teaspoons baking powder
1 cup sugar	1 teaspoon salt
1 teaspoon vanilla	1 cup milk

Put sugar in heavy skillet over low flame and beat slowly, stirring constantly with wooden spoon. When melted and smoking, remove from heat. Add boiling water very slowly—be careful—it spritzes (spatters)! Continue cooking and stirring until it has cooked down to ½ cup. Set aside to cool.

Cream shortening and sugar; add vanilla, then egg yolks, beating until fluffy. Stir in cooled syrup. Sift flour, baking powder, and salt together, and add to first mixture, alternately with milk. Beat egg whites until stiff, but not dry. Fold into first mixture.

Pour into 2 9-inch layer-cake pans which have been greased and floured. Bake at 350° for 20 to 25 minutes, or until top springs back at a touch. Ice with caramel or any good chocolate frosting.

Caramel Frosting:

2 tablespoons butter
½ cup heavy cream
⅔ cup brown sugar, firmly
  packed

⅛ teaspoon salt
½ teaspoon vanilla
1 pound confectioners'
  sugar

Mix butter, cream, sugar, and salt in saucepan. Bring to boil, stirring constantly. Remove from heat, and add vanilla. Add enough confectioners' sugar to give icing consistency to spread. Stir well to remove lumps, and spread over cake layers.   *Serves 8 to 12*

Quick Sponge Cake

We used this recipe in many ways—as a layer cake, with jelly between the layers, and iced with chocolate icing; as a jelly-roll base; and for what we called "little spunchers," baked in muffin tins lavishly greased with butter, with a little sugar sprinkled over the tops.

4 eggs, separated
1 cup sugar
3 tablespoons water
1½ tablespoons cornstarch

1 cup flour
1½ teaspoons baking powder
Pinch salt
½ teaspoon vanilla

Beat egg yolks until they begin to thicken, add sugar and then water. Put cornstarch in a cup, and fill it with flour; put in sifter, add baking powder, and salt and sift into egg-yolk mixture. Add vanilla. Beat whites until stiff, but not dry. Fold into batter. Bake at 350° for 15 or 20 minutes, or until top springs back at a touch.
Makes 1 layer cake or 24 sponge cakes

Hot-Water Sponge Cake

5 eggs, separated
1¾ cups sugar
½ cup lukewarm water
2 cups flour

Pinch of salt
2 teaspoons baking powder
1 cup coarsely chopped black
  walnuts

Beat egg yolks, add sugar, then water. Sift flour, salt, and baking powder together. Take out 1 tablespoonful of flour and sprinkle over nuts. Add sifted ingredients to yolk mixture. Beat egg whites until stiff and fold into batter. Lastly fold in floured nuts. Bake at 300°

in greased and floured tube pan, or in flat baking pan, for 40 to 50 minutes, or until cake pulls away from sides of pan, and springs back at a touch.   *Serves 12 to 15*

Chocolate Roll with Coffee Icing

4 eggs	¼ cup cocoa
¾ cup sugar	¼ teaspoon baking powder
¼ cup flour	¼ teaspoon salt
½ teaspoon vanilla	

Line a jelly-roll pan, 13½ by 15 inches, with waxed paper or aluminum foil; grease paper.

Beat eggs, add sugar gradually, and beat until thick. Sift dry ingredients together, and gently fold into eggs. Add vanilla. Pour into prepared pan, and bake at 350° for 25 minutes, or until it springs back at a touch. Turn out onto a clean towel sprinkled with a little confectioners' sugar. Peel off paper, and roll the cake right up, towel and all. Let cool.

Icing:

1 cup whipping cream, or 1 envelope topping mix	4 teaspoons instant coffee, or 6 tablespoons strong, cold coffee
6 tablespoons confectioners' sugar	1 teaspoon vanilla
	Chocolate sprinkle or 1 ounce bitter chocolate

Mix all ingredients except chocolate and beat at high speed until stiff enough to hold shape.

Unroll chocolate roll, spread with half the icing and roll up again (without the towel, of course!). Put on plate, seam side down, and ice with remaining frosting. May be decorated with chocolate sprinkles "for pretty," or with shavings made with a very sharp knife from an ounce of bitter chocolate.   *Serves 8 to 10*

Date-Nut Torte

½ cup flour	¾ cup chopped nuts (black walnuts, walnuts, or pecans)
½ teaspoon baking powder	
¼ teaspoon salt	3 eggs, separated
1 cup chopped dates	¾ cup sugar
1 teaspoon grated lemon peel	

Sift flour, baking powder, and salt together. Add dates and nuts and toss together to coat fruit. (Separate dates with your fingers if necessary.)

Separate eggs; beat whites, adding ½ cup sugar slowly, and beat until they form stiff peaks. Set aside.

Beat yolks with ¼ cup sugar until thick. Fold into flour mixture and add lemon peel. Add egg whites and fold again until no yellow streaks show.

Bake in square greased baking pan, 8 by 8 by 2 inches, at 325° for 45 to 50 minutes, or until surface springs back when pressed.

When cool, cut into squares. This is good served with vanilla ice cream, or topped with whipped cream.   *Serves 6 to 8*

Wassermelon Kucha
(WATERMELON CAKE)

Sometimes we got pretty fancy with our cakes in looking for something different. I remember one poor old soul who always colored her cakes a deep pink, and one time brought a purple cake to a church supper! They looked beautiful to her, no doubt, but there was a good deal of snickering among the women! To keep her feelings from being hurt, someone usually disposed of at least part of the cake deep down in the trash, because she was so proud of her beautiful products, and in her shy, modest way she would urge people "chust to try a bissel."

This watermelon cake is actually very delicious, and it is different looking. It was quite popular for a long time.

½ cup butter or margarine	2 teaspoons red sugar
1½ cups sugar	(add a few drops of red food
1 cup milk	coloring to granulated sugar)
3 cups flour	½ cup seedless raisins
2 teaspoons baking soda	(about)
4 egg whites, beaten stiff	

Cream butter and add sugar. Add milk alternately with flour and baking soda. Fold beaten whites into batter.

Take out ⅓ of the dough and carefully blend in the red sugar. Butter a jelly-roll pan (13½ by 9½ by 2 inches). Put half the white dough in it; then in the very center pour on half the pink mixture. On top of mixture, place raisins in a thick row (to look like seeds); pour on the rest of the pink dough, and cover with the rest of the white batter. Bake at 350° for 25 to 30 minutes, or until top springs back when touched. When cut, cake does resemble a slice of watermelon which has been peeled. *Serves 6 to 10*

Schaum Torte
(MERINGUE TORTE)

Schaum means "froth" or "bubbles." We baked this meringue in one large tube pan and filled the center with berries and ice cream, or we made individual meringues, topped with berries or sliced peaches and whipped cream.

7 egg whites	Ice cream
2¼ cups sugar	1 cup strawberries, raspberries,
⅛ teaspoon salt	or sliced peaches mixed with
1 teaspoon vanilla	½ cup of sugar

Whipped cream

Beat egg whites until frothy. Add 1½ cups sugar and beat until very stiff. Gently fold in salt, remaining ¾ cup sugar, and vanilla.

Cover a cookie sheet with brown paper. Make circles of whatever size you please, then build up sides to form a cup, with the back of a spoon. If you make one large torte, use a spring-form pan with a tube.

Bake at 275° for at least 1 hour. Turn off oven and leave meringues in for another 10 or 15 minutes to dry out. Cool and peel off brown paper. Wet bottom of paper, if it doesn't peel easily.

Fill with ice cream. Top with any sugared fruit which has been allowed to stand for 15 minutes and then add a dollop of whipped cream. The meringues freeze well, but are very fragile. Do not store in an airtight container or they will get sugary. *Serves 6 to 8*

CHAPTER IX

From the Berry Patch and Orchard (Fresh Fruit Desserts)

"Everything seems to come on all at vunst, so's abody ain't hardly got time to breathe in the spring, ain't?" This was the complaint of many farm wives. Indeed the work increased as June approached. Most farm families had berry patches of currants, raspberries, gooseberries, and strawberries. Blackberries, elderberries, and huckleberries grew wild, as did the tiny wild strawberries which were so delectable that we children put more in our mouths than in our pails. In addition, most families had grape arbors, with either Concord or white grapes, or both.

From the orchard came the cherries—black, red, sour and sweet, and sometimes oxhearts. On our farm we had four very old cherry trees which yielded buckets and buckets of sweet black cherries. There were so many of them that two Amish families came every year to pick them on the shares.

All sorts of apples grew in the orchard, from the early greenings to the winter apples of the fall. Pippins, Bellflower, Northern Spy, Russets, and the most delectable of all, Smokehouse, were picked for applesauce, cider, apple butter, or

schnitzing (drying). (Smokehouse apples may still be found
in some sections of Lancaster County, but because they don't
ship well they are never grown for commercial use. They have
a rare winy flavor that is irresistible.) Besides the apples,
there were plum, pear, and peach trees—not on every farm,
but one could always swap with a neighbor, or pick on the
shares.

Canning, preserving, and drying went on apace, as the
farmer's wife, female relatives, and children "worked away"
all the fruits and berries that couldn't be used at once. And the
food! Not only fresh fruit pies, but roly-polies, dumplings,
sauces, jams, jellies, and fritters of every sort. If there is anything a Dutch housewife can't throw into a fritter it's inedible!

Most families made wine "for the stomach's sake." When I
asked an old woman for her recipe for currant wine, she gave
it to me with the warning "It don't always make, but ven it
don't abody has vine winegar, not?" The recipe included here
will "make" because of the toast soaked in yeast—a secret which
apparently she didn't know.

Few Pennsylvania Dutch women baked only one pie. They
might have started out to use up some apples, but after they
had mixed up a batch of dough they kept on, until it was "all."
Of course pie was served for breakfast, lunch, and dinner, and
for the neun uhr stück (mid-morning coffee break), if nothing
else was available. This nine o'clock "piece" was taken out to
the fields, usually by the children, along with peppermint tea,
lemonade, or just plain cold water from the spring. The men
would stop their work just long enough to eat, and then go
back to their haying, mowing, plowing, or whatever they were
doing.

Baking day was usually on Thursday, especially if the family
"tended market," which meant the sale of baked goods as well
as other products. In that case, every available pie plate was
set out to be filled according to the housewife's fancy. Women
usually took great pride in the variety they were able to
produce.

Basic Pie Crust

1½ cups flour
½ cup lard, or ¼ cup lard and
  ¼ cup butter

½ teaspoon salt
⅛ to ½ cup cold water

Using your hands, work flour, lard, and salt together quickly, until the flour has taken up all the shortening. Add water, a little at a time, tossing with a fork until the dough leaves the bowl. (Use as little water as possible.) Roll out to ⅛ inch on floured surface. This recipe is enough to make 1 double 9-inch pie crust or 2 single 9-inch crusts. If you are making an open pie you can just halve the recipe.

Green Currant or Gooseberry Pie

The method is the same for both fruits. On our farm the currants were picked when they first showed the faintest blush of red.

Line a 9-inch pie plate with crust (see above), making a high border. Add enough washed currants or gooseberries, about 3 cups, to fill to the rim. Place 1 tablespoon flour in measuring cup, and fill with granulated sugar. Stir and pour over fruit. Bake at 400° for 50 minutes to 1 hour. If you like, you can put a lattice crust on top.

Serves 6

Rhubarb Pie

Pie:

Dough for 1 9-inch pie crust
  (see Index)
3 cups uncooked rhubarb,
  cut in ¼-inch slices

1 tablespoon flour
1 cup sugar

Line a deep 9-inch pie plate with crust. Fill with rhubarb. Mix flour and sugar and pour over.

Crumb Topping:

½ cup flour
⅛ teaspoon cinnamon
½ cup brown or granulated sugar

4 tablespoons butter or
  margarine

Combine ingredients and mix with fingers until crumbly. Beginning at center of pie, swirl crumbs over top in pinwheel pattern, leaving space for rhubarb to peep through.

Bake at 400° for 5 minutes, then lower heat to 350° and bake about 50 minutes more—until rhubarb is soft, and the crumbs brown and bubbling.   *Serves 6*

Apple Raisin Pie

Pie:

4 large cooking apples, chopped or cut into small pieces
½ cup chopped walnuts— black or English
¾ cup sugar
¼ cup raisins

¼ teaspoon cinnamon
¼ cup wine—any kind will do
Grated rind of one lemon
Dough for 1 9-inch pie crust (see Index)

Mix all ingredients (except crust) and cook for 5 minutes. (Taste —if apples are sweet, you may need to add lemon juice in addition to wine.) Let cool. Line 9-inch pie plate with crust, and fill with apple mixture. Bake at 350° for 30 to 40 minutes. Remove from oven and let cool while you make meringue.

Meringue:

1 egg white   2 tablespoons sugar

Beat egg white with sugar until forms stiff peaks. Turn oven up to 400°. Spread meringue over pie, being sure to bring it out to edge. Place in hot oven for 5 minutes, just until the meringue browns slightly.   *Serves 6*

Quick Lemon Custard

Dough for 1 8-inch pie crust (see Index)
2 eggs
1 cup sugar

¼ pound butter or margarine, melted
Juice and rind of 2 lemons

Line 8-inch pie plate with crust, fluting edges. Prick bottom of shell with a fork.

Beat eggs, add sugar, and melted butter, then juice and rind of lemons.

Bake 5 minutes at 450°. Reduce heat to 325° and bake 15 to 20 minutes more—until a knife inserted near the center comes out clean.   *Serves 4 to 6*

Sour Lemon Pie

Dough for 2 9-inch pie crusts
  (see Index)
3 eggs
1½ cups granulated sugar
3 tablespoons flour
¼ teaspoon salt

5 tablespoons butter or
  margarine, melted
2 tablespoons grated lemon rind
2 peeled lemons, sliced as thin as
  possible (be sure to remove all
  white rind)

½ cup cold water

Line 9-inch pie plate with crust, fluting edge. Prick bottom with fork. Using 8-inch pie plate to measure, roll out another circle of dough. Slice this into equal wedges—6 or 8—put on a lightly greased cookie sheet and sprinkle with sugar. Bake at 400° for 10 minutes. Set aside to cool.

Beat eggs, add sugar, then stir in rest of ingredients. Pour mixture into prepared crust. Bake 25 to 30 minutes at 400°. Remove from oven and carefully arrange wedges of cooked dough on top. Bake 10 more minutes. You may not be able to use all the wedges, but use at least three. This looks pretty and tastes wonderful—but it *is* sour!   *Serves 6*

Cherry Custard

1 baked pie crust (see Index)
4 cups cherries—sour or sweet,
  canned or fresh
3 tablespoons cornstarch
¾ cup sugar

1 tablespoon butter or
  margarine
1 tablespoon lemon juice
  (optional)

Drain cherries, saving 1 cup of juice. (If you are using fresh cherries you will have to crush a little to get juice.) Combine cornstarch and sugar. Gradually add cherry juice. Heat to boiling over low heat, stirring constantly, and boil 3 minutes. Add butter, lemon juice, and drained cherries. Cool thoroughly.

Custard:

2 tablespoons butter or margarine	2 cups milk
¼ cup cornstarch	2 egg yolks
¾ cup sugar	½ teaspoon water
½ teaspoon salt	½ teaspoon vanilla
	3 drops almond extract

Melt butter, add cornstarch, sugar, and salt. Gradually add milk. Bring to boiling, stirring constantly. Beat egg yolks with water. Add a little of the hot cornstarch mixture to eggs, then add yolks to the whole mixture. (This is to keep eggs from curdling.) Cook over low heat, stirring constantly. Add vanilla and almond extracts. Cool thoroughly.

When ready to serve, pour custard into baked pie shell (or a graham cracker crust) and top with cherry mixture.   *Serves 6*

Huckleberry Muffins

Huckleberries grew wild on what we called the "Welsh Mountain." It was six long miles away, but we always made the expedition because these small berries made such wonderful pies, roly-polies, and muffins.

2 eggs	2 teaspoons baking powder
¾ cup milk	Pinch of salt
1 cup sugar	1 cup huckleberries (blueberries
½ cup butter or margarine, melted	may be substituted)
1½ cups flour	¼ teaspoon vanilla

Beat eggs, add milk and sugar, then melted butter. Sift dry ingredients together, then add egg mixture, stirring just enough to moisten all ingredients. Fold in washed berries and add vanilla. Fill greased muffin cups about ¾ full. Bake at 400° for 20 minutes or until nicely browned.   *Makes 12 to 18 muffins*

Ebble, Kirsch, Parshung Kuchen und Pflaum Torte
(APPLE, CHERRY, PEACH CAKE, AND PLUM TART)

Kuchen or torten are open-faced pies with cake-like crusts made from sweet raised dough as in the recipe for Sticky buns (see Index) or as follows:

Crust for Fruit Kuchen and Torten

1 cup sifted flour	2 tablespoons butter or
½ teaspoon baking powder	margarine
¼ cup sugar	1 egg

Mix dry ingredients, then work in the butter with fingers, or cut in with two knives, until bits of batter are size of peas. Add egg and stir. Flour hands, and line 9-inch pie plate with pastry. Pat and press into shape, making a high, fluted crust, but keep shell fairly thin. (This dough is sticky.)

Short Cut:

Add 1 egg and ¼ cup sugar to 1 cup prepared biscuit mix, and proceed as above. *Makes 1 9-inch crust*

Ebble Kuchen
(APPLE KUCHEN)

Dough for 1 9-inch kuchen	1 cup granulated sugar
(see above)	⅛ teaspoon cinnamon
5 or 6 apples	¼ cup raisins or chopped
1 tablespoon flour	nuts (optional)
Lemon juice (optional)	

Line a 9-inch pie plate with dough. Pare apples and quarter. Arrange in circles in crust, pressing fruit into dough. You may have to piece a little, but keep fruit close together, as it shrinks in baking. If apples are not good and tart, add a few teaspoonfuls of lemon juice.

Put 1 tablespoonful of flour in a cup and add sugar and cinnamon. Stir and pour over fruit.

Either raisins, nuts, or both may be added to apple kuchen, if you want a rich party-like cake. Bake at 400° for 35 to 40 minutes, until apples are soft. *Serves 6*

Kirsch Kuchen
(CHERRY KUCHEN)

Dough for 1 9-inch kuchen
  (see Index)
1 can sour cherries, or
  2 or 3 cups fresh sour cherries,
  pitted and drained

1 tablespoon cornstarch or flour
1 cup granulated sugar
2 drops almond extract
  (optional)
1 tablespoon cherry juice

Line pie plate with dough. Arrange cherries in 1 layer in circular pattern. Mix cornstarch and sugar, and pour over cherries. Mix almond extract and cherry juice and dribble over top. Bake at 400° for 15 minutes, until crust is brown and cherries nicely glazed.

Serves 6

Parshung Kuchen
(PEACH CUSTARD KUCHEN)

Dough for 1 9-inch kuchen
  (see Index)
6 to 8 ripe peaches, or
  2 cups canned peach halves, or
  2 packages frozen peaches
2 eggs

¼ cup sugar
½ cup cream
1 tablespoon flour
⅛ teaspoon nutmeg
1 tablespoon lemon juice
  (optional)

Line pie plate with dough. If using fresh peaches, peel and cut in halves. Arrange fruit in circles on the dough. Beat eggs, add sugar, then cream, and finally flour and nutmeg. Pour this custard over the peaches. (If you use canned peaches, add lemon juice to give them tartness.)

Bake at 400° for 5 minutes; reduce heat to 350°, and bake 20 minutes more, until custard is set and peaches soft.   *Serves 6*

Plum Tart

Dough for 1 9-inch kuchen
  (see Index)
8 to 10 ripe plums
1 tablespoon flour

1 cup sugar
⅛ teaspoon cinnamon
2 tablespoons plum juice or
  lemon juice

Line pie plate with dough. Do not peel plums, but halve them, removing seed. Arrange in concentric circles on dough. Put 1 tablespoonful flour in cup, fill it with sugar and pour over fruit. Sprinkle with cinnamon, and then dribble fruit juice over top. Bake at 400° for 25 to 30 minutes.   *Serves 6*

Huckleberry Kuchen

Dough for 1 9-inch kuchen   ½ cup sugar
  (see Index)   2 tablespoons cornstarch
3 to 4 cups huckleberries (blue-   ⅛ teaspoon cinnamon
  berries may be substituted)   2 tablespoons lemon juice
½ cup water   2 tablespoons lemon rind

Line pie plate with dough. Wash berries, and bring to boil in water. Drain, saving 1 cup juice. Cool.

Mix dry ingredients in saucepan. Slowly add berries, lemon juice and rind, stirring constantly over low heat. Bring to boil, then cook 1 minute longer, until mixture just begins to thicken.

Line pie plate with kuchen dough, fill with berries, and pour cornstarch mixture over them. Bake at 400° for 5 minutes, then at 350° for about 20 minutes more, or until crust is nicely browned.

This is usually served with cream.   *Serves 6*

Deep-Dish Peach Pie

Filling:

6 to 8 peaches   1 tablespoon butter
¼ cup water   ½ teaspoon cinnamon or
1 cup sugar   nutmeg

Peel and quarter peaches. Boil with water and sugar until soft, but not mushy. Add butter and cinnamon or nutmeg. Pour into greased pan, 8 by 8 by 2 inches.

Dough:

1½ cups flour   Pinch salt
½ cup sugar   ½ to ¾ cup milk

Mix dough with just enough milk so that you can pull off small pieces. Pinch off about a teaspoonful at a time and drop on top of peaches. Bake at 350° for 15 to 20 minutes, just until dough is lightly browned.   *Serves 6*

Fruit Roly-Poly

As a child my favorite roly-polies were blackberry or black raspberry. This is a quickly made dessert, and is usually served with pitchers of heavy cream.

This is made with a very rich biscuit crust. (If you use prepared biscuit mix, add ¼ cup melted butter or margarine.)

2 cups flour	1 cup milk (approx.)
3 teaspoons baking powder	2 to 3 cups berries
½ teaspoon salt	(fresh, frozen, or unsweetened
3 tablespoons butter or other	canned)
shortening	1 cup sugar
1 egg	½ cup water

Sift flour, baking powder, and salt together. Work in shortening, either with two knives or hands. Add egg, then gradually add milk, and mix until it forms a soft dough. Roll out about ½ inch thick, pressing lightly. Roll the whole sheet of dough onto floured rolling pin and transfer to baking pan, 13 by 9 inches, or larger. (If dough breaks, you can piece it by patting it into shape.)

Mix berries with 1 cup sugar and spread over dough, leaving about 2 inches as a border. Fold dough over fruit, sealing edges well, and add ½ cup water to pan. Turn over, so that the seam side is down.

Bake at 350°, basting frequently, for about 30 to 40 minutes, until juices have thickened and crust is brown. *Serves 4 to 6*

Fruit Dumplings

For all dumplings roll out dough for pie crust (see Index) to about ½-inch thickness. (A packaged mix may be used instead.) Cut into squares, large enough to contain whatever fruit you are using—about 2 inches. Place fruit on the square and fold the corners up over the fruit. Transfer seam side down to baking pan—9 by 9 inches, or larger.

Apple Dumplings:

Peel and core 6 small apples. Place each apple on a 4- to 6-inch square of dough. Fill center with 1 teaspoon sugar and a dash of cinnamon. Fold the corners up over the apples.

In saucepan, mix together 1 cup dark brown sugar, 1 tablespoon butter, 2 tablespoons orange juice, and 1 teaspoon cinnamon. Bring just to a boil. Pour over dumplings. Bake at 400° for 30 to 40 minutes, until apples are tender. Baste with sauce every so often. Serve hot or warm, with hard sauce or cream.   *Serves 6*

Peach Dumplings:

Peel 6 peaches and cut in half. Remove pits and place a few nuts in each center, together with 1 tablespoon sugar and a pinch of nutmeg. Put halves back together, then place each piece on square of dough and fold up. Transfer to baking pan. Make syrup by boiling 1 cup sugar, 1 teaspoon butter, 1 drop of almond extract, and 2 teaspoons of lemon juice. Pour into pan. Bake at 400° for 25 to 30 minutes, until peaches are tender, basting with sauce several times.

Serves 6

PUDDINGS

Apple pudding was usually served with the main course, especially with ham or roast pork.

Apple Pudding

4 cups sliced apples	½ cup butter or margarine
1 cup sifted flour	1 tablespoon lemon juice
1 cup sugar	(optional)
1 teaspoon cinnamon	

Peel, core, and slice apples and put into 1-quart casserole, or 9-inch square baking pan. Mix dry ingredients and cut into butter until crumbly. Spread mixture over apple slices. If apples are not tart, add a tablespoonful of lemon juice. Bake at 375° between 50 and 60 minutes.   *Serves 4*

Pineapple Pudding

This is not an echt (true) Pennsylvania Dutch dish because canned pineapple was not available until recently. It is now very popular, and is served with ham or pork chops.

5 slices bread, cubed	¼ pound butter or margarine,
3 eggs	melted
½ cup sugar	1 can crushed pineapple

Cut bread into cubes, crust and all. Grease 1½-quart casserole or baking dish. Beat eggs, add sugar, then melted butter. Fold in crushed pineapple, and mix with bread cubes. Pour into casserole, and bake at 350° for 40 minutes. *Serves 6*

Raspberry Pudding

There were two ways to make this. One resembles a deep-dish pie, the other is a true pudding.

Deep-Dish Raspberry Pudding

2 or 3 cups fresh raspberries
1 cup sugar
½ cup butter or margarine
2 cups flour

1½ teaspoons baking powder
Dash of salt
2 eggs
¼ cup milk

Mix raspberries and sugar and place in deep dish. Cut butter into mixture of flour, baking powder and salt until fine as meal. Add 1 egg and stir. Roll out on slightly floured board to about ¼ inch. Cover berries with dough, pricking to allow steam to escape. Beat 1 egg in a cup and pour in milk. Spread over top of dough. Bake at 350° for 40 to 50 minutes. *Serves 4 to 6*

Raspberry Pudding

1 quart raspberries, red or black
½ cup sugar
1 envelope gelatine

2 tablespoons cold water
3 tablespoons boiling water
1 pint whipping cream

Wash berries and sugar them. Stir and let stand for at least ½ hour to draw the juice. Soak gelatine in cold water, then add boiling water and stir until dissolved. Cool until it just begins to set.

Whip the cream. Mix fruit and gelatine and fold in whipped cream. Refrigerate until completely set. *Serves 4*

Fruit Fritters

To make apple and other fruit fritters, use one of the following basic recipes, and add the other ingredients as indicated in the recipes that follow.

Batter for Fritters No. 1:

1 egg
1 cup flour
2 teaspoons baking powder

2 teaspoons sugar
½ teaspoon salt
⅔ cup milk (approx.)

Beat egg and add to dry ingredients. Pour in milk last. Stir well.
The amount of milk needed varies because of differences in eggs,
so you may not need all of it. The batter should have the consistency
of pancake batter.

Batter for Deep-Fried Fritters No. 2:

1 egg
¼ cup milk
1 tablespoon melted butter or
    margarine

¼ cup sugar
Dash of salt
¾ cup flour
½ teaspoon baking powder

Separate egg and beat the white until it holds a peak. Mix yolk,
milk, and melted butter with dry ingredients to make a smooth
dough. Fold in egg white. Batter should be quite stiff. (If too stiff,
add more milk, but be sure it holds its shape.)

Apple Fritters

2 or 3 sour apples
Powdered sugar
1 recipe batter No. 2
    (see above)

Shortening for deep frying
Cinnamon (optional)
Sugar (optional)

Peel and core apples and cut into thin, round slices. Dip in
powdered sugar, and let stand a few minutes. Then dip into batter.
Fry in deep fat until nicely browned on both sides. Place on paper
towel to absorb the grease. Mix cinnamon and sugar and sprinkle
on fritters, if desired. *Serves 4*

Apple Fritters, Pan Style

2 or 3 sour apples
1 recipe batter No. 2
    (see above)
Powdered sugar

1 teaspoon cinnamon
½ cup sugar
1 tablespoon shortening

Peel and core apples and slice thinly. Dip in batter and fry in a spider until browned, turning just once. Dust with mixture of cinnamon and sugar and serve at once. *Serves 4*

Cherry Fritters

2 cups drained sour or sweet cherries (canned or pitted fresh ones)

1 recipe batter No. 1 (see above)
1 tablespoon shortening

Add cherries to batter; mix thoroughly. Drop by the spoonful into a spider or griddle. Turn when they bubble all over. Serve with powdered sugar or syrup. *Serves 4*

Apple Dessert

4 eggs
3 cups sugar
2 teaspoons vanilla
½ cup butter, melted
4 cups diced apples, pared
1 cup nuts, coarsely chopped

2 cups flour
2 tablespoons baking powder
1 teaspoon salt
1 teaspoon cinnamon
1 teaspoon nutmeg (optional)

Beat eggs, then add sugar, vanilla, butter, apples, and nuts. Sift dry ingredients together, and add to first mixture. Bake in greased cake pan, 14½ by 10 inches, at 350° for 35 to 40 minutes. Serve warm. Delicious with vanilla ice cream. *Serves 6 to 8*

Porcupine Apples

1 cup sugar
2 cups water
1 tablespoon lemon juice
4 apples

2 egg whites
½ cup pecans, cut lengthwise into thin strips
Powdered sugar

Mix sugar, water, and lemon juice and put on to boil. Pare and core apples, but leave whole. Drop into boiling syrup and cook until tender. Remove from syrup and let drain. Beat egg whites until stiff. Coat each apple with meringue, then stick all over with pecans. Sprinkle liberally with powdered sugar, set in baking pan and brown for a minute or two in 350° oven. *Serves 4*

Baked Cherry Pudding

2 cups pitted sour cherries (may be canned)	¼ teaspoon salt
½ cup sugar	1 egg, well beaten
1½ cups flour	1 cup milk
1½ teaspoons baking powder	2 tablespoons melted butter or margarine

Mix well-drained cherries with sugar and set aside. Sift dry ingredients. Add milk, beaten egg, and melted butter. Mix well. Fold in sugared cherries.

Butter small pudding pan or casserole, pour in mixture. Bake at 350° for 45 minutes. Serve with cherry sauce.

Cherry Sauce:

Mix ½ cup finely chopped cherries and 4 tablespoons sugar; bring to a boil. Thicken with 1 teaspoon cornstarch mixed with a little cold water. Simmer gently 10 minutes, being careful to keep it from sticking.   *Serves 4*

Cherry Betty with Cherry Sauce

2 cups pitted pie cherries (canned cherries, sweet or sour)	1 tablespoon butter
	2 tablespoons cherry juice
1 cup sugar	1 recipe cherry sauce (see above)
2 cups diced bread (about 4 slices)	

Mix cherries and sugar. Drain, but save some juice. Butter small pudding pan or casserole, put in ½ cup diced bread, then 1 cup cherries. Repeat, making 3 layers of bread and 2 layers of cherries; dot with butter. Pour cherry juice over mixture. Cover and bake at 350° for 25 minutes. Remove cover and bake 20 minutes more. Serve with cherry sauce.   *Serves 4*

Persimmon Pudding

Persimmons grew down in the meadow and at the edge of the woods. They were small, and wonderfully sweet, but only if you waited until they had been touched by frost; if you couldn't contain your eagerness, you had a puckered mouth for quite a while. We gathered them in baskets and took them home—as many as were left, that is, after greedy children had dipped into them.

Fruit:

Wash persimmons and put them through a food mill or a sieve. You will need 1 cup of pulp.

Batter:

1 cup flour	2 eggs
½ teaspoon salt	2 tablespoons butter, melted
½ teaspoon baking soda	1 cup milk
¾ cup sugar	½ grated lemon rind

Mix dry ingredients. Beat eggs, add melted butter, then milk and dry ingredients alternately. Blend well. Fold in persimmon pulp and grated lemon rind. Bake in greased pan, 8 by 8 by 2 inches, at 350° for 50 minutes. Serve with plain or whipped cream.   *Serves 4 to 6*

Fruit Soup

Cold soups are nothing new in the Pennsylvania Dutch country. We made all sorts of fruit soups—raspberry, apple, blackberry, and cherry. The method is the same for all of them, and they "tasted us wery vell," on a hot summer evening.

6 or 8 sour apples, or	1 cup wine (currant, sherry, or
2 quarts berries	any sweet wine)
Water	2 tablespoons flour or corn-
1 stick cinnamon	starch, mixed with equal
1 cup sugar	amount of water
1 lemon, juice and grated rind	

Cut apples into quarters. Core but do not peel and cut into thin slices. If you use berries, just wash them. Cover fruit with boiling water and cook until soft. Strain through a sieve or food mill; add cinnamon, sugar, lemon, and wine. Bring to a boil again and thicken with flour and water.

Serve hot or cold. This is a refreshingly different dish—really more of a pudding than a soup, but we called it "sup."   *Serves 4 to 6*

Cider Time

Cider was made in the fall. There were two types of presses: one a round, barrel-like contrivance with a lid on it, which was turned by hand; and another, much larger and more complicated, which was worked by using a horse. Not every farm had a press, but most farms did. If you didn't have a press you could always take your apples to a neighbor. There were differing opinions about just how many sweet and how many sour apples gave just the right flavor, but most people used half and half. Cider making usually took place before sun-up, or after sundown, by the light of a lantern, to avoid the terrific nuisance of the bees and yellowjackets which swarmed around the sweet juice.

The cider was hauled home in two, three, or even four barrels. One or two of these were carried to the cellar and put on wooden blocks. A cupful of old vinegar, together with the "mother," a gelatinous mass of goo which had been carefully drained and saved from last year's batch, was added. A bung was placed loosely in the end of the barrel, and it was left for several months until the alchemy of nature turned it into vinegar, or, as we used to say, "it made." Our vinegar was strong and undiluted, far different from the kind that is bottled today. To taste it you had to be very careful and dilute it with water, else it would "kreistle" you (make you shudder!).

Some or all of the cider in another barrel was jugged or bottled for drinking or for selling at market. Pop seldom liked sweet cider; he preferred it to be "a bissel bitzlich" (with a little bite) or hard—not too hard, mind you, for then it tasted like vinegar, but just fermented enough to have a "little kick to it." Such an elixir, when the apples were properly blended, and such an aroma, as the tiny bubbles rose to the surface and tickled your nose! The poor man's champagne!

Cider Sup

Cider soup was a by-product of cider making. The cider was diluted with a little water, placed on the stove, and brought to a boil. It was then thickened with a thin paste of cornstarch or flour, and again brought just to a boil to thicken a bit more. Sweet cream and small pieces of toasted bread were added just before serving.

Molle Cider

The name "molle" is either a corruption of "mulled" or a borrowing from the German *Molle,* which is a kind of light table wine. This was served on cold days, but it is no longer well known.

Beat 3 eggs until light. Slowly add hot cider, reheat just to boiling, add a cinnamon stick to each mug, and pour in the hot cider. Sugar may be added, if the cider is too sour, but it is preferred "so." A sort of Pennsylvania Dutch zabaglione!   *Serves 4 to 6*

CHAPTER X

From the Canning Kettle
(Sweets and Sours)

Canning, preserving, pickling, and drying went on throughout the spring, summer, and fall. From the earliest green shoots of asparagus to the last of the late apples, sooner or later, the housewife got some of them into a crock, jar, or bag.

The origin of the custom of putting Seven Sweets and Seven Sours on the table is unknown, but the tradition prevails to this day. It wasn't absolutely necessary to have the exact number of each on the table, but the custom served as a yardstick to judge the abundance of the set-out.

Even today, not only on the farms but in the villages and towns, when it is no longer necessary or economical, Pennsylvania Dutch women put up fruits and vegetables, preferring the flavor of those they can and preserve at home to any others. Sauerkraut originally came from the need to preserve cabbage, but string beans were also salted down, and the bean seeds were dried. The two were sometimes combined for a sweet-and-sour dish that I still make. Corn is dried, as well as frozen or canned, because the flavor of dried corn makes it taste like a different vegetable. You can still find dried corn at market and in some grocery stores. Apples and peaches were dried or canned and also made into butter or jelly.

Sauerkraut

We used to pack kraut in big earthen crocks, weighed down with a clean stone, and keep it in the cellarway all winter.

Nowadays, however, we can it, and it takes up less room and is easier to care for, since there is no scum to remove and no stone to scrub once a week. It is just as delicious.

Before I give the recipe, a word of warning. The kraut boils up and spills over as it is fermenting, then subsides and seals itself. Don't worry about it. One friend of mine put up 24 quarts of it, but I forgot to warn her—she thought it was spoiled and threw out a good half-day's work!

2 or 3 heads of cabbage	Quart jars with old-fashioned
Salt	metal lids, sealed with
Boiling water	rubber rings

Cut the cabbage fine as for slaw. Pack into sterilized quart jars a little at a time, pressing down with a wooden spoon to "make chuice." Add 1 tablespoon salt to each jar. Fill the can with boiling water, leaving about 1 inch of head space. Close the jar, not too tightly, and put aside in a cool, dark place on a tray to catch any juice which might boil over. When the fermentation has subsided, check jars to be sure they are tightly sealed. This keeps well all winter.   *Makes about 6 quarts*

Pickled Tripe

This seems to be a purely masculine dish; most women won't touch it, but men are "so for it."

2 to 3 pounds honeycomb tripe	1 teaspoon horseradish
Salted water to cover	1 cup vinegar
1 small onion, sliced	4 whole cloves
1 small hot pepper, or 1	1 bay leaf
teaspoon Tabasco or hot	1 teaspoon mustard seeds
pepper sauce	½ cup water

¼ cup sugar

Wash tripe and cut into strips about 1½ inches wide. Put on to boil in salted water. Simmer at least 3 hours—longer, if you have time. Drain and add sliced onion. Mix rest of ingredients, bring to a boil, and pour over tripe. Bring to a boil again. Refrigerate in a glass or earthenware dish at least 1 week. Taste for seasoning. This recipe is good and scharf (sharp) so if you prefer a milder dish, decrease the horseradish and omit the Tabasco. Keeps for several weeks.

Serves 6 to 8

Mincemeat for Pies

2 pounds lean boiled beef, chopped fine	1 quart cider
	½ pint wine
4 pounds chopped tart apples	½ tablespoon salt
½ pound chopped beef suet	½ tablespoon allspice
1½ pounds seeded raisins	2 tablespoons cinnamon
1 pound dried currants	½ tablespoon mace
¼ pound candied citron, diced	1 tablespoon nutmeg
½ pound brown sugar	1 tablespoon cloves
1 pint cooking molasses	½ pint brandy

Mix thoroughly all ingredients except brandy and bring to a boil. Remove from fire, and stir in brandy. Put into sterilized quart jars and seal, leaving head space. This will keep a whole winter.

Makes about 5 quarts

Green Tomato Mincemeat

2 quarts green tomatoes	1 tablespoon allspice
2 cups cider	1 tablespoon cinnamon
4 pounds brown sugar	1 tablespoon ground cloves
1½ pounds seedless raisins	1 tablespoon salt

Chop tomatoes quite fine and drain in sieve. Boil in cider for 15 minutes, then add sugar, raisins, spices, and salt, and boil for 2 hours, stirring once in a while to prevent sticking. Pack into sterilized quart jars while hot.

When baking a pie, add one finely diced apple to the mincemeat, and the juice of half a lemon.

Makes about 2 quarts

Dried Corn

Use only fresh corn. With a sharp knife, cut corn from the cob. Spread kernels on cookie sheets or baking pans and dry slowly in a cool oven (300°), leaving oven door open. Or cover with cheesecloth and dry in the sun. Stir frequently until perfectly dry. Corn will rattle. Store in jars or cans or plastic bags. Keep in a cool, dry place.

To serve dried corn, prepare as follows:

2 cups dried corn	1 teaspoon salt
2 quarts cold water	1 tablespoon sugar
2 tablespoons butter	⅛ teaspoon pepper

Soak corn in water overnight. Next day bring to a boil in same water, then simmer 1 hour or until tender. Add rest of ingredients and boil a few minutes more. Taste to correct seasoning.

Dried corn is never completely tender, but it has a marvelously unique flavor. *Makes 1½ cups*

PICKLES

Dilled Green Tomatoes

10 to 12 green tomatoes	5 cups water
Brine made of ½ cup salt to 4 quarts water	Grape or cherry leaves
¼ cup salt	3 hot peppers
½ cup cider vinegar	6 to 8 sprigs of dill (seeds and stalks)
3 cloves garlic	

Wash tomatoes and remove stems. (They should be perfect, with no spots or soft places.) Place in brine overnight. Drain. Combine salt, vinegar, and water. Bring to a boil and then cool.

Use wide-mouth sterilized half-gallon or gallon jar. Put grape leaves on bottom, add tomatoes, red peppers, dill, and garlic. Pour vinegar solution into jar, making sure that all tomatoes are covered (add a little water if you don't have enough juice). Put plate over tomatoes and weight it down with a clean stone, or any weight (not metal) you can think of. Keep in dark, cool place at least 4 weeks, skimming about once a week, to remove any scum which rises to the top. (You can also use sterilized half-gallon jars which close with a rubber ring.) *Makes 1 gallon*

Dilled Beans

2 pounds very small green beans, or 2 cans whole green beans
Salted water to cover
1 small onion, sliced
⅛ cup salt

2½ cups water
¼ cup cider vinegar
Few sprigs dill (stalk and seeds), or 2 tablespoons dried dill seeds

1 clove garlic (optional)

If using fresh beans, string them, then cook in boiling, salted water until not quite tender—about 15 minutes. Drain. Slice onion into very thin slices and mix with beans.

Mix salt, water, and vinegar and bring to a boil. Pour over beans and onions, and pack into sterilized pint jars (into which you have put dill and garlic, if you like these flavors). Seal. This is ready in about 10 days but will keep indefinitely. *Makes 2 to 3 pints*

Pickled Onions

3 or 4 quarts tiny white onions
1 cup salt

¼ cup mixed pickle spice
2 cups sugar

2 quarts vinegar

Peel onions, add salt and let stand overnight. Drain and rinse thoroughly to remove salt. Tie spices in a cloth, add to sugar and vinegar and bring to a boil. Add onions, boil again, and pack into pint or quart sterilized jars. *Makes 6 to 8 pints*

Sweet Pickles
(QUICK METHOD)

6 sour pickles with juice (bought or homemade)

1½ cups sugar
1 teaspoon mixed pickling spices

Mix sugar and spices with pickle juice, bring to a boil and pour over pickles cut into 1-inch pieces. Let "set" overnight or longer. *Makes about 2 pints*

Pepper Hash

1 dozen sweet red peppers
1 dozen green peppers

Boiling water to cover
1 stalk celery, sliced

1 dozen onions, sliced

Wash peppers, remove seeds and pith, and cut into squares. Pour boiling water over them and let steep for 5 minutes. Drain. Add celery and onions. Let stand while you make the syrup, as follows:

3 pints vinegar	1 teaspoon dry mustard
2 tablespoons salt	2 cups sugar
	2 teaspoons celery seed

Boil all ingredients for 5 minutes. Pour over vegetables, bring to a boil, put into sterilized pint jars and seal. *Makes 2 to 3 pints*

Corn Pickle

1½ quarts vinegar	2 quarts of corn (cut from cob,
1¼ pounds sugar	or canned whole-kernel corn)
1½ tablespoons salt	2 quarts finely chopped cabbage
¼ cup dry mustard	4 green peppers, chopped

Mix vinegar, sugar, salt, and mustard, and pour over corn, cabbage, and peppers in a large kettle. Cook until corn is tender—about 15 minutes. Pour into sterilized pint jars and seal.

Makes about 6 pints

Corn Relish

5 sweet red peppers, chopped fine	2 cups water
5 green peppers, chopped fine	2 cups cider vinegar
2 stalks celery, sliced on a diagonal	1 cup sugar
2 medium-sized onions, chopped fine	1 tablespoon yellow mustard seed
2 tablespoons salt	½ tablespoon dry mustard
	12 ears of corn, or 3 cans whole-kernel corn, drained

Combine all ingredients except corn. Bring to a boil and boil 15 minutes, stirring frequently. Cut corn from the cob or drain canned corn and add to the mixture. Cook 10 minutes more. Pack into sterilized pint jars and seal. *Makes 5 to 6 pints*

Cucumber Sauce

2 tablespoons salt	1 cup sugar
3 quarts cucumbers, sliced thin	1 teaspoon celery seed
1 quart vinegar	1 teaspoon yellow mustard seed

Add salt to sliced cucumbers and let stand ½ hour. Combine other ingredients and bring to a boil. Add cucumbers and boil a few minutes until the cucumbers are heated through. Put in sterilized pint jars and seal.   *Makes 5 to 6 pints*

Kimmel Kirsche
(PICKLED CHERRIES)

8 cups seeded sour cherries	3 cups vinegar
8 cups sugar	

Cover cherries with vinegar and let stand overnight. Drain and add sugar. Place in deep bowl or crock and cover tightly. Let stand in cool place for 9 days, stirring once a day. Pack into pint jars (they need not be sterilized) and seal. Cherries are served as a relish and are especially toothsome with ham.   *Makes about 4 pints*

Brandied Cherries

Use the above recipe for kimmel cherries, but add ½ cup of good brandy before canning.

Pickled Filled Peppers

10 or 12 sweet peppers (red, green, or both)	4 cups vinegar
	½ cup sugar
Brine to cover (1 tablespoon salt to 1 quart water)	2 tablespoons whole yellow mustard seeds
1 large head cabbage	12 whole cloves
2 tablespoons salt	1 piece whole cinnamon stick

Cut tops off peppers, leaving stems on, and remove seeds and pith. Soak overnight in brine. Shred cabbage fine, sprinkle with salt, and also let stand overnight. The next day, squeeze all water from cabbage and fill peppers with it. Put tops back on peppers, and fasten with toothpicks.

Put filled peppers in stone crock or deep non-metal utensil, and cover with vinegar, sugar, and spices which have been brought to a boil. Cover with clean cloth, put a plate over it and weigh peppers down with a clean stone. They will be pickled in a week, but will keep for several months in unsealed jars. *Makes 10 to 12 pickles*

Bread and Butter Pickles

1 gallon cucumbers	2 green peppers, shredded
8 small onions	½ cup salt

Ice cubes

Wash cucumbers and slice ⅛ inch thick; slice onions; shred pepper. Sprinkle with salt, cover with ice and let stand 3 hours. (When there was no ice, we let them stand overnight.)

Syrup:

5 cups sugar	2 tablespoons yellow mustard
1½ teaspoons turmeric	seeds
½ teaspoon ground cloves	1 teaspoon celery seeds

5 cups vinegar—not too strong

Mix all ingredients together and bring to a boil.

Drain pickle mixture, add vegetables to hot syrup, heat to scalding, but do not boil or cucumbers will shrivel. Pack while hot into sterilized pint jars.

If vinegar is too strong it will also make the cucumbers shrivel, so if you are using homemade vinegar, dilute it with water. These are ready to eat in about 5 to 6 weeks, and are a delightful addition to any table. *Makes 8 to 10 pints*

Sign on door: "Bell don't make. Bump, or go around back."

Dill Pickles

My father considered himself the expert on dill pickles and made quantities in large crocks. Later I learned to make them in glass jars and am pleased to report that they are just as good as the old messy way. I use smaller cucumbers, which will fit in pint or quart jars, but you can use medium-sized ones, and put them in 2-quart jars. With these you must use the old-fashioned porcelain tops, with rubber jar rings.

50 to 100 cucumbers, depending on size	1 quart vinegar
	2 cups salt
Brine (½ cup salt to 4 quarts water)	Grape or cherry leaves
	Small red peppers (hot)
10 quarts water	Fresh dill stems and seeds

Garlic cloves

Wash cucumbers, cover with brine and let stand overnight. Boil water, vinegar, and salt, and let cool. Drain cucumbers. Put 1 grape or cherry leaf in bottom of each jar, together with 1 pepper, 1 piece of dill and a garlic clove. Pack each jar tightly with cucumbers, cover with vinegar-salt solution, and screw down cover, not too tightly. Put in a dark place, on a tray, so that they can effervesce. When they have stopped fermenting, close the cover tightly.

The very small pickles are ready to eat in 10 days.

Makes about 10 pints or 5 quarts

Catsup

8 quarts ripe tomatoes, quartered	Water
	½ teaspoon cayenne
Small bunch of parsley—stems and leaves	¼ teaspoon allspice
	1 teaspoon mace
4 medium-sized onions, peeled and quartered	1 teaspoon paprika
	1 teaspoon pepper
½ cup sugar	1 teaspoon celery seed
2 tablespoons salt	1 teaspoon whole cloves

1 cup vinegar

Place tomatoes, parsley, onions, sugar, and salt in water to cover and boil until soft and mushy. Strain well, using coarse sieve or food mill. Tie spices in a cloth; add to tomatoes along with vinegar. Boil slowly for several hours, stirring frequently until thick, or until a little catsup placed on a saucer shows no water running from it. Remove spice bag, taste for seasoning, add more salt if needed. Place in pint jars while hot, and seal. *Makes about 10 pints*

Apple Relish

2 dozen ripe tomatoes
1 dozen apples
6 green peppers
10 small onions
1 hot red pepper

3 cups sugar
2 cups vinegar
3 tablespoons salt
1 tablespoon pickling spices,
    tied in a bag

Wash tomatoes and dip into boiling water for about ½ minute. Put under cold water and peel. Pare apples and core them. Remove seeds and pith from green pepper. Peel onions.

Put all vegetables and the apples through a food grinder. Add rest of ingredients, cook gently for 1 hour. Pour into sterilized pint jars while hot, and seal. *Makes about 4 pints*

Watermelon Rind Pickle

1 medium-sized watermelon
Water
2 tablespoons slack lime
    (Lilly's lime—at all
    drugstores)

1 box white ginger root or
    ½ box cracked ginger

Peel rind of melon, cutting off all the pink part and the hard, green outer skin. Cut into squares or diamonds, or whatever shape you prefer. Put in a deep kettle, cover with water and add lime. Soak overnight.

Drain and soak in cold water 1 hour. Drain, cover with cold water; let it come to a rolling boil and boil ½ hour. Drain again, cover with cold water and add ginger root. Cook until tender when pierced with a fork. Drain for the last time.

Make a syrup by combining:

15 cups sugar
3 pints vinegar
1 box whole cloves

1 box mixed pickling spices,
    tied in a cloth

Pour syrup over rind and cook gently until rind is transparent and clear. Add a few drops of color, if desired. I like to make some red, and some green, because they are especially attractive at Christmas time. Pack into sterilized pint jars, pour the syrup over the rind and seal. *Makes 8 to 10 pints*

Muskmelon Preserves
(CANTELOUPE RIND)

Use partially green melons for this. Remove rind; peel and cut into uniform shapes and pieces. Soak overnight in salt water—1 cup salt to 8 cups water. Then proceed as for watermelon rind.

Plum Preserves

6 pints firm plums	9 cups sugar
	1 cup water

Wash plums, remove pits, cover with sugar and add water. Cover, and let stand overnight. Drain and boil juice for 5 minutes. Add plums and cook a few minutes until clear. (Do not overcook, as they jell after standing.) Pack into sterilized jars and seal.

Makes 4 to 6 pints

Hot Mustard Pickles

This is a short-cut method. We used to salt the cucumbers down for 3 to 6 days, with salt and vinegar, but now I use the commercially canned sour pickles.

4 large sour pickles, sliced into 1-inch pieces	¾ cup flour
	3 tablespoons dry mustard
4 or 5 stalks celery, sliced	¼ cup salt
1 pound small white onions, peeled	½ teaspoon turmeric
	¾ quart vinegar
2 large cauliflowers, broken into flowerets	1 tablespoon prepared horseradish
1 sweet green pepper, sliced	2 hot peppers, or
¾ cup sugar	1 teaspoon cayenne

Prepare vegetables and let stand in colander. Sift dry ingredients into a large kettle. Add vinegar gradually, stirring constantly to avoid lumps (I like a wooden spoon for this). Put over medium heat and cook, stirring constantly, just until mixture thickens. Add vegetables, horseradish, and peppers. Bring to a boil and cook gently for 5 minutes, stirring constantly to keep it from sticking. Pack into hot, sterilized pint jars.

If you do not like very hot pickles, omit the horseradish and hot pepper and add another cup of sugar. *Makes about 4 pints*

Spiced Peaches

Get small, firm peaches for this. I prefer the early or late clingstones, which are small enough to cook whole. You can use halves, but fruit must be firm.

4 cups sugar	4 pieces of stick cinnamon
1 quart vinegar	4 pounds peaches
	Whole cloves

Mix sugar, vinegar, and cinnamon and boil for 10 minutes. Peel peaches, stick two whole cloves in each, or in each half, if you halve them. After syrup has boiled for 10 minutes, add peaches and cook until just barely tender—about 4 or 5 minutes (they should stay firm). Remove from fire, and let stand in syrup overnight. Pack fruit into sterilized pint jars, boil syrup until thick and pour over the peaches. Seal. *Makes 6 to 7 pints*

Spiced Crabapples

4 pounds crabapples—not too ripe	1 quart vinegar
	2 teaspoons allspice
Whole cloves	10 to 12 drops red food
4 cups sugar	coloring

Wash crabapples, remove little black spot at bottom and insert a whole clove in its place. Do not remove stems. Set aside.

Mix rest of ingredients, and boil 10 minutes. Add crabapples and cook 10 to 15 minutes, until soft but not mushy. (The stage of ripeness has a great deal to do with how long you cook them.) Pack fruit into sterilized pint jars. Boil syrup until thick and pour over crabapples. Seal at once. (The amount of food coloring you use depends upon whether you like the fruit to be very red—I do.)

Makes about 6 pints

Spiced Pears

3 dozen Seckel pears	1 quart vinegar
Whole cloves	4 pieces stick cinnamon
4 cups sugar	Food coloring, if desired

These small, sweet little pears are just right for spicing. Peel them, remove the little brown part at the bottom, and replace it with a whole clove. Proceed as for spiced crabapples. *Makes about 6 pints*

Red and Green Piccalilli

3 pounds red tomatoes	3 pounds sugar
3 pounds green tomatoes	2 pounds yellow onions, peeled
3 sweet red peppers	1 medium head cabbage
3 green peppers	1 medium bunch celery
¼ cup pickling spices, tied in a cloth	½ cup salt
	½ cup yellow mustard seed
1½ quarts vinegar	½ teaspoon cinnamon

1 teaspoon ground cloves

Wash all vegetables, remove stems and seeds and put through a meat grinder. Add salt, and let stand overnight. Drain, and add rest of ingredients.

Place in a deep kettle, bring to a boil, then simmer 1 hour, stirring frequently. Pack at once into sterilized pint jars. *Makes 5 to 6 pints*

Chili Sauce

15 onions	1 teaspoon each ground cloves,
6 sweet red peppers	cinnamon and allspice, tied
4 sharp red peppers	in a cloth
8 quarts tomatoes	3 to 3½ cups sugar
2 cups vinegar	1 cup flour, mixed with
½ cup salt	1 cup water

Peel onions, seed peppers, and chop all vegetables. (They need not be too fine as they boil down during the long cooking.) Add rest of ingredients except flour and boil 1 hour, stirring frequently. Beat mixture of flour and water vigorously so that no lumps are left. Add some juice from kettle to flour mixture; stir again, then very carefully pour back into kettle, stirring furiously to avoid lumps. Boil gently 20 minutes longer, stirring constantly. Remove from fire, and pour into sterilized pint jars.   *Makes 8 to 10 pints*

Chow Chow
(MIXED PICKLES)

1 quart small cucumbers or sliced cucumbers, ⅛-inch thick
12 small white onions, peeled (optional)
Brine (1 cup salt to 1 gallon water)
4 cups string beans, sliced in 1-inch slices
1 quart corn (fresh or canned whole kernel)
1 small cauliflower, separated into flowerets
2 cups small lima beans
1 red pepper, seeds removed, and diced
2 green peppers, seeds removed, and diced
1 cup small carrots, scraped and sliced
4 tablespoons white mustard seed, or 2 tablespoons yellow mustard seed
2 tablespoons celery seed
1½ cups sugar
5 cups cider vinegar
4 tablespoons salt

Soak cucumbers and onions in brine overnight. Drain, cover with cold water and let soak 2 hours.

Cook string beans, corn, cauliflower, and lima beans in salted water until not quite tender—about 15 minutes. Drain.

Mix all vegetables together and add remaining ingredients.

Let stand overnight. Drain and heat liquid to boiling. Return vegetables and let simmer 15 minutes, stirring frequently. Pack chow chow into hot, sterilized pint jars, cover with liquid, and seal.
            Makes 6 to 8 pints

Grape Catsup

12 pounds Concord grapes
8 pounds sugar
3 pints vinegar
1 tablespoon cinnamon
1 tablespoon allspice
1 tablespoon ground cloves
½ tablespoon black pepper
¼ teaspoon cayenne

Weigh fruit, then stem and boil until quite soft. Rub through colander or food mill. Add sugar and boil until thick—until it jellies on a saucer. Add vinegar and spices and boil 15 minutes longer. Pack in sterilized pint jars.   *Makes 6 to 8 pints*

Raspberry Vinegar

4 quarts red raspberries   2 quarts vinegar
3 pounds sugar

Put berries in a large jar and cover with vinegar. Let stand for 10 days. Strain and measure juice. To every quart of juice add ¾ pound sugar. Bring to boiling; bottle in quart bottles or jars and seal.

To serve, put about 2 tablespoons of the vinegar in a glass, fill up with water, and add ice. Delicious on a hot day!

Makes about 4 quarts

JELLIES, JAMS, AND PRESERVES

Currant Jelly

Wash and pick over currants, but do not remove stems. Mash in a 6-quart kettle with spoon or potato masher. Add ½ cup water for each 2 quarts fruit, put on to boil and boil over a low fire for about 10 minutes, stirring frequently. Pour into a jelly bag and let it drain. (Do not squeeze, if you want a clear jelly.) After it has drained, measure juice and add 1 cup sugar for every cup of juice. Reheat slowly, skim, and begin to test for doneness.

The best test I know for jelly is when the mixture makes two separate, distinct drops when it is dropped from a spoon—the drops must not run together. Another test is when the jelly "sheets and tears" from the spoon in a distinct piece. If you're not sure, remove the jelly from the fire, put a small amount in a cold saucer, and see if it is as thick as you like it, remembering that it will thicken a little more as it stands.

Elderberry Jelly

Elderberry jelly is made exactly the same way as currant jelly.

Old-Fashioned Strawberry Jam

This is one of my favorite recipes. The strawberries remain whole and plump, and the juice pops out as you bite into them.

It takes a bit of doing but actually isn't very difficult. My children like to use it over ice cream, for strawberry sundaes.

Use firm, ripe strawberries, the larger the better. Wash, then hull and add sugar, cup for cup (which means 1 cup sugar to 1 cup fruit). Do not use more than 2 or 3 cups of fruit in any one batch. Put in a deep kettle (at least 6-quart capacity), stir gently, and let stand until strawberries draw juice—overnight is best. In the morning, stir gently to mix the sugar and berries, and put over low heat. Bring to a boil and boil 12 minutes, or until they are thickened. (These are a little on runny side but after the jar has been opened for a while they thicken up.)

Pour into shallow baking pans so that jam is no more than 2 inches deep. Let stand overnight. This distributes berries and juice, so berries don't go to bottom of jar. Pack into clean, sterilized jelly glasses and seal.

Cherry Preserves

Wash, stem and pit cherries. Measure the cherries, put into a deep kettle, and add 1 cup sugar for each cup of fruit. Let stand to draw the juices—at least several hours. Stir gently, bring to a boil and boil gently about 10 minutes or until thick and clear. Drain off juice from cherries and pack berries into hot, sterilized jars. Boil down juice until two separate drops fall from a spoon raised above it. Pour over cherries, and seal.

Orange Marmalade

3 large oranges	11 cups water
1 lemon	4 pounds sugar

Slice oranges and lemon thin, discarding pith but saving juice and seeds. Soak seeds overnight in 1 cup water. Add 10 cups water to sliced fruit and let stand overnight. Strain seeds, add water in which they were soaked to fruit, sugar and water. Cook gently until rind is tender, about 1½ hours. Let stand for another day. Bring to a boil and cook until it jells. (The whole process may be speeded up by the addition of ½ bottle of fruit pectin for the last boiling, in which case bring just to a boil, skim, and pour into sterilized glasses.)   *Makes about 6 jelly glasses*

Peach Preserves

1 lemon   4 quarts peaches
1 orange   4 cups sugar
2 cups hot water

Put orange and lemon through a food chopper, rind and all. Mix with sliced peaches, then add rest of ingredients. Put into a deep kettle, and cook slowly 1 hour, or until thick and jellied. Pour into sterilized glasses and seal.   *Makes about 6 pints*

Lemon Butter Spread

¼ pound butter   6 eggs
2 cups sugar   3 lemons—juice and grated rind

Cream butter and sugar together. Add eggs, one at a time, and continue beating. Fold in lemon juice and rind. Pack into sterilized pint jars or jelly glasses.   *Makes about 2 pints*

Peach, Pear, or Plum Butter

The texture of these fruit butters is similar, but the taste is as varied as that of the fresh fruits.

Wash fruits; do not pare, but remove seeds or cores and cut into quarters. Cover with water and boil until soft and mushy. Press through colander, measure pulp, add ½ as much sugar as you have pulp. Cook mixture slowly until thick and clear, stirring constantly. (We always added juice of half a lemon to pear butter to give it a little zip.) Pour a little fruit butter on a saucer and if it is thick, without thin juice trickling from the center, it is done. Pour into sterilized glasses or jars, and seal.

Grape Butter

1 quart Concord grapes, washed   3 tablespoons water
1 pound sugar

Mix all ingredients, bring to a boil, cook 20 minutes, then strain through sieve or food mill. Bring to a boil again, and pour into sterilized glasses.   *Makes 4 to 5 jelly glasses*

Candied Cherries

We made our own candied cherries. They were spread all over the place for days, it seems, but they were delicious!

Use sour cherries only. Wash and remove seeds, trying not to break fruit. Use 1 cup sugar for every cup of fruit. Add just enough water to sugar to keep it from caramelizing; stir and bring to a boil. Add cherries and cook slowly until clear. Drain cherries; spread on platters or baking tins and dry in a cool oven (or in the sun, covering the dishes with a pane of glass). Turn often. When they are dried, dust with granulated sugar, place in jars, and keep in a cool place. We made cherry jelly from the juice, by boiling it down until it was thick. (Nowadays we would add fruit pectin, according to directions on the package.)

Pear and Peach Conserve

2 cups peaches, peeled and diced
2 cups pears, peeled, cored, and diced
2 lemons—juice and rind, cut up very fine
3 cups sugar
⅔ cup walnuts

Mix fruits and sugar. Stir well. Place over flame and boil rapidly for 5 minutes. Add nuts, cook 10 minutes longer. Pour into sterilized glasses and seal. *Makes about 6 pints*

Spiced Strawberry Jam

1 quart strawberries
1 quart sugar
1 tablespoon vinegar
½ teaspoon ground cloves

Wash and hull strawberries. Mix well with sugar. Let stand 15 minutes to draw juice. Boil gently for 15 minutes. Add vinegar and cloves and remove from fire. Put into large jar, and several times a day for 2 or 3 days push the berries down into the syrup to "plump" them. Pour into sterilized glasses and cover with paraffin.
Makes 3 to 4 jelly glasses

Rhubarb Conserve

1 quart rhubarb, cut fine
2 oranges, juice and grated rind
1 lemon, juice and grated rind

1 pound raisins
1 pound English walnuts,
coarsely chopped

Sugar

Measure rhubarb, fruit, raisins, and walnuts. Add equal amount of sugar and mix thoroughly. Cook over low heat until mixture jells, or until two drops fall separately from a spoon held over kettle. Pour into sterilized glasses and seal.   *Makes 5 to 6 jelly glasses*

Plum Conserve

4 pounds plums
1 cup seeded raisins
2 oranges
1 lemon

1 cup water
¾ cup sugar for each cup
fruit
½ pound walnuts, chopped

Wash plums and remove pits. Put plums and raisins through coarse blade of food grinder. Add oranges and lemon, sliced very thin; add water. Measure. Add ¾ cup sugar to each cup of fruit and juice. Cook slowly in a deep kettle until thick, like jam, stirring constantly because it sticks easily. Add chopped walnuts and pour into sterilized pint jars or jelly glasses.   *Makes 6 to 7 pints*

Huckleberry Jam
(BLUEBERRIES MAY BE SUBSTITUTED)

3 cups sugar
1 cup water
3 tablespoons lemon juice

4 cups berries, washed and
drained

Boil sugar, water, and lemon juice until syrup spins a thread when dropped from a spoon. Add berries and boil 20 minutes. Pack in sterilized jelly glasses, and cover with "paraphene," as my old recipe says!   *Makes about 2 pints*

Cherry Cranberries

1 quart cranberries   ¼ cup water
2 cups sugar

Wash cranberries, add water, cover, and cook over low flame about 5 minutes, or until skins burst and pop. Pour sugar on top of berries, cover again, and let cook, very gently, for 20 minutes. Pour into sterilized jelly glasses and seal. These cranberries keep indefinitely and resemble candied cherries, hence the name.

Makes 1½ pints

CHAPTER XI

Feasts, Fairs, and Funerals
(Quantity Recipes)

FEEDING THE THRESHERS

Soon after dawn the men came to thresh the wheat. Far down the road, the little pot-bellied steam engine whistled to let the farmer know they were on the way. It was also a signal to the housewife to speed up her preparations for the day. The kitchen table was pulled out its full length, or if the kitchen wasn't large enough, a trestle table and benches were set up in the shade of a big tree in the yard.

Pies, cakes, and bread had been baked the day before, but there was still much to get ready for the mammoth noonday meal. Preparations began even before the men of the family had finished breakfast and left for the barn. Usually a neighbor woman or two came in to help, but the housewife wanted to "redd up" before *they* came, so everyone scurried around— the children washing and drying the breakfast dishes, and straightening up the bedrooms, while Mom began work on the dinner. Most farmhouses had a second, outside kitchen, which was used during the summer, and for this meal it was usually necessary to use both stoves. The meat, potatoes, and the vegetables were put on to cook. Pickles and jellies had to be fetched up from the cellar and dished up, the tables set, and the cooled slaw, applesauce, and butter brought up from the springhouse. Then there was the gravy to make, the bread to slice, and the final dishing up. The meal required what would seem like mountains of bread today, but hungry threshers ate three or four slices and used the last piece to wipe out their plates, as was only manners, before attacking the pies and cakes.

Each farm wife took great pride in her table and vied with the neighbors in providing the best meal for the thresher. Sometimes she would question the head man (usually the owner of the steam engine) about what he had been served at other homes. Since neighbors helped neighbors, Pop had probably already brought home news about some of the meals, and jokes were made at the expense of some of the poorer cooks —which tickled Mom. "Her bread was so heavy it woulda sunk a raft," made her snicker and proffer more of her own feather-light baking. The worst criticism was "Yes vell, at that house, ve had chust store bread and cold cuts, nothing like this here set-out."

Just before 9 o'clock, the older children were sent to the springhouse to bring up milk cans full of peppermint tea, which had been made the day before and put down to cool. These were carried out to the men in the barn, together with a can of fresh, cool pump water. Threshing was hot and dusty work, and the men stopped work whenever they could to quench their thirst and eat the big doughnuts or large, thick cookies which were also sent out in baskets lined with cloths.

At noon, the steam whistle blew, and everyone hurried to get all the food on the table. A fresh roller towel had been hung on the porch, next to the pump, and soap and tin basins were ready on a nearby bench, so that the men could wash. They came stomping in and joked and snorted in the icy water from the pump. After washing, they filed silently in to sit at the table, suddenly abashed in front of the women. They remained silent for the blessing, and from then on, only the noise of knives and forks and chewing was heard. Once in a long while Pop and the head thresher would speak to each other, but there was no general conversation.

The women started passing the heavy platters of food and saw to it that all dishes were filled. As soon as the plates were wiped clean, they quickly served the pies and cakes which were already on the table. Then one by one, as they finished, the men pushed back their plates, ducked their heads in thanks to the housewife and strode out.

When all the men had left, the women and children quickly cleared the tables, and finally sat down to "eat themselves." But there was no loitering—supper time would come before long. There were never as many men to feed in the evening, since many of them had to go home and do their own chores. In contrast to twelve or fourteen extra for dinner, there would be only five or six, besides the family, for supper.

TYPICAL DINNERS FOR THRESHERS

✿ ✿ ✿

Chicken Pie
Mashed Potatoes
Baked Beans
Apple Sauce
Cabbage Salad
Jelly, Pickles
Bread and butter

Peach Pie   Apple Pudding   Burnt Sugar Cake
Coffee

✿ ✿ ✿

The best bread and butter obtainable
Roast Beef with Browned Potatoes
Fried Sweet Potatoes

Cole Slaw   Pickled Beets

Pickles, Jelly
Schmierkäse mit Schnittlach
Apple Sauce

Cherry Pie   Shoofly Pie   Drop Cakes
Coffee

This meal usually consisted of cold sliced meat, fried potatoes or potato pancakes, coleslaw, red beet eggs, any leftover vegetables, bread, hot biscuits or muffins, fritters and the usual pickles, relishes, pie, cake, and coffee.

Nowadays feeding the threshers is not such a chore for the farm wife, since automobiles have lessened distances, and with automation, fewer extra hands are needed. But the housewife is never sure how many she will have to feed until she has sent the children out to the barn to find out from Pop, and meals are no less lavish than they used to be.

When we made pies for fairs or for the threshers, we baked the pastry separately, dished up the filling and topped it with a square of cooked crust. It not only looked nicer, it was quicker and easier to serve. I still use this method for our church suppers, but for a buffet I put the topping on the filling in the roasting pans, and set it out for each person to help himself.

Chicken Pie for 25 People

Chicken filling:

6 3-pound chickens
Water to cover
1 tablespoon salt
½ teaspoon pepper
Dash of paprika
3 celery stalks
1 small onion, sliced

1¼ cups butter, margarine, or
    chicken fat
4 cups flour
3½ quarts chicken stock
1¼ cans evaporated milk, or
    2¾ cups fresh milk

Cut chickens into serving pieces. Cover with cold water, add salt, pepper, paprika, celery, and onion. Cover, bring to a boil, and simmer until tender—about 2 to 2½ hours.

Remove chicken, cut into 1-inch cubes, discard skin and bones. Skim fat off broth and strain. Add enough butter to the fat to make about 1¼ cups fat. Heat fat, add flour, and blend. Gradually add chicken stock and milk. Cook until thickened—about 10 minutes, stirring constantly.

Place cubed chicken in 2 roasting pans. Pour about 2 quarts of sauce over chicken in each pan. Bake at 350°.

Pastry:

5 tablespoons salt
2½ quarts flour
3½ cups lard or other
  shortening

5 egg yolks
¾ cup cold water
  (approx.)

Sift salt and flour together. Mix in shortening until mixture has texture of coarse corn meal. Add egg yolks, then water (just until mixture leaves sides of the bowl and forms dough). Roll out to about ⅛-inch thickness. Cut into 3-inch squares, brush with cold water, and prick with a fork. Bake at 400° for 15 to 20 minutes, until nicely browned.

Allow about 1½ cups chicken to each serving. Top with squares of crust and serve.

Roast Beef for 25

2 tablespoons salt
1 teaspoon pepper
9½ to 10 pounds beef, rolled ribs,
  eye of the rump, or round
1 medium-sized onion
Meat tenderizer (optional)

7 pounds potatoes, peeled and
  quartered
4 tablespoons flour
1 cup water—or more, if needed
⅛ teaspoon paprika
⅛ teaspoon garlic salt

Salt and pepper beef. Put in roasting pan. Do not cover or add water. Peel onion and add to pan. Roast at 350° for 20 minutes per pound for rare; 25 minutes for medium rare; and 30 minutes for well done (which is the way we always cooked it).

If you are using a rolled round steak, put a piece of suet on top of it and tie it on. The fat will baste the meat. (You may want to use a tenderizer. If so, follow the package directions. We never did —if the meat wasn't well marbled, and looked tough, we made sauerbraten because the marinade served as a tenderizer.)

At least 1 hour before roast is done add potatoes. Turn to coat with fat so that they will brown nicely. Turn again, 2 or 3 times during cooking. At end of cooking time, remove meat and potatoes to warm platter. Put pan on top of stove over low heat. Add flour, stir to blend, then add water—just enough to make nice thick gravy. Stir to get all brown pieces off bottom of pan. Add paprika, garlic salt, and more salt if needed. Taste again. Strain and serve with the meat.

Apple Pudding for 25

8 or 9 pounds sour apples, or
  6 20-ounce cans apple slices
¼ cup lemon juice
3½ cups flour

3 cups brown sugar
1 teaspoon salt
1 tablespoon cinnamon
¾ pound butter or margarine

Ice cream or cream

The number of apples needed depends upon their size. Peel, core, and slice. Place in greased baking pan, 13 by 9 by 2 inches. Sprinkle with lemon juice. Mix dry ingredients, and work in the butter until crumbly. Sprinkle over apples, shaking pan so that some of mixture goes down into the apples. Bake at 375° for 30 minutes, or until the apples are soft and top is nicely browned. Serve warm with ice cream or cream.

Drop Cakes

½ cup lard
½ cup butter
3 cups white sugar
3 eggs

1 cup sour milk or buttermilk
1 teaspoon baking soda
1 teaspoon cream of tartar
4 cups flour

Cream lard, butter, and sugar together, add eggs. Dissolve baking soda in sour milk, and add. Mix cream of tartar and flour, and stir into first mixture.

Drop by spoonfuls onto ungreased cookie sheets and bake about 20 minutes, or until cakes spring back at a touch and are lightly browned. *Makes 4 to 6 dozen*

Returning Vacationer: "It spites me that my off is all. I ain't hardly overed it yet, vhen I hafta go back to work."

BARN RAISING

When a young farmer is just starting out, or when an older man decides he needs another barn, or when a barn has been destroyed by lightning or fire, all the neighbors in the Plain community join together to help build a new one. After the foundation is laid, a date is set for the raising, far enough in advance to suit everyone.

I can still remember when we had our barn raising, with people coming from miles around—the men with their tools, and some of the women to help with the dishing up and serving. Few came empty-handed. Some brought extra dishes and cutlery, others "chust a char of something." The materials were all assembled beforehand, and, as usual, one experienced builder was in charge, although in a close-knit community not much bossing actually is needed. Every man knows his own qualifications and limitations, and although there is a lot of commotion, hollering, and joking, the work goes on apace. In one day, the whole wooden structure was erected, the men staying until the barn was under cover, with the roof in place. It was exciting and amazing to see the steady progress.

Most of the old Swiss-type barns which still exist in the Dutch country were erected this way, and they remain sturdy and strong, even though there is no architect, contractor, or union labor. There is a union, true, but it is one of neighborliness and common need—a practical application of the Golden Rule.

There is a holiday air about a barn raising, and the food fits the occasion. The platters are laid out on the usual planks on trestles in the yard. The men eat first, of course, with the women waiting on them. They tuck away unbelievable quantities! "It wonders me that they don't have sick," as one woman remarked, "but they don't." And indeed, they seem no less active after the gargantuan meal.

In poorer families the set-out is never too elaborate, but when a farmer is well-to-do, the women really "put out." Meats, such as ham and roast beef, all sorts of salads, pickles, jams of every variety, and plenty of hot bread and butter. Several kinds of cakes, with as many kinds of pies as can be imagined. And always the ubiquitous coffee, made by the gallon; or if the weather is very hot, peppermint tea and lemonade.

When all the food is set out on the table, there is little room left for the dishes, knives and forks, and glasses. At our house we never needed anything fancy in the way of table settings— the food was decoration enough! When everything was ready, the children were sent either to ring the bell on top of the farmhouse or, if there was no bell, to run to the barn excitedly, calling, "Kum, esse!" (Come, eat!)

Baked Beans for 25

4 pounds dried navy or
  pea beans
6 quarts water
1 to 1½ pounds salt pork
3 small onions, stuck with cloves

4 teaspoons salt
2 cups molasses
2 tablespoons prepared mustard,
  or 1 teaspoon dry mustard
1 cup catsup
½ cup brown sugar

Pick over beans. Wash, cover with cold water, bring to a boil and boil for 2 or 3 minutes. Let stand at least 1 hour. Bring to a boil again and cook until skins burst, about 1 hour. Drain and reserve broth.

Slice pork thin and put half over bottoms of 3 roasting pans, 13 by 9 by 2 inches. Put an onion in each roasting pan, then divide and add drained beans. Add 4 cups bean liquor to rest of ingredients, except brown sugar; mix well and pour over beans. Be sure they are covered—add more bean liquid if needed. Sprinkle with brown sugar and top with rest of salt pork, arranged in rows. Cover tightly with aluminum foil. Bake at 325° for 6 to 7 hours, or at 250° overnight. Uncover during last hour to brown.

Macaroni Salad for 25

5 cups elbow macaroni
5 quarts boiling water
1¼ tablespoons salt
1 cup finely chopped onions
½ cup finely chopped green
  peppers
½ cup finely chopped sweet red
  peppers

2 teaspoons celery salt
5 hardboiled eggs, chopped
1 cup sweet pickles, chopped
½ pound cheese, cut in small
  cubes
3 cups salad dressing

Cook macaroni in water according to instructions on package. Drain and chill. Combine rest of ingredients with cold macaroni. Toss lightly until well mixed.

Pork Loaf for 25

2 quarts stale bread	3¾ pound ground lean pork
Water	3¾ pound ground beef
¼ cup lard or other shortening	2½ tablespoons salt
1 cup onions, chopped fine	1 teaspoon pepper
¾ cup celery, chopped fine	¼ cup parsley, minced or dried

4 eggs, beaten slightly

Moisten bread with water and squeeze dry. Melt lard; add onions and celery and brown lightly. Combine all ingredients, and lightly mix—don't mash. Shape into 2 or 3 loaves.

Grease 2 or 3 roasting pans, put in loaves, and bake at 325° about 1½ hours. Pour off all fat. Serve hot or cold.

"The cake is all, but the pie is yet."

FAIRS

Many of the "gay," "fancy," or "English" people in the Dutch country are descendants of the Plain People. Some, of course, are descendants of the Lutherans or German Reformed who all sought refuge from persecution. But almost all are pious and ardent church-goers, even if they don't assume or keep the Plain garb.

It seemed as if there was always some project for the church which required money—which doesn't differ too much from the present! In order to raise cash, the women of the various churches usually "took a stand" at local fairs, such as Farmer's Day, Fourth of July parades, auction sales, or even at political rallies. The stand, made of boards and trestles with benches for the customers, was erected on the main street. An oil stove and an ice chest were set up, and the ladies were in business.

As for the food! No hot dogs or hamburgers, but chicken corn soup; thick chicken sandwiches on homemade bread; deviled clams; pepper slaw; cakes and pies, and homemade ice cream.

Even on a hot day, chicken corn "sup" sold well. Sometimes fried chicken or chicken pot pie was the specialty of the stand. It was well to eat early, because when the homemade ice cream was "all" (gone), store ice cream was substituted.

Different churches became famous for special foods, and people said, "I believe I'll get some of that Reformed Chicken Corn Soup, then the Lutheran clams, and the Methodist pie." It was literally "a moveable feast."

The custom still prevails in some of the small towns in the Pennsylvania Dutch country, because churches still need money, and the women delight in showing off their cooking. But much commercialization has set in with the sale of hot dogs, hamburgers, and soft drinks, which are easier to prepare and which the children and their calorie-conscious parents seem to prefer to the heavier fare.

Deviled Clams for 50

100 clams	4 tablespoons Worcestershire sauce
1 large bunch celery, washed	
6 large onions, peeled	2 teaspoons salt
1 bunch parsley, minced	2 boxes bread crumbs
25 to 30 slices stale white bread	½ pound lard or other shortening
6 large eggs	

Open clams and save juice. Wash shells and let drain. Put clams, celery, and onions through food grinder. Add minced parsley. Put in large kettle, with clam juice. Add 25 slices of bread, and mix until all juice is absorbed. Add more bread if needed. Add eggs, Worcestershire sauce, and salt, and stir until thoroughly mixed. Add bread crumbs until mixture holds shape, being sure to save some to sprinkle on top of each clam.

Pile filling into clam shells, sprinkle with remaining bread crumbs. Fry in lard, crust side down, until lightly browned (fat should be fairly shallow). Put crust side up into large roasting pans and bake at 400° for 25 minutes or until puffed up.

Chicken Corn Soup for 25

4 3- to 4-pound chickens
Water
1 tablespoon salt
1 teaspoon sugar
½ teaspoon pepper
2 medium-sized onions, sliced
8 stalks celery, sliced

8 quarts corn—fresh, frozen, canned or whole-kernel
8 hardboiled eggs, chopped
½ cup parsley, chopped
1 teaspoon saffron
1 to 2 packages (10 ounces) fine noodles

½ teaspoon paprika

Wash and cut up fowl, including giblets. Put on to boil with about 8 cups of water per chicken. Add salt, sugar, pepper, onions, and celery. Bring to a boil, then lower heat and simmer until meat is tender. Strain broth. Cut chicken in bite-sized pieces. (If you want to, you can take out breasts and thighs for making chicken salad or chicken sandwiches.)

Return meat to broth; add corn, cut-up eggs, parsley and saffron. Taste and correct seasoning. Bring to a boil again to blend flavors. There should be about 1½ gallons of stock; if not, add water. Add noodles and boil 20 minutes, or until noodles are tender. Soup should be thick. (We used noodles when making chicken corn soup in quantity, since they are simpler than rivels and the taste is just as authentic.)

Sprinkle with paprika, and serve with hot, homemade bread, or crackers.

Chicken Salad Sandwiches for 25

3 quarts cooked, diced chicken
—meat from 3 to 5 chickens
Water to cover
1 small onion, sliced
10 hardboiled eggs, diced
1½ cups celery, finely diced
¼ cup parsley, finely chopped

2 teaspoons salt
½ teaspoon pepper
4 tablespoons lemon juice
4 to 5 cups mayonnaise
¼ cup chopped sweet pickle
(optional)
Bread

Lettuce

Cover chickens with cold water, bring to a boil, add onion, and simmer until meat is fork tender. (The number of chickens depends upon the size of the poultry. Three large fowl or 5 broilers will be needed.)

Remove chicken from broth and dice, discarding skin and bones. Broth should be reserved for soup. Add rest of ingredients except bread and lettuce. Mix well. Do not add too much mayonnaise, as mixture should not be runny. Taste and correct seasonings. Refrigerate.

Spread rather thickly on white or whole wheat bread, and add lettuce, if desired.

Iced Tea for 25

1 cup plus 2 tablespoons loose tea
1 quart freshly boiled water
1½ cups sugar (optional)

1 gallon plus 5 cups cold water
3 lemons, cut in eighths (optional)

Put tea in cloth bag large enough to allow for expansion. (I use an old, clean tea towel.) Tie with a string long enough to hang over side of kettle. (A very large tea bag!) Pour boiling water over tea bag, add sugar, if desired, and stir. Let steep for 5 minutes. Stir, remove bag. Add tea concentrate to cold water—don't add water to the tea, or it may cloud. Serve over ice with lemon wedges, if desired.

FUNERALS

No book on Pennsylvania Dutch cooking would be complete without the mention of funerals, since in the days when transportation was limited to horse and buggy, funeral preparations necessarily included food. Restaurants were few and far between; besides, who would eat in such fancy, dear, and sinful places when there was always some friend or freundschaft (relative) in any neighborhood?

The conduct of funerals differs among the various sects, but in most cases the same customs prevail even now, when there is no longer a transportation problem, except for those Plain

People to whom automobiles are forbidden. As soon as a death becomes known, all the neighbors, whether Plain or Fancy, come to the home to offer their condolences.

The nearest neighbor women and women relatives come to help "redd up." The house is scrubbed from attic to cellar, even if it is already immaculate. The grass is cut, raked, and the lawn swept, so that nary a random leaf or weed can be seen, and all is made sparkling clean so as not to shame the dead. When all this is done, the women set about preparing the food. The funeral meats, vegetables, pies, and cakes are baked, especially when a large congregation is expected. Near neighbors (within a radius of two miles is considered near) also bring dishes of their own concocting to eke out the larder. This custom is still followed in the area as it is in most of rural America.

There was little time between death and burial because embalming was not then practiced in most regions of the country. There was a viewing, to be sure, although it wasn't so designated. The coffin was placed in the "good room," and all acquaintances, friends, and relatives came to give a good-bye to the departed. They brought all their children, even babes in arms, to see the corpse, and the children gazed in awe and wonder at the strange sight.

There is an acceptance of death among these simple people, who sincerely and devoutly believe in a better life to come and who are familiar with death among the animals on the farm. It never occurs to them that there might be an emotional trauma for the children to meet death face to face; they are realists, knowing that "in the midst of life we are in death," and also that "our days are as the grass . . ."

The set-out at funerals is much the same as at other feasts—only the atmosphere is more subdued. But eating, like death, is a natural thing, and provision is made for all. I remember one time when my mother was helping prepare for a funeral and the oldest son came into the kitchen and said, "Be sure you put a plenty butter in the mashed potatoes—Mom always used lots of butter—and I shan't eat again in this house!" Mother was shocked, but it was his show of mourning, and nobody else thought anything about it.

Burial used to take place in the family plot, located on a hillside and carefully kept up by the family. After the procession returned, the food was set out, in the house if it was winter, or in the yard in warm weather. It was consumed quickly, with little conversation, and the men repaired to the barn while the women and children ate and then washed up the dishes.

At funerals, relatives from distances of more than twenty miles usually came to spend the night. The housewife eked out her dwindling stores of canned and dried fruits with raisin pie, which somehow became known as "funeral pie."

Raisin Pie

½ cup flour
¼ cup sugar
4 tablespoons butter
1½ cups raisins
1 cup sugar
1 cup water
1½ teaspoons cornstarch, dissolved in water

1 tablespoon butter
1 tablespoon lemon juice or vinegar
Dough for 1 9-inch pie (see Index)

Using hands, mix flour and ¼ cup sugar with butter until crumbly. Set aside.

Boil raisins with sugar and water for about 5 minutes. Add cornstarch which has been dissolved in a little water, butter, and lemon juice. Bring to a boil again, stirring constantly to avoid lumps.

Pour raisin mixture into a pie plate lined with pie crust. Sprinkle crumbs on top, and bake at 400° until nicely brown—about 40 minutes. We sometimes added a few chopped nuts, if they were available, to the mixture and these greatly improved the taste of the pie. *Serves 6*

Corn Bread for 24

3 cups sifted flour	2 tablespoons salt
4 tablespoons baking powder	4 eggs, beaten
1½ quarts corn meal	5 cups milk
½ cup sugar	1 cup shortening, melted

Sift flour and baking powder together. Add corn meal, sugar, and salt. Combine eggs, milk, and melted shortening, and add to dry ingredients. Stir just until all dry ingredients are mixed—do not beat. Pour into 2 greased baking pans, 12 by 8 inches, and bake at 400° about 20 minutes, or until top springs back at a touch and is well browned. Cut into squares and serve hot.

Pepper Slaw for 25

5 pounds cabbage	1 cup sugar
1 small green pepper	1 cup vinegar
1 small sweet red pepper	1 tablespoon salt
½ teaspoon pepper	

Wash cabbage and shred fine. Chop peppers and add to cabbage. Add rest of ingredients. Taste and correct seasonings. This does not keep well for more than 2 or 3 hours, as it turns dark, but you can prepare it in advance by shredding the cabbage and adding salt and pepper, and then adding sugar and vinegar at the last moment.

LUSCHDIGES DINGS
(MERRY THINGS)

Amusements were never lacking for the farm people in the days before radio, television, and cars. Usually their entertainment was a constituent of work, but make no mistake about it, they had a merry time. Corn huskings, quiltings (for the women), and apple-butter parties served a dual purpose.

At an apple-butter party every girl brought her own parer. The cider was already made, and the fellows made a fire to start boiling it down. While all this was going on, the young people sang, gossiped, and joked. Such parties were usually held in the kitchen, where the copper kettle was suspended from a crane over the open fire, but they were also sometimes held outdoors, which gave even greater privacy for schmooching. Everyone took a turn at the "schtirrer," and there was much interest in seeing just who would pair off. The girl took one side of the long handle, and her swain the other, and so they stood, facing each other, stirring Lattwarik (apple butter) and Liebe (love) at the same time.

When the work slackened, the games began. They played "Schtopper, Schtopper, Stänli," a version of Button, Button, Who's Got the Button?, during which a small stone or pebble (stänli) was passed from hand to hand around a circle, and the one who was "it" in the middle had to guess who was holding it. They played "Blindes Meizli" (Blind Man's Buff) and the old reliable, Spin the Platter, which gave a young man the right to buss the young lady before whom the plate stopped.

They also sang songs with their games, such as "Die Frohe Müller," the verses of which ended with, "Grab," whereupon the boy who was "it" was allowed to try to grab the girl of his choice and if he caught her was permitted a kiss.

Such merriment and drollery! Some of the songs became a little ribald as the evening progressed, since Dutch humor is pretty earthy. But the girls didn't seem to mind. Many of the lyrics had been brought over from the Rheinpfalz and a lot have been lost to posterity. The Pennsylvania Dutch still like to sing, and many parties end up, even to this day, with a group around a piano or a parlor organ, or just singing in close harmony.

The set-out for an apple-butter party was fairly simple—just a few cakes and pies to "go vis" the sweet cider, and perhaps some bread and butter for sampling the apple butter.

Lattwarik
(APPLE BUTTER)

2 quarts fresh cider	3 cups sugar
(without preservatives)	½ teaspoon cloves
4 quarts peeled apples, sliced	½ teaspoon allspice
1 teaspoon cinnamon	

Simmer cider in large kettle until it cooks down to about 1 quart. Meanwhile, pare and cut up apples, placing them in salted water to maintain their color. When cider is boiled down, "srow in" drained apples and cook until mushy, stirring constantly with a wooden spoon. Add sugar and spices, and boil until a dab of apple butter placed on a saucer shows no juice trickling from it. (This takes a good 2 hours, and it isn't the sort of thing you can put on and forget about—if it scorches, it just isn't fit to eat.) Pour into sterilized jars and seal. Serve hot if you want a taste sensation!

Makes about 8 pints

THE GLORIOUS FOURTH

For many, many years it was the custom for all the churches in the upper end of Lancaster County to get together for an annual picnic, usually held on the Fourth of July. An ecumenic and patriotic combination! The Plain people didn't participate, but as many as twenty or thirty other churches did.

The ones I remember best were held in the park at Lititz, where rows and rows of picnic tables and benches were added to the ones already there. Lititz (accent on the first syllable, please), originally a Moravian settlement, was noted for its piety, wonderful singing, and famous candle-lighting ceremonies.

At the park in Lititz there was a stream with a small waterfall and toward evening candles were floated out onto the water. As far as the eye could see, the little twinkling lights gave forth a festive glow, which was a sight to behold. This was an occasion for visiting from group to group, and table to table. In the days of limited travel, it was an opportunity to see freundschaft (relatives), to renew old friendships, and to meet new people. Many a marriage had its beginnings in this park.

The menfolk hauled to the tables baskets filled with jars, crocks, cake plates, dishes and cutlery, and also freezers of homemade ice cream. From there on it was up to the women— until it was time to eat, of course! Everything except the ice cream was dished up and set out, then covered with clean white cloths to keep off "them pesky flies." At noontime, the men and children were rounded up, the covers were removed, and the feasting began.

Plates were heaped high with ham, beef, souse (pickled pork), sausages, fried chicken, potato salad, coleslaw, pickled beets, tomatoes, red beet eggs, applesauce, a variety of cheeses, together with rolls, butter, and jelly. There was no hurry to finish—a meal could last for several hours, what with conversation and trying a little of Mrs. Zartman's salad or perhaps Mrs. Wenger's special piccalilli, or anything else one had overlooked.

When no one could possibly eat another bite, the tables were cleared of the soiled plates and cutlery but were left set up for the evening meal. Now the visiting began in earnest.

MENU FOR BASKET PICNIC

Fried Chicken
Cold Cuts:
Liverwurst, Plain Bologna, Lebanon Bologna, Baked Ham
or Boiled Smoked Tongue, Schmierkäse, Store Cheese,
and Corned Beef

Potato Salad
Deviled Eggs
Red Beet Eggs
Sliced Tomatoes
Pepper Slaw
Rolls, Homemade Bread
Bread and Butter Pickles
Dill Pickles
Piccalilli
Chow Chow

Large Sponge Cake   Molasses Layer Cake
Cookies   Pretzels   Ice Cream
Lemonade or Fruit Punch

After supper, as dusk came and the candles in the stream were lighted, the promenade began along one side to the little cascade of water, up the steps, and down the other side. People who hadn't attended the picnic arrived to view the sights and see friends. The climax of the day came when fireworks were set off in a nearby field. By this time all the baskets had been tucked back into the buggies and carriages, together with sleeping babies and the "young-uns" who couldn't stay awake.

After the fireworks the long ride home began. The children slept and the "old folks" quietly reviewed the excitement and the gossip of the day. As we drew near home, my mother often said, "I believe my potato salad [or whatever] was as good as any on the table." Pop would reply, "Better," and with this accolade Mom would say, "Yes vell," and snuggle closer to him. It had been a day to remember.

Potato Salad for 25

7 pounds potatoes (old potatoes are best)
5 tablespoons salad oil
1 tablespoon prepared mustard, or 1 teaspoon dry mustard
2 tablespoons vinegar
1 teaspoon sugar
2 tablespoons salt
¼ teaspoon pepper
Pinch cayenne

2 onions, minced
2 cups celery, thinly sliced
8 hardboiled eggs, chopped
½ cup parsley, chopped
3 tablespoons sweet red pepper, chopped (optional)
½ cup green pepper, chopped
1½ cups salad dressing, or 1½ to 2 cups mayonnaise
Paprika

Boil potatoes in their jackets. Peel as soon as cool enough to handle, and slice while still warm. Mix oil, mustard, vinegar, sugar, salt, pepper, and cayenne. Pour over potatoes. Let marinate 15 minutes.

Add onions, celery, chopped egg, parsley, and peppers to potatoes. Add just enough salad dressing to combine—it should not be runny. Mix gently but thoroughly. Sprinkle with paprika and chill.

Stuffed Tomato Salad for 25

25 washed ripe tomatoes	2 tablespoons sugar
4½ cups chopped cabbage	2 tablespoons salt
2 cups chopped celery	Juice of 2 lemons
½ cup salad dressing	

Remove stems from tomatoes. With sharp knife, partially cut tomato into 6 sections—don't cut all the way down. Invert to drain.

Spread chopped cabbage and celery in 2 large roasting pans. Sprinkle with sugar, salt, and lemon juice. Let stand for 5 minutes. Add salad dressing. Mix thoroughly.

Put about 2 tablespoonfuls of cabbage in each tomato. Serve cold.

Raspberry Ice

Fourth of July picnics are always associated in my mind with raspberry ice and blitzkuchen. Mother prepared the raspberry mixture, and we children took turns at the crank and at hammering the ice in a burlap bag with the flat blade of a hatchet. Cries of "It's ready!" were always greeted with "Turn a little more." It seemed forever until finally she would grasp the handle and test how hard it was herself. When she could just budge the handles she'd say, "Now ve're getting some-vheres. Turn chust a little more, but not too fast, mind," lest in a final spurt of enthusiasm and superhuman strength we might spoil it. (I know that ice cream should not be turned too fast because it gets buttery, but I never did understand what would happen to the ices if one handled them the same way.) She also had a theory that ices should be turned for 5 minutes, should rest for 5 minutes and then be turned again. I'm not sure what this does, but it works.

At last the chore was pronounced done, and cold water was carefully poured over the lid. Then the can was opened, and we were allowed to lick the sweet distillation from the dasher while she repacked the can in ice and salt. We made many

other ices and ice cream, but raspberry remains my favorite
to this day.

2 cups sugar
4 cups water
2 quarts red raspberries, or
   2 packages frozen raspberries,
   thawed

½ cup lemon juice
   (about 2 lemons)
Pinch of salt

Mix sugar and water in large kettle. Bring to a boil, stirring until
sugar is dissolved. Let boil, without stirring, for 5 minutes. Cool.
If berries are fresh, wash. Then mash and press through strainer or
food mill. Measure pulp and juice, adding enough cold water to
make 3 cups. Add cooled syrup, lemon juice, and salt. Chill. Freeze,
according to the directions for your electric or crank freezer.

This can also be frozen in a freezer tray. As soon as it becomes
firm all over, beat it with an electric or hand beater until all the
crystals have been broken up, but not until it's melted. Return to
freezer and freeze again until firm.   *Makes about 2½ quarts*

Lemon Ice

2 cups sugar
4 cups water

Yellow coloring
4 lemons—juice
Pinch of salt

Mix sugar, 2 cups water, and a few drops of yellow coloring together. Bring to a boil, stirring until sugar is dissolved, then boil
5 minutes without stirring. Add 2 cups water, lemon juice, and salt.
Cool and freeze according to directions for your electric or crank
freezer.   *Makes about 1½ quarts*

Fruit Ice

2 cups sugar
4 cups water
2 cups fruit juice, or
   2 cups mashed fruit and juice

Lemon juice to taste
Dash of salt

You can use any fruit alone, or fruit in combination. Black raspberry, currants, peaches, pineapple, or apricots make delicious ices.
Proceed as for raspberry ice.   *Makes about 1¾ quarts*

Vanilla Ice Cream

We always made a custard for any ice cream, and preferred it to the thinner mixtures which we disdainfully dismissed as "ice milk, not *cream*."

4 cups and 2 tablespoons milk	2 cups sugar
2 tablespoons cornstarch	1 tablespoon vanilla
2 eggs	Pinch of salt

2 cups heavy cream

Scald 4 cups milk—do not boil (scalding keeps the milk from expanding too rapidly in the freezer, and improves its texture). Mix cornstarch with 2 tablespoons cold milk, until completely smooth. Add to scalded milk, put over low heat and cook, stirring constantly, until it coats the spoon. Let cool while you beat eggs, sugar, salt, and vanilla together. Add cooled milk mixture to eggs slowly. Then add cream. Stir to mix completely. Chill. Put in freezer can, being careful to allow for expansion by never filling it more than two thirds full. Freeze and pack according to directions for your electric or crank freezer.   *Makes about 2 quarts*

Chocolate Ice Cream

4 ounces unsweetened chocolate   Recipe for vanilla ice cream

Melt chocolate over hot, not boiling water. Add to vanilla ice-cream mixture. Mix well, then freeze.   *Makes about 2 quarts*

Strawberry Ice Cream

1 box strawberries (1 quart)	2 eggs
2 cups sugar	Pinch salt
4 cups plus 2 tablespoons milk	2 cups heavy cream
2 tablespoons cornstarch	½ teaspoon vanilla (optional)

Wash strawberries, hull, and mash with 1 cup sugar. Let stand to draw juice, about 1 hour. Put through food mill or sieve.

Scald 4 cups milk. Mix cornstarch with 2 tablespoons cold milk, add to scalded milk, and cook over low heat, stirring constantly until it coats the spoon. Cool. Beat eggs and rest of sugar together. Add milk mixture, salt, cream, and the vanilla.

Put in freezer can, and following manufacturer's directions freeze to a good thick consistency. Remove lid, being careful not to get salt into can. Add fruit mixture, stir, replace lid, and freeze again until hard. Pack in ice and salt according to manufacturer's directions. *Makes about 1¾ quarts*

Peach Ice Cream

2 quarts ripe peaches	2 eggs
2 cups sugar	Pinch salt
4 cups plus 2 tablespoons milk	1 teaspoon lemon juice
2 tablespoons cornstarch	2 cups heavy cream

Peel peaches, slice thin, add 1 cup of sugar, lemon juice, and mash. Let stand until they draw juice, then put through a food mill.

Scald 4 cups milk. Mix cornstarch with 2 tablespoons cold milk, add to hot milk, and cook over low heat, stirring constantly, until it coats the spoon. Cool. Beat eggs, rest of sugar, and salt together. Add milk mixture and then cream. Chill.

Freeze according to the directions for your freezer, adding the peach pulp after the milk mixture is frozen, as for strawberry ice cream. *Makes about 1¾ quarts*

Banana Ice Cream

4 cups heavy cream	2 cups thin cream
1½ cups sugar	1 cup mashed banana
	¼ cup lemon juice

Scald heavy cream, add sugar, and stir until dissolved. Cool. Add thin cream and freeze. Mix banana and lemon juice, add to partially frozen mixture, and finish freezing. *Makes about 1¾ quarts*

Mocha Ice Cream

4 ounces sweet chocolate, or	Pinch salt
¼ cup cocoa	1 cup strong coffee, cold
1 cup sugar	4 eggs, separated
2 teaspoons cornstarch	2 cups heavy cream

Melt chocolate. (If you use cocoa instead, add it to dry ingredients.) Mix sugar, cornstarch, and salt. Gradually add cold coffee, stirring constantly until smooth. Cook over low heat, stirring constantly, until it coats the spoon. Add melted chocolate. Beat yolks, add to chocolate mixture. Beat whites until stiff, but not dry. Beat cream until stiff. Fold whites and whipped cream into chocolate mixture. Freeze according to directions for your freezer.

Makes about 1 quart

BEI'M VENDUE
(AT THE AUCTION)

One of the best places to observe the Pennsylvania Dutch people, other than at market, is at auction sales. Here all types of garb may be seen, from the colorful reds, greens, blues, and purples of the Amish, to the severe, undecorated dresses and bonnets of the new Mennonites and Brethren, or Dunkards (dubbed "Dunkers," which became "Dunkards," because of their practice of baptismal total immersion). Only the initiated can tell by the shape of the women's bonnets and little white caps to which sect they belong. The word "vendue," which is what they call sales, obviously derives from the French, as do many of the Dutch words. Vendues serve as gathering places for whole families. Although the occasion is usually a sad one, since it is occasioned by the dying out of part of a family, it's a good place for visiting and gossiping among the Plain folk. It served as well for the acquisition of some needed tools or machine parts for Pop and for additions to Mom's already well-filled china cupboard or collection of old furniture.

At a sale the women sit in the kitchen until the household goods are put up, while the men go around to the barnyard with the auctioneer to buy the farm equipment. The children are everywhere, shyly peeping from behind their mothers' skirts or playing boisterously out in the farmyard. When the bidding on the "haus schtuff" begins, the women come out and edge in to see, hear, and poke Pop to bid on any desired item. Everything that nobody bids on is knocked down to the "penny man," a second-hand dealer, who soon acquires a pile of "chunk."

Sales usually are held in the early spring before plowing begins and the work is slack, which is why they are so well attended. Every article is immaculately clean—no dust or cobwebs here, as in other sales. Would you want the family to have shame? Prices on furniture, dishes, glass, which often comes from a hundred years of discards in the attic, now run fairly high, which wasn't true in the old days. Antique dealers are quickly identified by the local folk, and their bidding is closely watched with some amusement. I remember acquiring a beautiful Staffordshire dog at what was to me a reasonable price for so rare a piece. The next morning when the butcher brought the wagon around, he said to me, "Roos, what fer dawk vas that that you gave $7.50 for?" and nothing would do but that I get it out and show it to him. A little later the rural mail carrier made the same request. It had "gone all over town" that I had given what seemed to them an outrageous sum for "such a little dawk!"

At most sales a food stand is set up, usually by the church women, and refreshments are offered. In the old days, pies, cakes, and coffee were available, with cookies "fur die Kinder," and at very large sales, which last all day, they are still available, together with sandwiches. But most stands nowadays serve the ubiquitous hot dogs and soft drinks, and perhaps pretzels. Everyone munches on something while following the bidding.

Two of the most delicious homemade foods sold at the summer auctions were, I remember, peach and cherry pie.

Deep-Dish Peach Pie for 25

Pie Crust:

2¾ cups shortening	1½ cups cold water
8 cups flour	(approx.)
2 tablespoons salt	1 egg white, beaten

Add shortening to flour and mix until combination has texture of coarse corn meal. Add salt to 1 cup cold water and slowly add to flour mixture. Then carefully add remaining water until dough is just formed. Chill at least 1 hour to make it easier to handle.

Roll out quite thin, about ⅛ inch thick, and cut into 3-inch squares. Brush with egg white, prick, and bake at 400° 12 to 20 minutes on cookie sheets. Reserve.

Peach Filling:

6 to 8 pounds peaches, or	1 teaspoon cinnamon
4 No. 2½ cans sliced peaches	3 tablespoons cornstarch or
3 tablespoons lemon juice	flour
2½ cups sugar	4 tablespoons water

Mix sliced peaches with other ingredients. Stir to be sure all sugar is dissolved. Place in 2 greased baking pans, 9 by 13 inches. Bake at 350° for 35 to 40 minutes, or until peaches are soft. (It will take a little longer for fresh peaches.)

Allow about ⅔ cup for each serving. Top with a square of the pie crust, and serve.

Cherry Crumb Pie for 25

8¾ cups sifted flour	2⅔ cups plus 2 tablespoons sugar
2¼ teaspoons salt	1 quart cherry juice
2¼ cups sugar	7 tablespoons cornstarch or
1½ cups lard or other	flour
shortening	½ cup cold water
10 quarts canned, pitted sour	2 tablespoons butter
cherries	Pinch of salt

Mix flour, salt, sugar, and lard to form a crumbly mixture. Put 1½ cups crumbs in each of 5 pie plates and press down to form a crust. Reserve remaining crumbs.

Drain cherries, saving juice. Add 1 cup 2 tablespoons sugar to cherries and stir. Spread 2 cups of cherries in each pie plate.

Combine cherry juice with remaining sugar, heat to boiling. Blend cornstarch with cold water and add to juice. Stirring constantly, cook until mixture is clear and smooth. Add butter and salt. Pour over cherries in pie pans, add 1 cup of crumb mixture to each pie, pressing it down slightly, so that some of the juice oozes up. Bake at 375° about 50 minutes, or until lightly browned and bubbling.

Short Cut:

Use 9 cans of prepared cherry pie mix. Distribute it between the pans which have been lined with the crumb mixture. Top with crumbs. Bake at 375° for 30 to 40 minutes, or until well browned.

Makes 5 9-inch pies

WEDDINGS

Weddings are joyous and sometimes raucous occasions among the Plain people. By tradition they are held in the fall, and are planned far in advance. Every Dutch girl, "plain" or "fancy," has a hope chest—drawers and chests filled with sheets, blankets, hand-embroidered pillow cases, beautifully embroidered towels, quilts of many different patterns, and china and glassware which she either has inherited or acquired against the day when she will set up housekeeping.

In earlier times, many of the young Plain girls worked as domestics—maids or nursemaids—in nearby towns or cities to earn enough money for a dowry. Nowadays they work in factories for the same purpose—to get "cash money" which is always hard to come by on the farm.

When the wedding date is set, a flock of turkeys is raised especially for the wedding feast, and extra hams and sides of beef are earmarked for the occasion. Members of the congregation and freundschaft from miles around will attend to give the bride their good wishes.

Some Amish weddings begin at dawn, with the singing of old hymns, and as the wagons and buggies begin to crowd the hitching rail in the yard, the work in the kitchen gains in intensity. The ovens of neighbors have been "borrowed" and all the turkeys, hams, and beef must be rounded up before the ceremony begins. Cakes and pies have been baked beforehand, as well as most of the other dishes.

In the other sects too, the wedding itself takes place in the forenoon, and there is much singing of the old German hymns, many of them written in the 1600's, both before and during the ceremony. There are no fancy bridal clothes, veils, nor any procession—that would be too worldly, but the sermon is usually a lengthy one, and there are many admonitions from the preacher, especially to the bride.

The usual planks on trestles have been set up in the yard if it is fine; if not, they are all over the house, both upstairs and down. Right after the marriage service is over, the food is set out. Hams, turkey with potato, chestnut, or bread stuffing, roast beef, cold tongues, mounds of mashed potatoes (did anyone mention calories?), dried corn, lima beans, corn pudding, peas, sweet and sour beets, pickles, chow chow, coleslaw, applesauce, and every kind of preserved and canned fruit that can be thought of. Then there are pies and many kinds of cakes, but no single wedding cake or cake to dream on. Sometimes there are freezers of homemade ice cream as well. All this appears on the tables at once, and disappears completely as the feasting, singing, and joking continue for hours.

Finally the bride and groom break loose to ride to their new home. (No honeymoon trip—setting up housekeeping is a serious business, and their new home is already furnished and ready for them.) But even then, they're not left at peace; as soon as dusk arrives, all the young men and some of the young women come to their door for a "shivaree," or serenade. They bring any kind of noise-makers they can find, and the whistling, singing, and yelling can be heard for miles around. They don't go away until the bridegroom appears, and offers them some refreshment—usually liquid—hard cider or schnapps. Thereupon they wax even noisier, and the jokes aren't always fit for the bride's ears, but she laughs and blushes and tells them to go away. This elicits more remarks, but finally the crowd dwindles and the couple are left alone.

The feasting doesn't end with the wedding. For months afterward, usually on Sundays, every member of the family must hold a dinner for the bride and groom, and each tries to outdo the other.

At large affairs like weddings, where there are sometimes as many as two hundred guests, the guests eat in shifts. The

important visitors or the men who have to get back to work are
served first. This custom is also followed in small houses where
there are large families. The plates of food are replenished, the
dinner plates are washed and replaced, the silver is quickly
wiped off and the glasses refilled, and the table is ready for the
next group. Even in these days of enlightened views on sanita-
tion there is no washing, let alone sterilizing, of the silver and
glasses. The plates are washed, but the fastidiousness doesn't
extend to anything else.

Smaller children usually eat with the women, and it is a mark
of manhood for a boy to be permitted to eat with the men.
Honored guests sometimes sit through more than one sitting,
and I can remember one time when the children, who were
seated last, stole envious glances at the adults' full plates.

Here are the recipes for some of the wedding cakes as well as
for a delicious and easy fruit punch.

Sponge Cake for Large Pan

9 eggs, separated	1½ teaspoons baking powder
1½ cups granulated sugar	1 teaspoon vanilla, or
1½ cups flour	1 teaspoon lemon extract

Beat egg whites until stiff, but not dry. Slowly fold in sugar. Beat
yolks and gently fold into whites. Sift flour and baking powder together, and fold into first mixture. Fold and turn bowl until no
white streaks are left. Add vanilla or lemon extract, and stir gently.
Bake in *ungreased* tube pan, at 300° for 1 hour, or until top springs
back when gently touched.   *Serves 16 to 20*

Schpeis Kucha
(SPICE CAKE)

2 teaspoons baking soda	2 cups sour milk or buttermilk
4 tablespoons molasses	4 cups flour
2 eggs	½ teaspoon cinnamon
2 cups sugar	½ teaspoon ground cloves
8 tablespoons lard or other shortening, melted	½ teaspoon ginger
	1 cup raisins, floured

Mix baking soda with molasses and stir well. Put into mixing bowl; add eggs, sugar, melted shortening, sour milk, flour, and spices. Mix raisins with about 1 tablespoon of flour, being sure to coat them (so that they will not sink to the bottom of the cake), and fold in. Pour batter into greased and floured baking pan. Bake at 350° for 25 to 30 minutes, or until top springs back when touched.

Serves 16

Nut Cake

2 cups sugar	Pinch of salt
¾ cup lard or shortening	1 cup milk
4 eggs, separated	1 teaspoon almond extract
3 cups sifted flour	1 cup ground nuts (hazelnuts,
3 teaspoons baking powder	black walnuts, or pecans)

Beat sugar and shortening together until light and fluffy, then add egg yolks. Sift flour, baking powder, and salt together, and add to first mixture, alternately with milk. Add almond extract and nuts. Beat egg whites until stiff, but not dry. Fold into first mixture. Bake in greased and floured tube pan at 375° for 45 minutes; just until it springs back when touched; do not overbake. Do not invert the pan.

It isn't necessary to ice this cake, but if you wish to do so, use a butter cream frosting made of confectioners' sugar and colored a pale yellow.

Butter Cream Icing:

3 to 4 tablespoons cream	½ teaspoon almond extract
2 tablespoons butter	⅛ teaspoon salt
1 pound confectioners' sugar	2 to 3 drops yellow food coloring

Heat cream and butter, bring just to a boil and add to confectioners' sugar. Add rest of ingredients, using just enough cream to achieve desired spreading consistency.

Serves 10 to 16

Fruit Punch for 25

5 cups sugar	1 pint grape juice
5 cups water	1 large can pineapple juice
2 dozen oranges	Juice from 1-quart jar sour
1½ dozen lemons	cherries

Mix sugar and water, bring to a boil and boil for 5 minutes. Cool. Squeeze oranges and lemons and add with other juices to sugar and water. If you want to, you can slice one orange and one lemon very fine and add to mixture. Let stand to blend flavors. Serve over ice in a large bowl.

Short Cut:

4 cups sugar
4 cups water
3 cans frozen lemonade mix
3 cans frozen orange juice
1 large can pineapple juice

1 pint grape juice, canned or frozen (optional)
1 medium-sized bottle maraschino cherries

Mix sugar and water and boil 5 minutes. This simple syrup brings out all the fruit flavors. Follow directions on the cans of frozen mixes. Mix all together, and let stand to blend. Serve over ice.

CHAPTER XII

Set-Outs

Why not try a Pennsylvania Dutch set-out? Here are six I've tried successfully. If you wish to copy one, remember that these menus are intended only as guides to offer ideas that you can change, shorten, or increase. Substitutions may be necessary, according to what is available in your locality, and omissions may be made for the calorie-conscious. The main thing, if you want to be echt Deitsch, is to have a lot of different dishes, especially seven sweets and sours, and to put the desserts on the table together with the other food.

SUMMER SET-OUT—FOR 6 TO 8
WITH
SEVEN SWEETS AND SEVEN SOURS

Deviled Clams
Baked Ham

Potato Salad   Pepper Slaw
Gurken Salat (Cucumber Salad)   Red Beet Eggs
Dried Lima Beans mit Schpeck
Semmel Rolls
Pineapple Pudding

Apple Butter   Strawberry Jam
Assorted Pickles, Chow Chow, Spiced Peaches,
Corn Relish, Watermelon Rind
Schticky Buns

Peach Kuchen   Shoofly Pie   Chocolate Cake
Coffee   Peppermint or Iced Tea
(See Index for recipes.)

Not much decorating is necessary, since the food is the main attraction, but if you have any peasant pottery, this is the time to use it. Pennsylvania Dutch decorations are colorful—hearts, birds, tulips, "anchels," six- and eight-pointed stars, and hex signs, which are stars and circles geometrically arranged. You can find Dutch paper napkins and paper plates in many of the variety stores. Hearts, tulips, and birds may be cut out of cardboard and colored, and put on the table, if you wish.

The beauty of this summer set-out or buffet is that you do most of the cooking beforehand and only need to "hotten things up" at the last minute. The ham, rolls, pies, and cakes can be baked the day before; the vegetables cooked; the potato salad and eggs prepared. If you have a freezer, you can bake the rolls, schticky buns, and chocolate cake as much as a week in advance.

Day Before: Bake the ham, glaze it, and refrigerate. Mix the clams, fry them, and refrigerate. Make the potato salad and red beet eggs. Cook the lima beans until just barely tender. Bake the rolls, pies, and cakes, if you haven't already done so. Mix the pineapple pudding and refrigerate.

Day of the Set-Out:

Morning: Dish up the assorted pickles and preserves. Remove the rolls, pies, and cakes from the freezer, and allow to thaw. Peel the tomatoes. Make the pepper slaw and refrigerate. Set the tables. (I like to use one table for the food, with small tables or a large one to "eat off'n.") Set out all serving dishes. Slice the eggs. Make the tea, cut slices of lemon if you're not making peppermint.

About 1½ hours before Serving: Heat the oven to 400°. Put the pie in for 25 minutes, remove it, and lower the heat to 350°. Put in the pineapple pudding. (It must bake for 40 minutes, but it keeps hot for a good long while.)

Dish up the potato salad and pepper slaw, put on the table, together with the pickles, relishes, and preserves. Cut the pie and cake into serving pieces, if you wish, but put the whole pie and cake on the table. Get out the ice cubes and lemon for the tea.

Put the clams and ham in the oven. While the ham is heating through, and the clams are puffing up—about 25 minutes, add the cream and vinegar to the cucumbers, and serve. Heat the lima beans. Cut up the tomatoes and make the tomato salad. Make the coffee.

Take the ham, clams, and pineapple pudding out of the oven and put in the rolls, which have been thawed. Slice the ham, surround the platter with the red beet eggs; put the clams on another platter, and garnish with parsley. Put clams, the ham, limas, and the pudding on the table.

Take the rolls from the oven, "up-dump" the schticky buns, and serve them, covered with a napkin.

Don't forget butter, sugar and cream, salt and pepper, and slices of lemon, if you are serving iced tea. Check your list to be sure everything is on the table, and then call, "Kum, Esse!"

WINTER SET-OUT—FOR 8 TO 10

Hinkel Bot Bei
(Chicken Pot Pie)
Sauerbraten mit Grumbere Kloess
(Sauerbraten with Potato Dumplings)
Sweet and Sour Sugar Peas
Mashed Turnips
Dried Corn
Assorted Rolls

Seven Sours:
Chow Chow, Dill Pickles, Corn Relish, Pepper Slaw,
Watermelon Pickles, Bread and Butter Pickles,
Spiced Peaches

Seven Sweets:
Strawberry Jam, Apple Sauce, Apple Butter, Currant Jelly,
Montgomery Pie, Mince Pie, Chocolate Cake
Coffee

(See Index for recipes.)

Before the Dinner: Cook the chicken, cut it up, refrigerate in its broth. Cook the beef, refrigerate. Cook all vegetables, rolls, and pies.

Morning of the Day of the Dinner: Mix the doughs for both dumplings and refrigerate. Set the table, dish up the relishes, cover with transparent wrap and refrigerate. Set out all serving dishes. Remove rolls, pies, and cakes from the freezer, if frozen. Make the pepper slaw.

Two Hours before the Dinner: Heat the chicken to boiling. Roll out the dumplings, cut them, and drop into the boiling chicken stock. (They will keep for several hours at low heat, without losing any of their quality.)

Put the beef on to boil in its broth. Shape the kloess into balls.

Put out all the sweets and sours. Heat the mince pie. Put all vegetables into kettles for last-minute heating. Cut the butter; make a pitcher of iced water. Cut the pies and cakes.

Twenty Minutes before Serving: Make the coffee. Drop the kloess into the boiling beef broth. Heat the rolls. Heat the vegetables.

SET-OUT OF FRUITS OF THE SEA—FOR 6 TO 8

Creamed Seafood in Patty Shells

Deviled Crabs

Deviled Clams

Pepper Slaw in Tomato Shells

Creamed Dried Corn or Canned Corn

Hot Rolls   Zwievelkuche (Onion Cake)

Assorted Relishes

Cucumber Salad

Nut Cake with Butter Frosting

Lemon Custard

Coffee

(See Index for recipes.)

Put the chicken on a large platter, surrounded by the dumplings. Dish up the vegetables and rolls. Pour the iced water. Slice the beef, put it on another platter, and surround with kloess.

Check your list to be sure you haven't forgotten anything. Then, eat yourself full!

Day or Days before the Dinner: Bake the cake, rolls, and onion cake. Soak the dried corn and cook. Make the deviled clams, fry them, and refrigerate. Make the patty shells. Make the lemon custard.

Day of the Set-Out: Make the pepper slaw, and hollow out the tomatoes. Let them drain. Mix the creamed seafood, put in a casserole, and refrigerate. Mix the deviled crab and refrigerate. Take rolls out of the freezer, if frozen. Set the table, cut the butter, arrange the relishes. Slice the cucumbers, and salt down.

One Hour before the Dinner: Set the oven at 375°. Put in the creamed seafood, crabs, and clams. Put all relishes on the table. Cut the cake, set out the lemon custard, and the butter. Pile the pepper slaw in the tomatoes and serve. Make coffee.

When the seafood is nicely browned, and the clams and crabs are puffed up, remove them from the oven and put in the rolls and patty shells. Arrange the clams and crabs on a large platter, garnish with parsley and serve. Put the patty shells on a large plate, and put them and the seafood on the table. Take out the rolls, put in a basket or dish covered with a cloth. Dish up the corn.

Check the table to be sure you have served everything, including pepper and salt, sugar and cream, butter and iced water.

COMPANY BREAKFAST OR BRUNCH—FOR 8 TO 12

This is an easy way to entertain, and one of the few occasions when the children can be included comfortably. Set up a table for the children, one for the adults, and a third for the food. Use peasant pottery and decorations, and be sure to put everything on the table at once.

MENU

Porcupine Apples   Canned Sweet Cherries
Blackberry Mush   Cider or Fruit Juice
Fried Ham Slices
Pawn Hase (Scrapple)
Pork Sausage Patties
Hashed Brown Potatoes
Waffles with Molasses and Syrup
Schticky Buns
Shoofly Pie
Butter Rolls
Scrambled Eggs with Cheese
Assorted Jams and Jellies
Cup Cheese
Sliced Peaches   Watermelon Rind Pickles
Coffee   Milk
(See Index for recipes.)

Day before the Breakfast: Bake the schticky buns, butter rolls, and shoofly pie. Bake the porcupine apples, make the blackberry mush, and refrigerate in serving dishes. Mix the waffle batter, cover closely and refrigerate. Set up the tables, with the sugar, pepper and salt, glasses for the milk and juices, if you plan to serve them, and cups for the coffee. Put the waffle iron on the table. Boil enough potatoes for the hashed brown potatoes.

About One Hour before Serving: Put the fruits on the table, the fruit juices in small pitchers or in glasses, and the milk in a large pitcher. Set the tables, not forgetting cream, butter, syrup, molasses, and the jams and jellies. Get out all serving plates.

About a half hour before serving, heat the rolls, buns and shoofly pie in a 350° oven for at least 25 minutes. Fry the ham slices, scrapple, and the pork sausage. Keep warm. Chop boiled potatoes into small pieces. Fry in lard and butter, adding ¼ teaspoon pepper, one teaspoon salt, and one table-spoon chopped parsley. (Just before serving add 2 tablespoons of cream.) Make the coffee.

Mix the number of eggs you will need (two to a person, at least) with 1 tablespoon of cream, and add ⅛ pound of very mild cheese (Velveeta, Chateau, or the like) cut in very small pieces. Beat enough to mix thoroughly, and add salt and pepper.

Ten Minutes before Serving: Dish up the rolls, "up-dump" the schticky buns, and cut the pie into small wedges. Cover with a napkin and put on the table. Begin heating the waffle iron, and when it is hot put in the batter for one waffle. Recruit someone to watch it for you. Now begin scrambling the eggs. Put a heaping tablespoonful of butter into a large spider, and when it is sizzling, add the egg-cheese mixture. Immediately lower the heat. Use a tablespoon to stir the eggs, and cook them until they are thoroughly cooked, but not dry. In the meantime, put the meats around the edge of a large platter, leaving space for the eggs in the center. Dish up the potatoes, garnish with parsley. By this time the eggs should be done. Put them in the center of the meat platter. Pour the coffee. Check your waffle assistant and your list to be sure you haven't forgotten anything, and then mahlzeit (mealtime)!

At a large family gathering, everyone brings something, and the hostess supplies the meats, breads, and beverages. This system simplifies things, and yet it requires some management. We never did end up with everyone bringing potato salad, because we usually decided beforehand what each one should bring. The suggested menu can be varied according to the skills of your guests. If anyone has a beloved specialty, of course she can substitute it. But your answer to "What shall I bring?" should be fairly definite, and if you have a menu in mind, your suggestions will avoid confusion.

Day before the Feast: Roast two pork loins and refrigerate to be heated the next day. Cook the tongue, and refrigerate it in some of the broth. (Save the rest of the broth for another day.) Set up the tables. (The porch or a shady place is wonderful in the summertime.) Make pineapple pudding and put in a baking pan and refrigerate.

COVERED-DISH DINNER FOR A FAMILY REUNION
FOR 15 TO 20

Rack of Pork with Cider Sauce   Boiled Tongue
Macaronie und Schinken or Ham and Macaroni (double the recipe)
Pineapple Pudding
(double the recipe and bake in a pan 10 by 14 inches)
Dried Lima Beans mit Schpeck (double the recipe)
Pickled Beets (double the recipe)
Pepper Slaw (double the recipe)
Potato Salad (double the recipe)
Rainbow Egg Platter
Corn bread (double the recipe)
Cheese Biscuits (double the recipe)
Assorted Relishes and Preserves
Burnt Sugar Cake with Caramel Frosting
Cherry Kuchen (make two)
Raisin Pie (make two)
Coffee   Iced Tea   Milk
(See Index for recipes.)

Morning of the Dinner: Mix the corn bread and biscuits and bake them, to reheat later. Prepare macaroni and cheese and the beans. Slice the tongue, and arrange it attractively on a platter. Cover with transparent wrap and refrigerate. Dish up the relishes and preserves, ready to put on the table. Cut the butter, put the milk in a pitcher, and make the iced tea. Slice lemons. Get out all serving plates and set the tables.

One Hour before the Dinner: Heat the oven to 350°, and put pork on to reheat. (Needs a full hour.) Put the pineapple pudding and macaroni in the oven. Put the rolls and biscuits on a baking sheet or baking pan, ready to reheat.

Put the iced tea on the table, together with the lemon, sugar, pepper and salt. Put the cream in a pitcher and refrigerate. Set out all pickles and preserves. Put out hot plates for the macaroni and pudding. Make the coffee.

When Guests Arrive: Decide beforehand upon the arrangement of the buffet (I sometimes draw a chart) and as your guests arrive, have them place their dishes right on the buffet table. Let each cook cut her pie or cake, while you carve the pork, reheat the rolls, and put the pineapple pudding on the table. Check your list, put the rolls in a dish covered with a napkin, bring out the milk and cream, and you should be all set for a real reunion, without being exhausted.

SUNDAY COMPANY DINNER—FOR 6 OR 8

Roast Chicken with Potato Filling
Ham Loaf (served hot)
Dried Corn
Rotkraut (Red Cabbage)
Sweet Potato Fluff
Buttermilk Biscuits
Gurken Salat (Cucumber Salad)
Amish Vanilla Pie
Montgomery Pie
Devil's Food Cake
Assorted Sweets and Sours (Preserves and Relishes)
Coffee

(See Index for recipes.)

You will do most of the cooking the day before. I feel that this is by far the easiest way to entertain. For roast chicken, I like to use two 2½ pound broiler-fryers, rather than one large chicken. If you prefer a large one, get at least a 6 to 6½ pound roasting chicken or capon.

Day Before: Wash the chicken, remove the giblets, and make a broth of them, together with a slice of onion, one stalk of celery, salt and pepper and a little parsley. Refrigerate to use in making the gravy. Mix the potato filling (see Index), and refrigerate in a bowl. Mix the ham loaf, and refrigerate in the pan in which it is to be cooked.

Bake the pies and cake. Cook the vegetables, both of which improve upon being reheated. Mix the potato fluff, and put it in a casserole ready for baking. Refrigerate.

Two Hours before the Meal: Heat the oven to 350°. Put the chicken in a roasting pan and stuff it with the potato filling. (If you have any leftover filling, put it in a casserole, and bake it too.) Salt and pepper and butter the breast. (Do not cover, and do not add water.) Put in oven to bake.

Set the tables, putting on the relishes and preserves, salt and pepper, sugar and butter, etc. Get out all serving dishes.

Mix the biscuits and put them on a baking sheet, ready for last-minute baking. Make the tomato salad and refrigerate. Cut the pies and cake and put them on the serving table.

One Hour before Serving: Put the sweet potatoes and ham loaf and any remaining potato filling in the oven. Begin basting the chicken, and baste every 15 minutes or so for this last hour. Heat the corn and red cabbage, and keep hot over low heat. Put the salad on the table. Make the coffee.

25 Minutes before Serving: Remove chicken, sweet potatoes, and ham loaf from the oven. Turn heat up to 400° and put in the biscuits. Put ham on a small platter, carved or not, as you please. Carve the chicken, put it on a large platter with the filling in the center. Dish up vegetables. Make gravy, using giblet broth you have prepared.

Take out biscuits, serve them covered with a napkin. Put cream on the table, and call your guests. Check your list.

Mother to son: "You chust better mind, else the Belsnickel von't come!" "Belsnickel" is Pennsylvania Dutch for Santa Claus. *Nickel* in German is a diminutive for Nicholas, hence a Nicholas mit bells—so, vas iss selbe letz? or what's wrong with that?

CHAPTER XIII

"Oh Weinachtszeit!"
(Sweets for Christmas)

While there are numerous occasions for "fressing," Christmas is the time for the greatest feast of all. When I was young, preparations usually began in the summer, when the nicest jars of vegetables and fruits were put aside for this glorious occasion, along with bottles of the best wine which "made." Geese and ducks were fattened, always with the thought of saving the best for Christmas. But the actual preparations began the day after Thanksgiving, the traditional time for the housewife to make fruit cakes, which were then wrapped in wine-soaked cloths and stored in the cellar to ripen in covered crocks or lard cans.

On fruit cake-baking day, all the women helped. Some cut up and floured the preserved fruit rinds and nuts, others greased and lined the pans with brown paper carefully saved from market, still others beat the eggs or creamed the butter, and many hands were needed to stir the final mixture in a large tub. The kitchen boiled with activity, and no one who wasn't helping was allowed underfoot. When the cakes were finally in the oven, the tantalizing odors of cinnamon, ginger, and nutmeg spread throughout the house, and small heads peeked around the door to get a better lungful. "Shut the door to, you'll make them fall—but don't bang," they were told. It was a great honor to be considered old enough to help, even if it was only to do the menial job of washing up the many bowls, spoons, and utensils. Later, good children were given the brown papers to lick, after they had been carefully peeled from the cooled cakes.

Both dark and light fruit cakes were baked in the more affluent homes, and even the poorest housewife, in both senses of the word, at least had an apple sauce cake on hand for Christmas visitors. "Boughten" fruit cake, except that bought at market, was unheard of. Smaller cakes were rewrapped at Christmas and given as gifts to those who weren't fortunate enough to have anyone to bake for them.

Nowadays, most Dutch housewives still bake their own fruit cakes. It is a lonely task for me now, and a mixer is a poor substitute for the many willing and able hands of my childhood, but I would be even more desolate if I didn't bake fruit cakes on the Friday after Thanksgiving. The recipes given here are those of my grandmother, and goodness knows how far they preceded her! Fruit cakes are not difficult to make—just messy —and the end result is a great satisfaction.

After the fruit cake came the plum puddings and the mince-meat, all of which had to ripen to achieve the best flavor. The plum pudding recipe is the only one I have from my paternal grandmother, and it is the best I have ever eaten. It is a source of great satisfaction to me that my daughter makes plum puddings at Christmas to give to close friends, and even in the Deep South they are greatly appreciated.

In the first weeks of December there was a lull in the cooking activities, but it was the time to "redd up" (clean) for the advent of the Christ child or "Gristkind." Every room was thoroughly scrubbed—walls, woodwork, and furniture—and polished to a shine. The ornaments for the tree were brought out and refurbished, if necessary. Many of them had been handed down for generations, and some are still used today.

After the house was in perfect order, it was time to begin

the cookie making. Most of these were for the family or for "set-outs" for guests, but others were arranged "fancy" on plates to be given friends, relatives, and neighbors. We didn't send Christmas cards when I was a child—a box or plate of cookies was the customary greeting. If you didn't care too much for some of your neighbor's cookies, you could always pass them on, but you had to be very careful about this, lest she found out. Some of them were "somesing fierce"! Smaller children, however, would eat almost everything in the cookie line, so few were wasted.

Although we do not bake in the quantity of yesteryear, the present Pennsylvania Dutch housewife still prides herself on the variety she turns out. My mother baked over twenty different kinds, and I still bake at least twelve varieties, because each member of the family has a special favorite which must not be omitted.

Preparations for Christmas were not confined to the kitchen, nor yet to the women. When the spicy smells from the kitchen began to permeate the house, Father and the boys usually stole up to the attic to hunt for the carefully stored parts of the "Putz" (pronounced like "puts"). *Putz* means "ornament" in German, but a Pennsylvania Dutch Putz is "somesing else again." The origin of the Putz is unknown but it probably began as a simple manger scene, or crèche, and grew and grew, until now it consists of whole villages, with mountains, valleys, and waterfalls carefully carved and painted. Most "fancy"— not Plain people—have a Putz, and these creations seem to grow more elaborate every year. At first the place for the Putz was under the tree, but it became so elaborate that in many homes a special platform is built for it. Men try to show their ingenuity and spend hours with their sons on these sometimes handsome, but often garish, displays. In the manner of true artists, no one seems to be satisfied with his efforts from the year before, and so there is much changing and improvisation.

Families visit each other to see the various Putz, some of which have become so famous that the public is invited in to see them. At every house there is always a "set-out." Cookies, candies, fruit cake, with wine, punch, or soft drinks are served to each visitor and after a round of Putz viewing, the children can scarcely move!

Grandma's Plum Pudding

Although this plum pudding is not Pennsylvania Dutch in origin, it is delicious; it is my grandmother's recipe. It makes a delightful gift at Christmas, especially if accompanied by a jar of hard sauce.

1 pound beef suet, ground	1 pound seeded raisins
8 eggs	1 pound currants
1½ cups brown sugar	½ pound citron
4 cups dry bread crumbs	¼ pound chopped nuts
½ teaspoon cinnamon	½ pound chopped figs
½ teaspoon ground cloves	Dash of salt
1 cup wine, or wine and brandy mixed	½ cup sifted flour
	Water

Have the butcher grind the suet for you. Grease 4 1-quart molds well. If you use a tube pan, be sure to cork the hole.

Beat eggs until light, add sugar and suet, then crumbs, spices and wine. Mix fruits, nuts, and figs with salt and flour, then add to egg mixture. Fill pans almost to the top, since this does not rise. Cover tightly with foil or mold lids. Place on rack in a large roasting pan, and pour in water to ¾ of height of molds. Steam for fully 5 to 6 hours, depending upon size of mold. Check water level at intervals, to be sure puddings are steaming.

This may be made weeks ahead of the holidays and frozen. To serve, it should be steamed again, for at least 1 hour. Serve with hard sauce. *Makes 4 large or 6 small puddings*

Hard Sauce

½ cup butter	1 pound confectioners' sugar
	1 tablespoon brandy

Cream butter, then add sugar and brandy. If brandy is unavailable, use 1 tablespoon of vanilla. This keeps very well, if refrigerated, for several months. *Makes about ¾ cup*

White Fruit Cake

2 cups almonds, blanched and slivered
1½ cups thinly sliced citron (9¾ ounces)
1½ cups thinly sliced candied orange peel (3½ ounces)
½ cup thinly sliced candied lemon peel (3½ ounces)
1½ cups candied cherries, halved (10½ ounces)
1½ cups white raisins (8 ounces)

4 cups sifted flour
½ teaspoon salt
½ teaspoon nutmeg
1 pound butter—at room temperature
1 pound granulated sugar
9 large or 10 medium eggs
¾ teaspoon vanilla
¾ teaspoon lemon extract
2 tablespoons brandy (optional)

Prepare nuts and fruits and place in deep kettle. Grease 2 medium-sized loaf pans and 4 small loaf pans, or 4 1-pound coffee cans. Line with double thickness of waxed paper and grease the paper. Cover only bottom of tube pan, but be sure to grease sides well.

Sift flour, salt, and nutmeg together. Take out ½ cup and add to the cut-up fruits and nuts, mixing well, to insure that each piece is well coated. Using a mixer, cream the butter, add sugar gradually and cream well. Add eggs, one at a time, and beat until mixture is light and fluffy. Add flavorings and brandy, if desired. Add flour, about ½ cup at a time, beating at low speed after each addition.

Add batter to floured nuts in deep kettle, and stir until you can't see any more flour—takes time and muscle too, but don't get too vigorous about it; just keep turning and folding.

Put a shallow pan of water on oven floor and heat to 300°. Bake fruit cakes about 3 hours, or until a straw stuck in the middle comes out clean. (Smaller cakes naturally take less time.)

Let cool completely. Turn out of pans onto a board or clean surface, and gently peel off waxed paper. Wrap in cloths soaked in brandy or wine, then in aluminum foil, and store in a cool, dark place. These keep for over a year, if you can keep them from your family! Slice quite thin when serving. If you want to decorate the tops, use corn syrup as glue, and stick on candied cherries, pineapple, or whatever. *Makes 4 large or 6 small cakes*

Dark Fruit Cake

1 pound seeded raisins	1 teaspoon ground cloves
1 pound currants	½ teaspoon allspice
1 pound yellow raisins	½ teaspon nutmeg
¼ pound citron	1 teaspoon baking powder
¼ pound candied lemon peel	¾ pound butter
¼ pound candied orange peel	1 pound sugar
½ pound dried figs	8 eggs
½ pound candied cherries	1 small cup strong coffee
½ pound candied pineapple	(or brandy)
½ pound mixed nuts	1 large glass strawberry
4 cups flour	preserves
1 teaspoon cinnamon	

Cut up fruits, not too fine, and add nuts. (In cutting up sticky fruits, dip your knife into very hot water, and they won't stick so much.) Mix flour, spices, and baking powder and add to fruits and nuts. Mix thoroughly.

Cream butter, add sugar and eggs, and beat until very light and fluffy. Add coffee (or brandy) and jam; mix thoroughly. Add to cut-up fruit and mix well.

Prepare pans by greasing them first, then lining with a double thickness of waxed paper, and greasing the paper. Use loaf pans, molds, or coffee cans. (Recipe will make from 5 to 7 cakes, depending on the size of the pans.)

Fill pans ¾ full, pressing down with the back of a spoon to be sure they are thoroughly filled. Put a pan of hot water on oven floor, and heat to 300°. Bake about 2½ hours, or until a straw inserted in middle of cakes comes out clean. Let cool, then invert on a clean board. Peel off waxed paper. Wrap each cake in a clean cloth soaked in wine or brandy, then wrap in aluminum foil, and store in a dark, cool place. Will keep for 1 year.

Makes 4 large or 6 medium-sized cakes

COOKIES

Kisses

These little bits of sweetness are still popular in the Dutch country. I remember as a girl going into the local confectionery store and buying a bag of kisses to eat at the movies, much as children munch popcorn today. There were all sorts and varieties, and it was hard to choose among them.

Vanilla Kisses

4 whites of eggs   4 cups granulated sugar
                                 1 teaspoon vanilla

Let whites of eggs stand in bowl to reach room temperature. Beat at high speed until they stand in soft peaks. Add sugar slowly, dribbling it in from a tablespoon. Then add vanilla. Beat until "it stands by itself," or until very high, stiff peaks are formed. Drop by teaspoonfuls onto ungreased cookie sheet. Bake in very slow oven (250°), about 1 hour, until they are a very *light* brown and can be moved around on the cookie sheet.   *Makes about 3 dozen*

Hazel Nut or Black Walnut or Coconut Kisses

Add 3 tablespoons lightly ground nuts or shredded coconut to the vanilla kisses recipe (see above). You may have to lower the heat a little for these, as coconut tends to scorch if it isn't watched carefully.   *Makes about 3 dozen*

Chocolate Kisses

6 egg whites   4 cups granulated sugar
1 ounce grated chocolate, or   3 cups ground nuts
   3 tablespoons cocoa   1 teaspoon vanilla

Beat egg whites until very stiff. Mix chocolate or cocoa with sugar, and add gradually to eggs while continuing to beat. Fold in ground nuts. (You may use any variety, but black walnuts are superb.) Add vanilla. Drop by teaspoonfuls onto ungreased cookie sheet and bake about 1 hour, or until kisses can be moved freely on cookie sheet.   *Makes 4 to 5 dozen*

Anise Seed Cakes

1 teaspoon cold water   1 cup granulated sugar
4 egg yolks   1 cup flour
                1 teaspoon anise seed

Add cold water to egg yolks and beat until just mixed. Add sugar; place over hot (but not boiling) water and beat until mixture begins to thicken. Remove from fire, and add flour and anise seed. Drop by spoonfuls onto a greased cookie sheet, and let stand overnight in a cold oven, to dry out. Next day, remove from oven; heat oven to 300°, then bake just until cookies begin to brown around edges—from 15 to 20 minutes.   *Makes 3 dozen*

Quick Animal Cookies

In our family these have become known as "people cookies," because when the twins were small I put eyes and a mouth with cinnamon candies on round cookies and handed them to the twin of the appropriate sex, saying, "This is a boy cookie," or "This is a girl cookie." When they finally asked, "What's the difference between a boy cookie and a girl cookie?" it was as though they had found out about Santa Claus. We called them "people cookies" from then on. I make them frequently because they are quick, easy, and delicious.

1 cup melted shortening   3½ cups flour—about
  (half butter)   2 eggs, beaten
2 cups granulated sugar   Nuts, chocolate bits, cinnamon
½ teaspoon baking soda   candy, and beaten egg white
1 teaspoon cream of tartar   for decoration
1 teaspoon vanilla

Add melted shortening, sugar, baking soda, cream of tartar, vanilla, and flour to beaten eggs, using just enough flour to make a thick but not really stiff batter. Let cool an hour or so. Roll out very thin and cut into shapes. Paint with beaten white of egg, decorate with nuts, chocolate bits, cinnamon candies, or whatever you like. Bake at 350° for 5 to 10 minutes, watching carefully, as cookies brown quickly.   *Makes about 10 dozen*

Spicy Drop Cookies

3 eggs	2 tablespoons hot water
2 cups brown sugar	1 cup chopped raisins
1 cup melted shortening	3 cups flour—about
(half butter)	Dash of ground ginger,
1 teaspoon baking soda	cinnamon, cloves, and nutmeg

Beat eggs, add brown sugar, butter, and baking soda dissolved in water. Fold in chopped raisins; add flour, enough to make the dough quite stiff. (It may not be necessary to use all the flour, since eggs differ in moisture content, so go slowly with the last cup.) Add spices—the amount of spice depends upon whether you want cookies very spicy, or not.

Drop by teaspoonfuls onto an ungreased cookie sheet. Bake at 350° for 10 to 15 minutes until nicely browned and tops spring back at a touch. *Makes 4 dozen*

Honey Nuggets

These are made two or three weeks before Christmas, as the flavor improves and mellows while waiting.

½ cup shortening (lard or	1 teaspoon baking powder
vegetable)	¼ teaspoon salt
½ cup clear honey	½ teaspoon vanilla
1 egg	½ cup shaved dark chocolate,
1 cup flour, sifted	or chocolate bits
¼ cup chopped nuts	

Cream shortening and honey together, add egg, and beat until light and fluffy. Sift dry ingredients and add to mixture. Stir in vanilla, chocolate, and nuts. Chill dough for several hours or overnight. Drop by teaspoonfuls onto greased cookie sheet. Bake at 375° for 10 to 12 minutes. *Makes 3 dozen*

Mandel Schnits
(ALMOND BITS)

These delicate cookies are mixed in an iron spider. They are easy to make and look as beautiful as they taste.

⅔ cup blanched almonds,
   ground
½ cup butter or margarine

½ cup granulated sugar
2 tablespoons milk
1 tablespoon flour

Grease and flour several cookie sheets. Heat oven to 350°. In a large iron frying pan, combine all ingredients, cooking and stirring until butter has melted and the mixture is mushy—a very short time. Drop by heaping teaspoonfuls about 2 inches apart. Bake 8 to 10 minutes, until a light golden brown. They brown quickly, so keep your eye on them! Remove from cookie sheet and quickly roll each one around the handle of a wooden spoon. They are very fragile, so store carefully. *Makes 2 to 3 dozen*

Walnut Drop Cookies

1½ cups sugar
½ cup margarine
½ cup sour milk or buttermilk
2 eggs
½ teaspoon baking soda,
   dissolved in a little vinegar

2½ cups flour
½ cup black walnuts, ground
Colored sugar or dragees for
   decoration (optional)

Cream sugar and margarine, add milk and eggs, and beat until thoroughly mixed. Add baking soda, then flour, and lastly the walnuts. Drop from teaspoon onto ungreased cookie sheet. Decorate with colored sugar or tiny dragees "for pretty." Bake at 350° about 10 minutes—or until nicely browned. *Makes 4 dozen*

Date Cookies

5 tablespoons flour
Dash of salt
2 tablespoons baking powder
1 pound chopped dates
1 cup chopped nuts

¾ cup sugar
2 tablespoons confectioners'
   sugar (approx.)
1 tablespoon vanilla
3 eggs

Mix flour, salt, and baking powder, and combine with chopped dates and nuts. Add sugar, vanilla, and eggs. Stir to mix well. Put in greased baking dish 10½ by 11½ inches. Spread well with spatula. Bake at 350° about 20 minutes, until top springs back at a touch and is nicely browned. Cut into bars while still warm, but not hot.

Ice with confectioners' sugar and water, keeping icing quite thin—
you only need a little on each cookie.   *Makes 4 to 5 dozen*

Fudge Cookies

This is a modern version of our old-fashioned chocolate cookies,
in which we used cocoa or shaved chocolate.

2 tablespoons butter	1 cup flour
1½ packages chocolate chips	1 cup chopped walnuts
1 can condensed milk	1 teaspoon vanilla

Melt butter and chocolate over boiling water. Remove from stove
and stir in milk, then flour, nuts, and vanilla. Drop from teaspoon
onto ungreased cookie sheets. Bake at 325° 15 to 20 minutes, or
until nicely browned.   *Makes 2 to 3 dozen*

Decorated Butter Cookies

These cookies were usually a family project. One person
rolled and cut out the cookies, another painted them with egg
white, and the older children decorated them.

We used special shapes for these cookies—the reindeer and
rabbit cookie cutters that had belonged to Greatgrandmother,
the heart with corrugated edges, and the long-necked goose
that came from Grandmother. The most popular shape with the
children was a Christmas tree, sprinkled with colored sugar,
because it was pretty, but also, I suspect, because it was the
largest!

¾ pound butter	2 teaspoons vanilla
1 pound sugar	Beaten egg white
2 eggs	Nuts, colored sugar, for
4 cups flour	decorating
1 teaspoon baking powder	

Cream butter and sugar, add eggs, and beat a little more, until
mixture is light and fluffy. Mix flour and baking powder and add
alternately with vanilla to creamed mixture. Mix well. The dough
will be quite stiff. Chill for several hours or overnight.

Roll out very thin on floured board or cloth. Cut into shapes, paint with beaten egg white, decorate with nuts, colored sugar, or in any way you like. Bake at 375° for 5 to 8 minutes or until a very light brown. Watch carefully because they brown quickly.

Makes 10 to 11 dozen

Mandel Kuchen
(ALMOND CAKE)

Filling:

2 cans almond paste

2 cups sugar

3 eggs, slightly beaten

Blend almond paste and sugar. This takes a bit of doing because the paste is so sticky. Add eggs and mix well. Chill overnight.

Crust:

4 cups flour

½ teaspoon cream of tartar

1 pound butter or margarine

1 cup cold water

1 egg white

Colored sugar, or sprinkles

Sift flour and cream of tartar together. Cut in butter until mixture is as fine as meal. Add water gradually, and mix to a smooth dough. Chill overnight.

Divide dough into 8 pieces. Roll each piece into a rectangle 10 by 6 inches, and about ¼ inch thick. Spread each rectangle with about 3 tablespoons filling, and roll up like a jelly roll, sealing as tightly as possible. Place rolls straight on greased cookie sheet or shape into a ring, pressing the ends tightly together. Brush tops with slightly beaten egg white, and sprinkle with colored sugar or sprinkles.

Bake at 425° for 25 to 30 minutes, until just golden brown.

These are served in ½-inch slices, but don't cut them until ready to eat, so that they don't dry out. They freeze very well, but should be heated after freezing. They look and taste like fine Danish pastry, and of course they are very rich.

Makes 4 large rings or 8 rolls

Pfeffernüss
(PEPPER NUTS)

1 pound mixture of lard and butter
1 pound sugar
3 eggs
½ tablespoon baking soda
½ cup sour cream
½ cup sweet cream
3 to 4 cups flour
½ teaspoon coarsely ground or cracked pepper
½ teaspoon cinnamon

Cream shortening and sugar, add eggs, and beat a little more, until well blended. Dissolve baking soda in sour cream, and add alternately with sweet cream and flour to creamed mixture until the dough is stiff enough to roll out. (The amount of flour needed differs with the quality of the eggs and the texture of the cream, so add it slowly after the first 2 cups.) Add seasoning and roll out on floured board about ⅛ inch thick. Cut into shapes, and bake at 375° for 5 to 8 minutes, just until nicely brown.   *Makes 4 dozen*

Ox Zunge
(OX TONGUE COOKIES)

These cookies were made on specially prepared sheets of corrugated tin, which had accordion pleats in them. You can simulate these rare old sheets by taking heavy-duty aluminum foil, the size of a cookie sheet, and folding it into deep pleats at least an inch high. The cookies are dropped into the valleys of the pleats, and you can put two in every other pleat. They resemble ox tongues when they are baked, hence the name. They are unusual looking, and they are my husband's favorite cookie because they are moist, but not too rich.

¾ teaspoon baking soda
½ cup sour milk or buttermilk
½ cup shortening
1 cup sugar
2 eggs
1¾ cups flour
¼ teaspoon salt
1 teaspoon cinnamon
1 cup raisins
1 cup oatmeal

Add baking soda to milk and stir to dissolve. Cream shortening with sugar, add eggs. Then mix flour, salt, and cinnamon. Then alternately add flour and milk mixture to sugar. Blend thoroughly. Add raisins and oatmeal, and stir again. Drop by teaspoonfuls onto special pans, or just drop onto unbuttered cookie sheets by teaspoonfuls and press with your fingers to make them resemble ox tongues. Bake at 350° for 25 to 30 minutes, or until they spring back at a touch. *Makes 4 dozen*

Nut Crisps

2 tablespoons water
1½ cups brown sugar
¼ cup butter
1 cup finely chopped nuts (English walnuts are wonderful)

1 teaspoon cinnamon
1 teaspoon vanilla
⅛ teaspoon salt
1 cup flour

Mix water and sugar. Cream with butter. Stir in nuts, flavorings, then salt and flour. Work dough until completely mixed. Shape into small balls and place several inches apart on greased cookie sheet. Bake at 350° for 10 to 12 minutes, until they show bubbles all over, but don't let them get too brown. Very easy to make and indescribably good—but fragile. *Makes 3 dozen*

Quick Drop Cookies

½ cup sugar and 1 teaspoon cinnamon, mixed
½ cup butter or margarine
⅔ cup sugar
1 egg

2 cups flour
2 teaspoons baking powder
⅓ cup milk
Dash of nutmeg
½ teaspoon vanilla

Cream butter and sugar, add egg. Mix flour and baking powder, and add alternately with milk to creamed mixture. Add nutmeg and vanilla. Drop by teaspoonfuls on unbuttered cookie tins; sprinkle with sugar and cinnamon. Bake at 400° for 10 to 12 minutes, until nicely browned and the top springs back at a touch.

Makes 4 to 5 dozen

Nut Butter Balls

2 cups sifted flour
¼ cup granulated sugar
½ teaspoon salt
1 cup butter

2 teaspoons vanilla
3 cups (approx.) finely chopped
  nuts (shellbarks, pecans or
  walnuts)

Sift flour, sugar, and salt together. Cut butter into small pieces and work into flour with your fingers until fine as meal. Add vanilla, then 2 cups of nuts (you can get by with fewer nuts—I often use only ½ cup; the cookies are not as rich, but they are still delicious).

Shape in 1-inch balls; roll in remaining nuts, pressing them to cover completely. Bake on ungreased cookie sheets at 325° for about 25 minutes, or until a delicate golden brown. *Makes 4 dozen*

Walnut Squares

⅓ cup lard or other shortening
1½ cups dark brown sugar
½ teaspoon salt
1¼ teaspoons vanilla
1 egg, separated

¾ cup flour
1 teaspoon baking powder
¾ cup chopped black walnuts
  (or English walnuts)

Cream shortening, add 1 cup of sugar, salt, 1 teaspoon vanilla, and egg yolk. Beat until smooth. Sift flour and baking powder together, then beat into mixture. Fold in ½ cup chopped walnuts. Spoon into a greased baking pan, 7 by 11 inches.

Beat egg white until stiff, then beat into it the remaining sugar and vanilla. Spread over top of batter. Sprinkle with remaining walnuts, and bake at 325° for 35 to 40 minutes. Cut into squares when cool. *Makes 2 dozen*

Basler Lebkuchen
(LOVE CAKES FROM BASLE)

This is my grandmother's recipe. It is quite different from the Nuremberg lebkuchen, which are far too dry for my taste. These are moist, delicate, and keep for months, and they may also be frozen.

3 eggs
1 pound dark brown sugar
¼ pound each: orange, lemon, and citron peels
¼ pound ground nuts (preferably almonds, but may be a mixture)

1 teaspoon cinnamon
½ teaspoon cloves
1 teaspoon baking soda, dissolved in 1 tablespoon vinegar
1 tablespoon strong coffee
2½ cups flour—enough to stiffen

Cream eggs and sugar together. Add rest of ingredients and mix well. Use enough flour to make a fairly stiff dough. Refrigerate overnight—Grandmother's recipe says "Let rest overnight!" Roll out into small squares, about ½ inch thick. Bake at 350° for 25 to 30 minutes, or until they spring back when pressed.

Ice very thinly with:

2 tablespoons confectioners' sugar

½ teaspoon vanilla
Water

Mix sugar and vanilla with just enough water to make a thin, runny icing. Drizzle over the lebkuchen while still warm.

Makes 4 to 5 dozen

Moravian Lace Cookies

This is one of the oldest recipes I have. These cookies are still found at market at Christmastime, and they are very popular. My daughter, when she was very young, called them "windows," because they look like the candy windows in Hansel and Gretel's house.

The only time I ever remember hearing my mother swear was when she was baking these cookies. If you start to take them off the pans when they are too hot, they stick to the spatula, and if you wait too long, they break. So when we heard her saying "Dammit, dammit," we knew she was making lace cookies. I don't have as much trouble, since I've discovered that if you use all butter, instead of half butter and half lard, they are easier to handle.

1 cup New Orleans molasses, light
1¼ cups light brown sugar
¼ pound butter
¼ teaspoon baking soda
¼ teaspoon cinnamon
1 can moist coconut, or 1 cup fresh grated coconut
2 cups flour

Mix molasses, sugar, butter, baking soda, and cinnamon in a saucepan, and melt over very low heat. After it is thoroughly mixed, add coconut, then flour. Chill.

Form into small balls, and place quite far apart on ungreased cookie tins, not more than 6 on a tin. Bake at 350° until they have spread and have little bubbles all over. Let cool just a little, and remove quickly from the pan with a sharp spatula. If they crack, return to the oven for a second to soften.   *Makes 4 to 5 dozen*

Mondsichellin
(MOON CRESCENTS)

1½ cups butter or margarine
2 tablespoons confectioners' sugar
1 egg yolk, beaten
3¼ cups flour
1 cup finely chopped walnuts or almonds
Confectioners' sugar

Cream butter and beat in sugar and egg yolk. Add nuts. Gradually work in the flour (you have to use your hands for this!). Form small pieces of dough into crescent shapes and place on cookie sheets.

Bake at 275° for 30 to 40 minutes until light brown. Spread bottom of roasting pan with confectioners' sugar, and place cookies on this. Sift a little more on top, and let stand until cool. Melt-in-your-mouth goodness, and a must for Christmas at our house.

Makes 3 dozen

Woman looking at her crowded icebox: "Ay grunt,
ve are getting a little behind in our eating."

CANDY

Candied Nuts

½ cup brown sugar
¼ cup white sugar
¼ cup sour cream

1 teaspoon vanilla
1½ cups unbroken walnuts or
  other nuts

Cook sugar and cream over low heat until it forms a soft ball in water (236° on a candy thermometer). Add vanilla and stir until it begins to sugar. Quickly stir nuts into mixture and pour on waxed paper. *Makes about 1 pound*

Nut Patties

1 cup granulated sugar
2 cups light brown sugar,
  firmly packed
¼ cup light corn syrup
⅛ teaspoon salt

1¼ cups milk
1 teaspoon vanilla
1½ cups unbroken nut meats
  (walnuts, almonds, or pecans)

Combine all ingredients except vanilla and nuts. Cook, without stirring, until it forms a soft ball (236° on a candy thermometer). Let stand until lukewarm. Add vanilla and nuts, and beat until mixture loses its gloss. Drop from a tablespoon onto waxed paper, spreading to form patties about 4 inches in diameter. Let stand until firm, then wrap in transparent wrap. *Makes 20 to 24 patties*

Fondant

At Easter time we used to make our own Easter eggs out of fondant which was allowed to ripen and then dipped into dark chocolate. I like the fondant just plain, perhaps with a nut or cherry on top. Either way, it's well worth the effort.

4 tablespoons butter
¼ cup cream
⅛ teaspoon salt

1 teaspoon vanilla
4 cups plus 2 tablespoons
   confectioners' sugar
Food coloring

Mix butter and cream, and melt in a double boiler. Add salt and vanilla and pour slowly over 4 cups sugar. Stir. Sprinkle remaining confectioners' sugar on a board, and knead mixture until it is thoroughly pliable. If you are going to add food coloring, this is the time to do it. To keep pastel shades, drop coloring from a toothpick and mix, so that it doesn't get too bright. Store in tightly covered bowl in a cool place, for at least 3 days, to ripen. Then form into shapes, and decorate as you wish, or add coconut, shape into eggs, and dip into melted chocolate. You can make mint patties by omitting the vanilla and adding 2 drops of oil of peppermint.

Makes about 1 pound

Peppermint Patties

These are the granular, old-fashioned kind of peppermint patties.

1½ cups sugar
½ cup boiling water
6 drops oil of peppermint

Put sugar and water in saucepan and stir until sugar is dissolved. Boil until it forms a thread or a soft ball in cold water (236° on a candy thermometer). Remove from fire, add peppermint, and beat until mixture begins to thicken and look cloudy. Drop from tip of spoon onto waxed paper. *Makes about 24 small patties*

Candied Citron, Lemon, Orange or Grapefruit Peel

2 citrons, or
   2 grapefruit, or
   4 oranges, or
   8 lemons

Water
½ teaspoon baking soda
1 cup sugar
2 tablespoons light corn syrup
Sugar

Peel fruit, taking care to remove all white or pithy part. Cut into strips of any length you desire, cover with cold water and baking soda. Bring to a boil and boil 10 minutes. Drain. Cover again with cold water and boil for 30 to 40 minutes. Drain again. If any white still adheres to the rind, now is the time to remove it. (Some people wait until this stage to remove the pith instead of doing it at the start, but I think boiling the skins with the pith makes the peel too bitter.)

Combine sugar, ½ cup water, and corn syrup and boil until mixture spins a thread (228° on a candy thermometer). Add peel and cook very gently until the peel becomes transparent. Drain and spread on cookie sheet covered with waxed paper to cool. When cool, dip each piece in sugar, rolling to be sure it is completely covered. Let dry again, then store in a tightly covered container. May be eaten "so," or used in fruit cakes.   *Makes about 1½ pounds*

Pulled Mints

2 cups sugar
1 cup water
4 tablespoons butter

½ teaspoon peppermint
  extract
Powdered sugar

Combine sugar, water, and butter. Boil to hard-ball stage (260° on a candy thermometer). Add peppermint extract, pour into buttered pan to cool. As soon as it is cool enough to handle, pull until brittle. Cut into 1-inch pieces and place in a dish of powdered sugar, covering the mints with the sugar, until the mints become creamy. Store in jars. Sometimes we colored these pink or green and red, "for pretty" for Christmas.   *Makes about 1 pound*

Molasses Candy

2 cups dark molasses
2 cups granulated sugar
½ cup hot water
⅓ cup vinegar

1 tablespoon butter
¼ teaspoon baking soda
3 cups black walnuts,
  coarsely chopped

Mix and boil first 4 ingredients. Boil to the crack stage (266° on a candy thermometer). Then add butter, baking soda, and walnuts. Pour into buttered pan. When cool, break into pieces.

Makes about 1 pound

Honey Taffy

1 cup brown sugar
½ cup strained honey
½ cup cream
1 tablespoon butter
Pinch of cream of tartar

Mix all ingredients and cook until mixture forms a hard ball in cold water (260° on a candy thermometer). Pour into buttered platter. When cool enough to handle, grease your hands and pull until taffy is white and looks like milk. Form into a long rope, or a braid if you prefer, then cut into pieces about 2 inches long—you'll have to whack it! Wrap in waxed paper or transparent wrap, and store in a covered container. *Makes about 1 pound*

Vinegar Taffy

2 cups heavy corn syrup
1 cup sugar
2 tablespoons butter
1 tablespoon vinegar
¼ teaspoon baking soda
1 teaspoon vanilla

Combine first 4 ingredients in saucepan and bring to a boil, stirring constantly until sugar dissolves. Continue cooking to hard-boil stage (260° on a candy thermometer), or until a small amount forms a hard ball in cold water. Remove from heat, stir in soda and vanilla, and beat until smooth and creamy. Pour onto buttered, heat-resistant platter. When cool enough to handle, pull with fingers until satiny and light-colored. Pull into long strips, about ¼ inch in diameter. Cut into 1-inch pieces with scissors.

Makes about 1 pound

Chocolate Vinegar Taffy

Add 3 squares of unsweetened chocolate to syrup, sugar, butter, and vinegar, following directions and quantities in recipe for vanilla taffy.

Stuffed Dates

1 package dried dates
½ to 1 cup whole nutmeats
Granulated sugar

Make a slit in the side of each date and remove seed. Fill hole with a half a walnut or any nut you prefer, press to close, and roll in granulated sugar to cover. Sometimes I put together two dates, pressing them closely around the nutmeat. *Makes 1 pound*

CHAPTER XIV

Wine, Mush, and Miscellaneous

There are many recipes in use in Pennsylvania Dutch cookery which are hard to classify, but which I felt should be included here because they are unique and definitely characteristic of the region. I have placed them all together here along with some cooking hints that my grandmother found indispensable.

Homemade Yeast

The following recipe for homemade yeast was given to my mother years ago, and she kept it, but to my knowledge never used it. It is included verbatim, for the sake of interest only, since the commercial yeasts are just about perfect. "What wonders me" is where they got the starter for the yeast in the first place; it's rather like fire—when the fire went out in pioneer days, they sent to a neighbor's for coal—but where did the first yeast come from?

Boil 6 large potatoes in 3 pints of water. Tie a large handful of hops in a small muslin bag and boil with the potatoes. When thoroughly cooked, drain the water and add enough flour to make a thin batter. Set this on the stove long enough to scald the flour (this makes the yeast keep longer). Remove from the fire, and when cool enough add the potatoes mashed, along with ½ cup sugar, ½ tablespoon ginger, 2 tablespoons salt, and a teacup of saved yeast. Let it stand in a warm place until it has thoroughly risen. Then put it in a large pan, add 1 pint of flour to enough corn meal to stiffen, so it will crumble up. Spread out to dry on a cloth in a warm place and dry quickly in the shade. One teacup will make 8 loaves of bread. Yeast will keep 5 or 6 months.

WINE

There are many different "receipts" for wine, and each family swears by its own. "You must chust try my vine," they say proudly, and there is great variation in the results! Wild elderberries, wild cherries, currants, peaches, cherries, rhubarb, dandelions, and of course grapes were the fruits most used for wine—if you can call dandelion flowers a fruit! The trick in getting wine to "make" is to use yeast in some form and to prevent the mixture from turning into vinegar (and pretty inferior vinegar at that!).

Dandelion Flower Wine

4 quarts boiling water
4 pounds sugar
4 quarts dandelion flowers
  (no stems)
2 oranges, juice and rind
1 lemon, juice and rind

1 small piece of ginger root
  (optional)
1 slice toast
¼ of a yeast cake, or
  ¼ envelope dried yeast

Pour boiling water on flowers and let stand 24 hours, stirring several times. Strain through colander, then put into kettle with orange and lemon rinds (save the juice) and ginger, if you like. Boil gently 30 minutes. Add sugar and stir until it dissolves, then add fruit juices. When liquid has cooled to lukewarm, pour it into a crock or glass, or enameled container (avoid metal utensils). Spread the yeast on the toast and float it on top. (Some people just add 1 tablespoon yeast, stir and let it stand, but I prefer the toast method.) Let it stand for 1 week. Strain through a cloth, and let stand for at least 1 month more. Bottle and cork tightly.

Fruit Wine

3 pounds sugar
3 quarts water
1 quart juice
  (raspberry, blackberry, peach,
  cherry, or grape)

1 slice toast, spread with
  ¼ cake of yeast

Dissolve sugar in water, then mix with juice. Put in a large gallon jug, preferably wide-mouthed. Float toast spread with yeast on top. Set in warm place at least 4 days. Strain and let stand 3 or 4 weeks. When it has stopped effervescing, bottle and cork tightly.

Currant Wine

4 quarts boiling water
4 pounds currants, or any other ripe fruit
4 oranges, sliced and peeled
4 lemons, sliced and peeled

4 pounds of sugar
¼ cup cold water
¼ yeast cake, spread on 1 slice toast

This is sometimes called "the rule of four," since everything is done by fours. Pour boiling water over fruit and let stand for 4 days, stirring twice a day. Strain; add sugar and cold water and stir until dissolved. Spread toast with yeast and float on top. Let stand for 4 days. Bottle, but not tightly, so that it can work. (I put it on an old tray, so that if it boils over, nothing is stained.) It takes 4 months to ripen.

MUSH
Corn Meal Mush

1 teaspoon salt

1 quart water
2 cups yellow corn meal

Bring salt and water to a boil in 2-quart saucepan. Slowly sprinkle corn meal into water (this takes two hands—sift it through your fingers with one hand, and stir constantly with the spoon in the other). Boil 10 minutes, lower heat, and let simmer at least 30 minutes longer. Serve hot with rich milk and sugar.   *Serves 4 to 6*

Fried Mush

Pour hot corn meal mush into greased bread pan. Cool. When cold, slice and fry in bacon fat or butter until brown, turn and brown other side. Serve with sugar, syrup, or molasses. *Serves 6 to 8*

Oatmeal Fritters

Put leftover oatmeal into greased bread pan or mold. Cool. When cold, cut into slices about ½ inch thick. Dip in beaten egg, roll in dry bread crumbs, and fry quickly on both sides. Serve with molasses, syrup, or powdered sugar.

Blackberry or Blueberry Mush

1 quart berries
Water
1 cup sugar
¼ teaspoon cinnamon

1 tablespoon cornstarch
1 tablespoon lemon juice
(optional)

Bring berries to a boil with as little water as possible. Cook gently until just soft. Add sugar and cinnamon. Mix cornstarch with ¼ cup cold water, and add to berries. Cook just until it thickens. Taste and correct the sugar content because berries vary in their tartness. I like to add lemon juice, especially to blueberries. Serve warm or cold with cream.   *Serves 4*

Clerk to Plain Woman entering store: "May I help you?"
Woman: "Ach, I chust came in to go out. Do you haf such a place?"

HOUSEHOLD HINTS

Anyone who keeps house learns short-cuts and miscellaneous operations which help to make her a better cook and house-keeper. Some of these hints are very old indeed, others are comparatively new. Some of the phraseology in my mother's cookbook, assiduously put down in her own hand, is—to me, anyway—hilarious. For example, she has: "To get rid of red ants, sprinkle generously with sulphur!" What you sprinkle on *she* knew, so she didn't bother to tell you!

Others include:

To get rid of flies, simmer a cup of vinegar on the kitchen range.

Wilted vegetables will freshen if you soak them in slightly vinegared water.

If you sprinkle the top of your cake with a light feathering of flour, the icing won't slip off.

To clean porcelain, rub with kerosene on a dampened cloth.

Boil oranges for salads 5 minutes. When you peel the orange, the white part also comes off.

You will get more juice from an orange or a lemon if you first soak it in warm water for a few minutes.

When washing windows, use a newspaper for drying them. The paper absorbs the water, and the ink from the newspaper serves as a polish and makes the windows shine.

Grease the top of your kettle about an inch deep to prevent boiling over.

Leftover egg yolks may be kept fresh if covered with cold water. Pour the water over gently, that they may not be broken. By changing the water every day they may be kept sweet for two or three days, even in hot weather.

When soup is poor, add a little grated cheese to make it rich.

To cook an old fowl, put it on to boil with cold water, with a tablespoon of good vinegar added. As the water boils down, add more cold water. It is much better than to use boiling water, as most cooks do.

Scorch stains can be removed by laying in bright sun on the grass.

Lemon and salt will remove iron rust. Apply and lay in sun on the grass.

To remove mildew, wet stain with peroxide, pour boiling water over and repeat until stain disappears.

White Liniment

1 pint vinegar   1 pint turpentine
Whites of 3 eggs

Put in a bottle, shake well until mixed. (If this didn't take your skin off, I'm sure it created heat!)

Baking Powder

1 pound cream of tartar   ½ pound bicarbonate of soda
½ pound cornstarch

Use flour sifter and sift through. Makes 2 pounds.

Hand Lotion

Simmer 1 tablespoon quince seed in 1 pint of water; strain. Add 1 gill Bay Rum, one gill Rose Water, ½ gill glycerine.

Put a piece of bread on the tip of your knife when peeling onions to keep the juice from getting in your eyes.

If you lay a piece of stale bread on cauliflower, onions, or cabbage when they are cooking, you will not have any of their odor in the house.

To remove a bad odor in the kitchen, pour a little coffee on the range, or put several slices of apples on the stove lid.

Add a little lard to starch when boiling it to keep the iron from sticking.

Rolling-pin cover: Buy a pair of child's cotton stockings at any variety store. Cut off the feet and you have an inexpensive and easily washed rolling-pin cover.

Glossary

Ach du lieber *or* Ach du lieber Gott—Oh, dear God!
All—all gone; used up
Allaveil—literally, all the while; these days or nowadays
Alles—everything
Anderes—another
Arlich, arlich gut—pretty, pretty good
Aufschnitt—cut off

Bei—legs
Bei'm—at the
Bissel—a little
Bitzlich—tangy; with a bite
Blindes Meizli—Blind Man's Buff
Blitz—lightning
Blotch—flat
Bot Bei—pot pie
Bouva Shenkel—beef shanks; literally, boy's legs, meaning legs for
  the boys to chew on
Brot—bread
Brust—breast
Bube, also spelled bouva—boys

Change around—change the outer clothes, in contrast to *schtrip
  around,* which means "to change from the skin out"
Cup Cheese—cooked cheese, cooled and served in cups

Dampf Nudelen—literally, damp noodles; steamed dumplings
Dier—door
Dings—things
Distelfink—thistle finch (much used in Dutch decorations)

Do—here; *also* there
Donnervetter—thunderstorm
Donnervetter nochamal—an expletive; literally, thunderstorm again
Doppich, or dopplich—clumsy
Dreck—dirt
Drei—three
Dumm—stupid
Dummkopf—stupid person

Ebble or Ebbel—apple
Echt—true
Eier—eggs
Einlauf—to pour in
Eins—one
Essen—to eat

Fancy—not belonging to any of the Plain Sects—not wearing garb
Fassnacht—literally, Fast Night; Shrove Tuesday
Feinschmecker—one who appreciates good food
Fershtay—to understand
Fershtay'sht?—Do you understand?
Fiel—a lot
Flaisch—(from the German *fleisch*), meat
Fra—(from the German *Frau*), wife
Frauenleit—the womenfolk
Fressen—to eat a lot
Fresser—a gourmand
Freundschaft—relatives
Fricadellen—fried meat
Frohe—happy

Gaul—horse
Gay—not Plain
Gehs'tmit?—Do you want to go along?
Gelb—gold
Geschlopped—slopped
Geschmeltze—buttered or greased
Geschtuffte—stuffed
Gristkind—The Christ Child
Grossmutter—Grandmother

Grossvater—Grandfather
Grumbere *or* grumberre—potatoes

Hahn—rooster
Halt—stop
Hase, hasen—rabbit, rabbits
Hauschtuff—furnishings
Henna—to have
Henner—Henry
Herz—heart
Hinkle—hen; poultry
Hoch Deitsch or Hoch Deutsch—High German, in contrast to collo-
    quial German
Hommy—calf

It hungers me—I'm hungry
It makes down—It's raining
It ouches somesing fierce—It hurts terribly
It spites me—It makes me mad
It wonders me—It puzzles me

Jetz—now

Kalb—veal; calf
Kalte aufschnitt—cold cuts
Karupss *or* Karps—turnips
Käse—cheese
Kastanie—chestnuts
Kennst—Can you, or do you know
Kerl—fellow
Kirsch, kirsche—cherry, cherries
Kloess—dumplings
Klopps—meat balls; also known as Koenigsberg Klops, from the city
    of their origin
Knepp *or* Knoepp—literally, buttons; small dumplings
Kochkäse—cooked cheese
Kraut—cabbage
Kreistle—to shudder
Kuchen—cake, cakes
Kum, esse—Come, eat

Laesen—to read
Lattwarik, Lattwerk, or Lottwerk—apple butter
Leber—liver
Leberwurst—liverwurst
Leit—people
Letz—wrong
Liebe—love
Luschdiges—merry

Mädl—girl
Mal—a minute
Mann—man, husband
Mehl—flour
Mennerleit—the menfolk, or people
Mir—we
Miss *or* muss—must
Mittgehe—to go with
Müller—miller

Nacht—night
Near—stingy
Nix *or* Nichte—nothing
Nicht war?—Isn't that so?
Nochamal—again
Nur a bissel—just a little

Over—to get over something
Ox *or* Oxe—beef
Ox Zunge—beef tongue for meat, but ox tongue for cookies

Pälzer—as in the Palatinate
Pälzer Wei—Rhine Wine
Parrer—(from German *Pfarrer*), preacher, minister
Parshung—peach; peaches
Passa mal auf—look out, beware
Patrich—partridge
Pawn Hase—scrapple
Peffer *or* pfeffer—pepper
Pfalz—Palatinate
Pflaum—plum

Pfund—pound
Puddings—meat pudding
Putz—Christmas decorations

Red Beet—beets; a literal translation from the German *rote Rübe*
Rheinpfalz—The Palatinate
Rivels—flour and egg rubbed together
Rutsch—wiggle

Sauer—sour
Sauerbraten—sour roast meat
Sawge, sawgen—(from the German *sagen*), to say
Sawgst—you say, they say
Schaum—froth or bubbles
Schellhase—lobster
Schinken—ham
Schmecken—to taste
Schmecks't gut?—Does it taste good?
Schnittlach—literally, cut back; chives (chives grow back after
    cutting)
Schnitz—to cut; dried apples; a little piece
Schnitzel—a slice
Schmutz—dirt
Schmutzig—dirty
Schpeck—fat; bacon; salt pork; ham
Schtrip around—to change one's clothes, including underwear
Schusselly—sloppy
Schwetz (en)—to speak
Sei—pigs; pork
Seiflaisch—pork
Selbe—that
Sella—that, or those
Semmel—white flour
Set-out—a company meal
Shivaree—a wedding serenade
Sou—pig, or sow
Sou's Maw—pig's stomach
Souse *or* Sulz—pickled pig's feet
Spätzele—dumplings, usually egg dumplings

Spread—a lavish meal; anything you can spread on bread
Spritz—splash, spatter
Stänli—little stone
Streisen—to strew
Streisel Kuchen—crumb cake, in which you strew the crumbs on top
Strubbly—unkempt hair
Stück—a piece of, a slice
Süss *or* süsse—sweet

Thank yourself—(from the German *Ich bedanke mich*), say
  "thank you"
Tutts—paper bag

Unterhose(n)—underwear

Vas is letz?—What's the matter?
Vas sagsts?—What do you say?
Vat amal—wait a minute
Vendue—(from the French *vendre*), auction sale
Verdammt—damned
Verdutz—bewildered
Verhuddled—mixed up
Versteht's?—Understand?
Vie bischt?—How are you?
Vie gehts?—How goes it?

Wass is letz?—What's the matter?
Wassermelon—watermelon
Weinachtszeit—Christmas
Wellar—which
Welsch Hahn—tom turkey
Welsch Hinkle—hen turkey; turkeys
Welsch Karn or Korn—sweet corn
What fer—what kind

Younguns—children
You-uns—you

Zwei—two
Zwievel(e) *or* swivel(e)—onion(s)

Index

For the convenience of users of *Eat Yourself Full* a special short Index of the Pennsylvania Dutch titles for the recipes has been added at end of this Index. See page 274.

PENNSYLVANIA DUTCH INDEX